Parent Yourself First

Parent Yourself First

Raise Confident, Compassionate Kids by Becoming the Parent You Wish You'd Had

• • • • • • •

Bryana Kappadakunnel, LMFT

G. P. Putnam's Sons
New York

PUTNAM
— EST. 1838 —

G. P. Putnam's Sons
Publishers Since 1838
An imprint of Penguin Random House LLC
penguinrandomhouse.com

Graphic on p. 139 based on the "Ladder of Needs" created by Conscious Mommy, LLC,
copyright © 2023 Conscious Mommy, LLC. All rights reserved.

Hardcover ISBN 9780593716519
Ebook ISBN 9780593716526

Printed in the United States of America
1st Printing

Book design by Daniel Brount

All names and identifying characteristics have been changed
to protect the privacy of the individuals involved.

To my children, whose laughter is my favorite sound, and to my husband, who saw in me what I failed to see in myself

CONTENTS

• • • • • •

Contents

Parent Yourself First

INTRODUCTION

• • • • • •

KNOW WHY I WROTE THIS BOOK. (MORE ON THAT IN A MINUTE.)
But why did *you* pick up this book?

You may have picked up this book because parenting is hard, because you're exhausted by all the demands, because you feel triggered by your child's behaviors, or because you're scared you're becoming your parents (although you promised yourself you never would). I'm here to tell you: it's *normal* to struggle with parenting. It is one of the hardest things you'll ever do. And parenting is especially challenging if you're trying to heal from your past hurts while also showing up for your child in a whole, healed way.

Every family is different. Your parents may have been strict, or permissive, or absent, or abusive, or overwhelmed. Maybe they were caught up in their own personal struggles. Or perhaps they just didn't show up for you in the way you needed as a child. Whatever the cause, the result was likely the same: you didn't have the most effective model to follow as far as parenting goes.

Here's my promise to you: you don't have to have *had* a good parent to *be* a good parent.

● ● ● ● ● ●

MICHELLE ARRIVES AT MY OFFICE, PUT TOGETHER ON THE OUTSIDE but disheveled on the inside. She's thirty years old with two kids, ages four and three. She's here because she's identified a problem: she doesn't know how to communicate with her children in a way that is supportive or healthy, particularly when she's set off by their behavior.

"They just don't do what they're told," she says, her voice quavering with sadness and frustration. She tells me she erupts at them almost daily and cries herself to sleep most nights. It's clear from her puffy eyes that she is exhausted. She knows there must be a better way, something that goes beyond simply doing the opposite of what her parents did when she was a kid (which was, she says, mostly nothing—they were very hands-off in a way that used to drive Michelle crazy). She is determined to be a constant, involved presence in her children's lives. But she can't get a handle on herself when the kids push her past her breaking point.

Michelle wants me to fix her kids. She fears something is wrong with them. Or worse, something is wrong with *her*. She has convinced herself that everyone else has it all together. Why doesn't she?

I'm a licensed marriage and family therapist with a unique specialization in infant, family, and early-childhood mental health. I see a lot of moms like Michelle—tired, overwhelmed, and at their breaking point. They're convinced they're failing and that nothing they do is enough for their families. In their quest to make everything appear effortless, they end up crumbling beneath the illusion of perfection.

Michelle is not a "bad" mom. She is a loving mom who is having a hard time. When we have difficult and challenging experiences, we want to place blame on someone or something else. This is particularly true if we grew up with parents who struggled with accountability and made their problems our problems. Michelle must learn that her children's job isn't to stop triggering her. It's *her* job to recognize that she's triggered and not make those triggers her children's problems. Michelle loves her kids, but she's terrified she's going to give them a traumatic childhood just like hers. She, like many of my clients, believes she is an utter failure.

Michelle's story is very common in my practice. She didn't have parents who were present or attuned to her when she was growing up, so she doesn't innately possess these skills. Fortunately, for her and everyone who resonates with her story, those skills can be learned. No matter where you are on your parenting journey— from toddlers to teens—you can make changes that will help you become the parent you always needed for yourself while also becoming the parent your kids need you to be for them.

Perhaps you're parenting from a place of fear—what if I screw them up? What if I'm just like my parents? What if my kids end up resenting me? What if they end up leaving me like everyone else does? What if they don't like me? The trick to getting to this place of fear-free parenting is to start with yourself first.

That's right: parenting your kids starts with *you*, not with them.

Most parenting books will convince you that something is wrong with your child's behavior and give you guidelines on how to deal with tantrums, back talk, defiance, aggression, and other common issues. A lot of those books put the parent in the position of fixing the child, falsely promising lasting change to their behaviors. In real life, these approaches teach parents how to exert control over their children in their formative years . . . and then parents act surprised when teenagers rebel and try to take back control. Parents then often respond by becoming stricter and punishing the behavior. It's a vicious cycle, and one that perpetuates the dysfunction to a new generation.

You have the power to stop that cycle. When you focus your efforts on supporting the child-parent relationship, not only will you see behavioral changes, but more important, you'll see more trust, emotional safety, connection, and joy shared between you and your child. This translates to more cooperation and more collaboration, two essential factors for running a (relatively) peaceful home.

To get inside your child's mind and understand them better, you need to do a deep dive into your own life story and discover why you act the way you do and how you came to be. In this book, you will examine your core life narrative: What happened to you in your childhood that remains unresolved today? You'll understand what patterns have emerged from your upbringing that continue to impact you in the present moment with your children. You'll discover the social and cultural influences that imprison your psyche, dictating how you should think, feel, and act based on factors that are largely outside your control.

Ultimately, you will learn to liberate yourself from the beliefs and behavior patterns that no longer serve you. You will learn to step confidently into the unknown and overcome past influences that wreak havoc on your day-to-day life of raising your children. Through this experience, you will become the parent you were always meant to be—grounded, present, intentional, and confident. What's more, you will become the parent you never had and give your children the opportunity of being raised without having to carry your baggage for you.

· · · · · ·

I'VE BEEN A THERAPIST FOR MORE THAN THIRTEEN YEARS. AND I know this material intimately not only because of my professional role but also because I am a survivor of childhood trauma myself.

It took me a while to admit—or even understand—that trauma.

(And I'm a professional!) The first time I had an inkling of it was when I left home for the first time and started comparing my childhood experiences with others'. I remember standing in line at a pizza shop with my brand-new college friend, Juliette. I had just moved to New York City from a small town outside of Pittsburgh, Pennsylvania, to go to New York University's Tisch School of the Arts. A very ambitious eighteen-year-old, I was going to be a Broadway actress.

Juliette ordered a salad and asked me, "What are you gonna eat?"

I told her, "Oh, I don't eat lunch."

She looked at me like I had just grown another head. "What do you mean, you don't eat lunch?"

Puzzled by her reaction, I responded, "Well, my mom said that eating lunch is bad for you, it makes you fat, and you should only eat once a day."

She rolled her eyes. "Your mother's crazy."

What did she mean, my mother was crazy? Wasn't this advice what every mother told their children? If something so normalized in my youth was obviously dysfunctional to my friend, what was going on? That was the day my eyes began to open . . . and my personal healing journey began.

I now have two children, and let me tell you that these kids reveal the wounds in me I didn't know needed healing . . . Every. Single. Day. As a professional, I've helped people from a variety of cultural and socioeconomic backgrounds become more conscious and more effective parents—by examining the received wisdom and inherited "truths" about themselves that were passed down from their parents. Some of that heritage is worth keeping and sharing with the next generation. Much of it just doesn't work for them anymore—and they need to find a new way to parent that is more in line with their values, principles, and personal beliefs. That's what we'll do, together, in this book.

Throughout *Parent Yourself First*, I will draw on my professional and personal experiences to guide you. I will share the real-life experiences of my clients (with identifying information obscured to protect their confidentiality), who have been where you are—with the hope that their stories will inspire you to heal your past wounds and make the changes in your family life that you need. You'll be given exercises and self-reflection prompts to examine your past and make an intentional plan of action to heal and grow. I ask that you keep a journal as you read through this book, so you can write out your responses to the exercises and any personal reflections you have along the way. You will be given the guidance, tools, and encouragement to open yourself up to learning about yourself first. But it doesn't stop there.

I also will give you the information and tools to pave the way to a future that allows you to connect with your children, be a better communicator, discipline with love and respect, and give your children the skills they need to go out into the world—without saddling them with the baggage you've been carrying from your own childhood. As a mother, I know how hard it is to change the way you parent, but I also know how satisfying it feels to become the parent you want to be. The cycle of family dysfunction can be strong, but it can also be broken. You can change the trajectory of your child's life by how you choose to show up in relationship with them. This is the true power you possess as a parent.

It all starts with *you*.

PART ONE

• • • • • •

Caring for the Child Within You

CHAPTER 1

Say Hello to Your Inner Child

How Your Past Shapes Your Present

JESSICA BELIEVED HER FIVE-YEAR-OLD DAUGHTER, DANI, WAS an "angry, rude kid" who couldn't make friends and never listened. Dani did what she wanted, *when* she wanted, and didn't seem to care about the consequences.

"I honestly question if I even like being around her," said Jessica. "Is that a terrible thing to say?"

Jessica wanted to feel close to Dani. She loved her. She just struggled to *like* her sometimes. It wasn't how Jessica wanted to be as a parent, but she wasn't sure how to break out of this cycle.

Shortly into our work together, Jessica revealed that, as a child, she had always struggled to feel close to her own parents. "I felt like an inconvenience to them. I even wondered sometimes why they had me," she admitted. Jessica summed up her childhood with one word: lonely. She'd thought that having a child would heal that loneliness, but now she had a child of her own and felt more alone than ever.

It was no surprise that Jessica struggled to support Dani. She was still carrying some heavy emotional baggage from her own childhood, specifically the abandonment she experienced from her parents. And it was distorting how she saw her own daughter. The more Dani embodied the anger Jessica had for years learned to repress and deny, the more Jessica found herself rejecting Dani altogether. Jessica was locked in a cycle of loneliness and shame she desperately wished she could break. But she just didn't know how.

"It's so painful to think about," Jessica admitted to me. "Not feeling wanted—that's how I felt my entire childhood. It's something I never wanted my child to feel. But I'm doing it all over again to Dani. And I'm afraid I've already done the damage." Jessica was drowning in her own fears of inadequacy, which had been sown and grown long before Dani even existed.

For things to really change with Dani, Jessica had to be willing to explore the trapped child within who felt too scared to make a fuss. She had to parent *herself* first before she could be a better parent to Dani.

Listening to Your Inner Child

How you show up as a parent is influenced by your childhood experiences—both the painful and the positive. This sounds simple, but too many of us gloss over the effect our own childhood has on our parenting style today. I get it. It can be extremely challenging to look back and recall what you went through as a child, and you might find this process really difficult at times. Be gentle with yourself. You're here to break the cycles of shame and parent your children with intention and connection. This is a noble effort. No matter how tough this road may be, I want you to remember that you're built for this.

I'll talk a lot in these pages about your "inner child." What do I mean by that? Your inner child is a psychological representation of your deepest fears and anxieties, as well as your unmet childhood needs. This inner child has been listening and learning since before you were even conscious of your surroundings, and it has picked up a lot of information (some that might not even be directly known to you) about who you are and what you require. Experiences in our past inform our inner child, even as we age. Some of us have a loud, needy, demanding inner child who takes the wheel at any opportunity. Others have learned to silence our inner child altogether, only for it to rage with potentially self-destructive consequences. Our inner child is particularly loud during times of conflict and strife! But by listening to our inner child, we'll unlock truths about our own past—as well as insights about how we relate to the children in our life today.

As we work through this book, we'll learn more about how to hear and heal that inner child within us to be a better parent to the kid in front of us. It can be challenging work. Remember: be gentle with that childlike voice inside you. Just like you would never consciously reject your own child, your inner child longs (and deserves) to feel accepted for who they are.

To feel safe, your inner child requires gentleness, kindness, and compassion. We all deserve that, no matter what our age, don't we? Yet many of us have internalized a harsh, critical voice when we speak to and about ourselves, which only further demeans our inner child. Have you ever wondered why you get hung up on feeling like a failure? Chronically guilty? Perpetually unlovable? Never enough? Misunderstood? These fears are all attached to your inner child and the "wounds" you inflict upon yourself when you don't treat them with compassion. When left unexamined and unhealed, these wounds become your core inner child narrative, the unconscious story that colors how you perceive yourself and everyone around you.

Children are not born defeated and disheartened. In its pure form, the inner child is curious, observant, self-accepting, totally present, trusting, open to taking risks, unafraid of failure, persistent, and joyful. But it has been said that children are the canvas upon which parents paint their unrealized hopes and dreams, and as a result many children suffer under the weight of their parents' expectations. They lose the free spirit of the inner child and replace it with survival skills such as competition, comparison, perfectionism, people pleasing, judgment, imposter syndrome, and more.

The inner child is not a rational thinker but an emotional one. When your inner child is triggered, it's often an indication of a need that is not being adequately attended to. So, if you're feeling empty and aren't sure that your needs will be promptly met, maybe you'll get angry, anxious, or nervous. You may run away, hide, or retreat. Perhaps you'll be rendered speechless, panicked, frozen, or stuck. Maybe you'll pretend like everything is perfectly fine, but behind the facade of your smile, you're slowly withering away inside. When these patterns emerge, know that it is your inner child speaking and your wounds are asking for healing.

By the time we grow up, a lot of these patterns forged in childhood have become automatic. But by taking the time to consider the thoughts, feelings, and needs of your inner child, you'll facilitate a deeper connection with the child in front of you. By intentionally making space for your inner child, you begin to mature as an adult—and as a parent.

Practically no one gets out of childhood without inner child wounding. My client Russ had never been to therapy, and he was quick to inform me that his wife "dragged" him into my office to get help with parenting their four kids. They would misbehave, he would explode, she would cry. Wash, rinse, repeat. The cycle was exhausting and unproductive. But no one could figure out how to break out of it. When I asked Russ what I could do for him, he lowered his gaze.

"I'm not used to asking for help. So, I really don't know where to begin." Russ was a fireman and a paramedic, so his ambivalence toward receiving help made sense. As a wounded healer myself, I knew that many people with difficult pasts were drawn to the helping professions. I wondered if Russ could relate.

Russ shared that his mother had been easily overwhelmed by parenting him and his sister, and as a result she hadn't been consistently emotionally available. She had yelled a lot and often reminded him of the ways he wasn't living up to her expectations. His father had threatened him with punishments and consequences if he didn't obey, and he'd often spanked him when Russ defied him. Russ felt voiceless beneath their authoritarian control. And these patterns continued into adulthood. His parents lived nearby, and even though Russ was a husband and father himself, he still felt pressure to comply with his parents' increasingly urgent demands on his time and attention, as if he were still a child. He always did what his parents asked . . . and then found himself having a shorter and shorter fuse with his own family.

"My kids call me Scary Daddy," Russ admitted, with tears welling in the corners of his eyes. "My fear was that I would be overbearing just like my parents, and it seems I've succeeded." Russ was unconsciously repeating the patterns that were conditioned within him: he yelled when he was frustrated, and he threatened when he didn't get his way. He had broken one cycle, though. He had sworn never to hit his children, and he'd kept that promise.

Because Russ's job often required him to be away for days at a time, when he *was* home, he wanted his time with his family to be free from chaos. Quite an expectation for a home with four young children! He wiped his tears, then asked me for the secret to getting his kids to listen to him.

Like many parents, Russ had bought into the delusion that getting his kids to "comply" is the definition of good parenting. *Maybe if they just listen*, we think, *that will prove that I'm not completely terrible at this whole "raising a child" thing.* But then, by extension, if your kids *don't* behave, that means you, as a parent, are not worthy. So when Russ's four young kids got rambunctious—as all young kids do—his inner child told him that not only was he a bad dad, but he was also a bad person.

Here's the thing: it's not your child's job to confirm that you are good. It's their job to show up as themselves. And it's your job, as a fully realized adult, to meet them where they are. To do that, you must unlearn the patterns that have filled you with self-doubt and find self-acceptance. And if you didn't have parents who could show you how to do this, you have to find your way there by yourself.

How do you do that? It starts by going inward and reflecting on what your inner child is really asking for. Even as an adult, you still have an inner child, and your inner child longs to feel seen, heard, understood, and safe. Russ's inner child had been raised on the idea that to "earn" love he had to comply with his parents' wishes, no matter what they were. And he was still doing it, decades later! It had worked, in a way. When he did whatever his demanding parents asked for (even when it inconvenienced him and his family), doing so kept the peace. But at what cost? What lesson was he reinforcing with his parents—and passing down to his kids—about what it takes to feel "safe" in their family?

Russ came to me insisting that it was his children's defiance that blocked a nurturing, emotionally safe connection between them. The more he clings to this belief, the more he reenacts the familiar pattern that his children are the problem. This is what his parents had done—and continued to do—to him. Just as he internalized that *he* must be defective every time he asserted his own free will, his children will likely internalize that they, too, are the problem whenever they want something different than their dad.

To overcome the unconscious urges to turn his inner child

problems into his kids' problems, Russ must notice that his inner child longs to feel heard and respected . . . while understanding that his kids cannot resolve that longing. Russ needs to do the work now for his inner child, who needed patience, grace, and compassion as well as nurturance, predictability, and clear boundaries. In Russ's case, that might mean setting some boundaries with his parents, not expecting them to change their behavior—and maintaining his composure when his kids start to push back on *him*, which is only natural as children grow up! Russ is forty-two years old and cannot expect to be the child in the family dynamic forever (even if his parents continue to see him that way!). And he definitely cannot expect his children to parent him, by asking them to manage and be responsible for his emotions. It's never a child's responsibility to parent a parent. Russ needs to heal the wounds within himself so that he can try to establish a new relational dynamic with his parents—and show up as the parent he wants to be for his kids.

When Your Inner Child Is Hurt

Modern parents are sold a myth. We're told that if we take every opportunity we can to stimulate our child's brain—dance classes! Foreign languages! Extra sports!—then our child will be superior. And if they are superior, they will live a better life.

I can promise you, despite the flash cards and aspirations, you'll have a kid who wipes their boogers on the wall at night before bed. They'll say "poo poo face" at the dinner table and think it's hilarious. They'll deal with rejection, pain, and disappointment . . . and they'll probably make some risky choices.

Our desire to control our children's lives comes from a place of fear. We are afraid that if we let go, then we might be letting go of ourselves. We cannot resist projecting our dreams and hopes onto our children. It's not wrong to want to share our love of music; it's another thing to expect our children to love music because we do. It's not wrong to want our children to enjoy a successful career; it's another thing to limit our children's vocational opportunities to only law or medicine because we believe doing so is what's best for them.

Sometimes, a child's own dreams and abilities can conflict with parental fantasies. Inner child wounding begins when children hear things like:

- It's not nice for girls to act like that.
- Be a big boy! You need to be tough; you don't want to look like a sissy.
- Don't just lay around and be lazy. Get up and do something!
- You need to tone it down. Enough with the drama!
- No one is going to like you if you keep acting like that.

The inner child becomes conditioned to learn *I cannot be who I feel driven to be, because it hurts too many people. I need to be who others need me to be. This is how I'll survive.*

Your inner child wounding may have been more overt. Perhaps you experienced an aggressive, harsh, traumatic, or otherwise harmful upbringing. Maybe you endured corporal punishment, violence and chaos, addiction in the home, abuse and neglect, or serious mental instability. Your inner child may feel more vulnerable to stress, more reactive, or dissociative—a psychological state in which you feel frozen or shut down, as if you were mentally transported to another time and place.

Your inner child longs to feel seen, heard, understood, and safe. In childhood, we rely on our parents to provide us with an environment that allows these vital needs to be met consistently, so we can form a healthy sense of self-esteem and confidence. Our core belief system accepts that although the world may be imperfect, we have safe, reliable, predictable people to connect with in our time of need. As a result, we may develop a generally quiet inner child, allowing for emotional maturity, perspective taking, and direct communication to guide us in times of conflict, struggle, or distress.

When these basic emotional needs are repeatedly ignored, repressed, silenced, punished, dismissed, shamed, or rejected, children form wounded inner child belief systems. These systems get rooted into their core sense of self and become the compass for their future relationships.

EXERCISE: IS YOUR INNER CHILD HURTING?

Take a moment and reflect on the following statements.

- I'm not enough.
- I'm bad.
- I'm a failure.
- I'm not lovable.
- Nobody wants me.

Do any of these statements feel familiar to you? If they resonate, you likely developed a wounded belief system in response to the emotionally repressed environment of your youth. This is how you learned to survive, and now, as a parent, you're acting out these survival patterns with your kids, although they don't serve you anymore. It doesn't have to be this way!

When Russ's daughter called him Scary Daddy after he erupted following his tenth request that she clean up her toys, his core inner child wound of *"You're bad, and you deserve punishment"* was activated. Instantly, he blamed her for his outburst, which was a projection of the shame his inner child had learned to repress. He didn't need judgment and self-rejection, but he couldn't resist going there as the fear of failure flooded him. He had learned to survive his childhood home by judging himself harshly and, in doing so, maybe shaping up and improving. His inner child was sounding the alarm, and he needed to defend his honor or totally shrink.

Suddenly he had a moment of clarity. He realized that he was hard on his kids because he had always been hard on *himself*. His inner child needed the reassurance that mistakes aren't fatal, ruptures can be repaired, and his children weren't punishing him for being a "bad dad." He was punishing himself with his impossible, militant standards that left no room for his humanity.

Like many of the clients I work with, Russ learned that his need for a perfect, chaos-free home was not only impossible but unnecessary. Our children need us to be imperfect, so they can learn how to exist in an imperfect world. They need us to be gentle, so they can learn how to be tender in a tough world. They need us to show nuance, so they can think more critically in a black-and-white world. They need us to heal, so they can be the healing for the world.

Before you had kids, it's possible these inner child belief systems weren't so loud and disruptive. I'm sure you've noticed that having kids pushes you to look in the mirror and see yourself in a new light. Having children makes your inner child wounds impossible to ignore. Your children may embody what you refuse to see within yourself.

This work isn't easy. You may find yourself lying awake in bed at night replaying all your missteps and "should haves." Or burdening yourself with so much guilt and shame about the mistakes you've made—as a parent and as a person—that you can't see your way through. That's information. It's a sign there's something you need to heal within. Be curious and open to discovering what that might be. These emotional wounds will cause you more pain if they are left unattended and unresolved. When you shine a light on your pain today and see that it is a shadow of your experiences in your past, something amazing can happen: You can make different choices. You can decide to parent differently than you were parented.

EXERCISE: WHAT DOES YOUR INNER CHILD NEED?

To gain an understanding of what you most needed as a child (and what your inner child needs now), consider the following and write your responses in your journal.

- What did your parents see in you? Does what they saw align with how you see yourself?

- In what ways did you feel heard in childhood? How did you feel unheard?

- In what ways did you feel understood by your parents? What moments didn't they "get" you?

- In what ways did you feel safe and secure? When you didn't feel safe or secure, what would have felt protective and supportive?

When you are faced with a difficult moment with your kid, go inward with these questions:

- What core inner child wound is being activated in the here and now?
- What does your inner child need right now?
- What are those needs about exactly? Why this moment?
- What do you need to feel safe in the here and now?

Pondering these questions will help you integrate the wisdom of the inner adult into your life, even if you didn't have parents who supported you in the ways you needed. This is how you shift from the feisty, triggered, anxious, scared inner child (who often speaks from a place of fear and inadequacy) into the steady, curious, clearheaded, and regulated inner adult who comes from a place of curiosity and wholeness.

Finding Your Authentic Self

As you embark upon deconstructing your inner child and begin to gain an understanding of what happened to you, you may be filled with a whole spectrum of emotions. Some of my clients feel confused; some find relief. Others feel like their life is falling apart. If you're feeling unraveled by this process of looking inward, I want you to know that this is normal. It does not mean you're so defective or broken that healing is impossible. Instead, all these difficult, painful feelings may reveal just how hard you've been working to keep it together! It takes enormous effort to suppress the fears, shame, and wounds we're used to running away from. You're not falling apart. This is what healing your inner child feels like. You can finally embody the sad, lonely, hurt, rejected, and ashamed parts of yourself that you learned to muscle through and smile over. They don't call them growing pains for nothing.

You're not alone in this process. Trust that the more you crack open your heart, the easier it will be for you to accept and support your—and your child's—true essence. But embarking on this work often makes people realize something upsetting: they have been hiding who they really are (what I call their Authentic Self) for far too long. When that disconnect between your inauthentic Masked Self and your true Authentic Self starts to become evident, some people have a crisis of confidence.

Sheena, a mother of two, was tightly wound, never allowing anyone to peek beneath her mask. She learned at a rather young age, after living with the chaos of substance-addicted parents, that survival meant never burdening anyone with her wants or needs. Sheena feared vulnerability and intimacy; with a deadpan sense of humor and a somewhat monotonous tone, she told tales of her contentious divorce and challenging emotional issues with one of her children. Her telling displayed an obvious disconnect from the reality of her situation. She wore the Stuff It All Down Mask, which she felt allowed her to earn more favor from everyone in her life. Although this mask had once ensured she survived her traumatic upbringing, it was now wreaking havoc on her family life.

Zayne, Sheena's nine-year-old son, had an unexplained, intense aversion to vomiting. He panicked at the thought of potentially becoming ill and would often say, "I don't want to throw up! I'm too scared!" Not only was he terrified of his own bodily turmoil, but he couldn't tolerate the sound of someone else throwing up. Sheena initially sought treatment for Zayne's anxiety, but we quickly learned his anxiety was a mirror of her own inner turmoil. Because Sheena was afraid of revealing all the complicated emotions that she had been hiding from for decades, Zayne was unconsciously being conditioned to stuff it all down, too. For Zayne's fear of vomiting to disappear, Sheena had to be willing to pull down the mask . . . and allow what she felt was "ugly and unacceptable" about herself to finally be revealed.

Just like Sheena, many of us have become so used to masking our emotions that we almost don't realize we're doing so. But not showing up authentically doesn't just harm us; it impacts our kids, too.

Our Masked Self vs. Our Authentic Self

The Authentic Self is the limitless expression of the complexity of this human experience: joy, love, empathy, compassion, selfishness, anger, rebellion, discontent, and so on. But just because these feelings are normal doesn't necessarily mean it's *easy* to show up as your Authentic Self. From a societal perspective, aspects of the Authentic Self are often unwanted and rejected. If you're a woman, your authentic feelings of rage or your tendency toward uncomfortable truth-telling could be unwelcome to some. If you're a man, your authentic feelings of gentleness or nurturing may not be embraced or supported by some—after all, are you even a real man? When you hide these aspects of your personality, you're going through the world as your Masked Self. By instead coming to terms with your Authentic Self, you'll gain a newfound freedom to exist in alignment with who you feel you are, rather than who society, culture, or even your family has indoctrinated you into being.

If you have ever watched little kids play, they exist fully within their Authentic Selves. They don't look for validation, reassurance, or approval from their peers—at least not at first. Rather, they *learn* to seek these things because we condition our children's psyche to need them. As parents, if we aren't living in our Authentic

Selves, we project this anxious need for validation, reassurance, and approval onto our kids.

The world conspires to repress the authentic nature of the soul. Your parents probably thought it was best for you to be tamed or controlled so you could fit in. The result: you go through life as your Masked Self, which conceals your Authentic Self. The Masked Self represents the limited vision that society, culture, and your family find acceptable for who you should be. You adopt masks to survive whatever restrictive environment you find yourself in; they are protection, armor. We often adopt masks in response to our parents, who say, one way or another, *I know you better than you know yourself.*

The Masked Self learns

- I must be pleasing.
- I must serve others' needs.
- I must deny myself for the convenience of others.
- My needs aren't as important as the needs of others.
- I cannot be wrong.
- I cannot look like a failure.
- I cannot be a disappointment.
- I must make others proud.
- I am my accomplishments.
- If I cannot do, then I am not worthy.
- I need the approval of others.

It takes a great deal of effort to be someone we're not. The emotional toll is hefty. Often it is not only us, but also our children, who pay the price.

Elsa, of the movie *Frozen*, is a great example of someone who had to suppress her Authentic Self. At a very young age, Elsa was told that her magical power could be dangerous, and in order to keep her (and others) safe, her parents taught her how to mask her Authentic Self. The deeper Elsa went into her Masked Self, the lonelier, more isolated, and more depressed she became.

When she could no longer maintain this false version of herself and realized that in her effort to please and serve others she was denying herself inner peace, true joy, and deep connection, she disrupted her community and caused a lot of harm. The Masked Self was not the "more desirable" or safer version of Elsa. Because she was not given permission to be her Authentic Self, she didn't know how to operate in a world that expected her to be something she was not. In the anthem "Let It Go" (c'mon, parents, sing it with me!), Elsa had to escape the world she hid behind to find her Authentic Self.

Although Elsa is a fictional character, her story is not unfamiliar—absent the magical powers. Perhaps you relate to the struggle of being something you're not just to keep the peace or to make others appreciate you. Just like Elsa, you'll never be enough if you keep trying to be what you think others need you to be. You have to let it go. I bet there are some masks you're desperate to let go of, too. Just like Elsa, you are learning to walk away from all that you've been told is true about you. You're stepping into something brand-new but true to your inner being.

Shadows and Stars

Adriana, an adult client who was suffering from postpartum depression, was the child of a nasty, contentious divorce. Her parents had been unable to co-parent in any amicable way, and as a result, Adriana had assumed the emotional burden of responsibility and maturity for her entire family. As the oldest child, she had shouldered the expectation that she should take care of her mother's and her siblings' emotional needs. Although she had been applauded for her intelligence and "grown-up" demeanor, she had felt dead inside throughout most of her childhood. It's no surprise that, when hit with the extreme responsibilities of new motherhood many years later, Adriana finally caved under all the pressure. Masking was no longer an option. She couldn't think her way out of her emotions. Adriana's new baby forced her to confront what she had been hiding from all along: her true self.

You also probably had experiences that forced you to mask. These experiences are your Shadows. Shadows are those life experiences and people who made you feel unsafe, unseen, misunderstood, or hurt you in some way. Shadows are those memories, feelings, and experiences that you would prefer to keep hidden. Most of my clients wish to repress their Shadows; they don't want to think about them, let alone talk about them. But Shadows cannot be avoided. They follow us and are always lurking in the background. The best way to deal with Shadows is to face them, bravely and tenaciously.

We all have Shadows. Often, we can see that the Shadows from our childhood experiences are Shadows from our parents' childhood experiences. If there is something about your child, partner, or family member that you find triggering and difficult, there is most likely a Shadow hidden there, awaiting acknowledgment and deconstruction. Your Shadows exist to protect your inner child from reexperiencing whatever pain and harm you endured in your early years. In fact, it's the Shadow—the unresolved, fearful experience—that keeps the inner child feeling inadequate, insecure, and unprotected.

Whether or not recalling the Shadows of your life experience is a challenge for you depends on your history. If you have experienced significant trauma, you may find it easy—albeit overwhelming—to bring your Shadows to the light. If you have been conditioned to protect your family of origin at all costs, you may struggle to recall any Shadows at all. Or you may have concluded, *What's done is done. If it's in the past, it's of no concern to me today.* While it's true that the past cannot be changed, denying its relevance to the present only sets the stage for history to repeat itself. Resist the urge to ignore your Shadows, because there is a wealth of self-knowledge you can uncover simply by allowing yourself to observe them without judgment or criticism.

In addition to Shadows, we have Stars. Our Stars are those life experiences and people who have helped us feel seen, heard, understood, and safe. While I have a lot of Shadows from my upbringing, I have one very important Star from my early childhood years. If it wasn't for her influence, it's highly unlikely I would be sharing this wisdom with you today.

I was a rambunctious, uncontrollable child who was quite challenging for the adults in my life. I was loud—I literally didn't know how to whisper—feisty, spunky, and not like other children. Doctors believed I had ADHD and wanted to medicate me. My mom was not interested in taking that route, and so she sent me off to kindergarten with a warning for my teacher, Mrs. Bunnel, *She can't shut up.*

Mrs. Bunnel could have given me an F for behavior or enacted punishments such as denying me social engagements like recess that I so desperately craved and needed. Fortunately for me, Mrs. Bunnel was an attuned and evolved teacher who may have been ahead of her time. She was undoubtedly a Star in my life.

I was lucky. Mrs. Bunnel chose to honor me. She put my desk next to hers and gave me the role of teacher's helper for the entire year. She determined that the best way to nurture my boundless energy was to put me in a position where I could chat with kids who needed help. She saw something inside me that my parents couldn't. She saw a nurturer and a leader, and she took it upon herself to encourage these innate skills, something every educator should aspire to do with all their students.

I distinctly recall beginning kindergarten feeling like a bad kid. Internally I was anxious and angry; externally I was bubbly and desperate for positive attention and real connection. Although I didn't formally set foot onstage until I was sixteen years old, I was already a master performer. My year with Mrs. Bunnel gave me the important perspective that I could be accepted as I was, and I didn't need to be perfect to be loved. While I still wrestle with this wounded inner child narrative, keeping the Star memories fresh helps to keep salt out of those wounds.

If you have a history significantly steeped in trauma, it might be hard to envision a Star in your life. Keep in mind that a Star does not have to be a consistent presence—even a small moment or encounter can serve as a Star. If you cannot think of a Star or a Star moment, I encourage you to consider doing some grief work with a professional therapist. Not only will doing so help you mourn the loss of something that is integral to your soul's development, but it may also help you to discover some Stars buried deep beneath the Shadows of your pain and life challenges.

EXERCISE: DISCOVERING YOUR INNER CHILD

Use your journal to explore the Authentic Self versus the Masked Self, and your Shadows and Stars. What do you discover about your inner child?

- In what ways do you believe your childhood experiences shaped your Masked Self and dismantled your Authentic Self?
- In your primary relationships, are you in Authentic Self or Masked Self? How do you believe this impacts you as a parent, partner, and so on?
- If you were to no longer live imprisoned by your Masked Self, what would your life be like?
- Who or what were your Shadow influences?
- Who or what were your Star influences?
- How do your Shadow and Star experiences influence you today as a parent?

If you cannot remember specific instances, that's okay. Try to focus on general feelings and general sensations instead and see what comes up for you. Sometimes (not always), not feeling or remembering anything is a sign that you learned to survive by avoiding or dissociating. This is a common theme for many people. So please be kind and gentle with yourself as you become more aware of your patterns.

Understanding more about your inner child will allow you to reflect on your past and connect with what is happening in the present moment with your child. This is just the beginning of becoming the parent you never had and transforming your relationship with your child.

CHAPTER 2

Break Unhealthy Family Cycles

GROWING UP AS AN ITALIAN-AMERICAN IN A SMALL TOWN, I absorbed an unspoken rule about family: whatever happens at home stays at home. Otherwise, you're betraying your people . . . and if you betray us, *you're* the problem. There was little to no self-reflection, accountability, or desire to grow or change, which was a tough combination for a quirky child like me who hadn't yet learned to silence her spunky self. I assumed that every family operated the way mine did—happy, functional, and smiling on the outside but depressed, chaotic, and violent on the inside.

Let's put your past under a microscope and examine how you were conditioned to think, feel, and act. This step takes courage, as you'll likely feel that you're violating unspoken rules about family loyalty. Perhaps those rules were applicable in childhood and possibly necessary for your psychological survival. But that contract has long since expired, and you can now heal from the pain, sadness, grief, or shame you so expertly learned to conceal.

The Best of Intentions

Your parents are not to blame for all your hardships. Blaming them is another way of trying to escape the personal responsibility we have to feel our feelings, heal our wounds, and grow beyond our pain. It's vital that you hold this in your heart: (nearly) all parents have good intentions. Even when those intentions are not executed in a functional, healthy way, practically every parent I've ever met wants their children to have a happy, successful life.

However, as you may already be aware, positive intentions do not automatically result in positive impact. When my client Tammy repeatedly spanked her three-year-old son, Carson, for getting out of bed, her intention was to teach him to stay in bed, which she believed was best for him. In her mind, Carson was smart enough to recognize he was being spanked for getting out of bed, which should have encouraged him to choose to avoid the painful experience and allow them both to get a good night's rest. That didn't happen. Carson continued to get out of bed, only to be met with repeated swats across his bottom. He cried, wiped his tears, and was returned to his room. Sure enough, the moment Mom stepped away, there he was again . . . directly behind her.

Tammy didn't realize that Carson wasn't motivated to avoid pain. He wanted her comfort, even if it hurt. Tammy, so consumed by the grief of suddenly losing her husband, Carson's father, just months prior, was too exhausted to fully assess the impact of her actions. With every spank, she confirmed for Carson that safety was unpredictable and asking for support was painful.

The problem escalated when Carson began getting physical with peers at his preschool. Every time Tammy received a report that he had hit another child, she punished him—by spanking him. Of course, her intention was to teach Carson to control his body and use his words. But she was unintentionally reinforcing the message that hitting was how you communicated that something was wrong. Carson was smart. He was picking up a lot of information from his interactions with his mom. Just not the lessons she wanted him to learn.

When Carson's behaviors intensified at home and school, Tammy grew more concerned. This was the point at which I met them. Tammy came to me, frustrated. "Why can't you just teach him to stop hitting?" she asked. But she was asking the wrong questions. She was worried about having the kid who hits. But the deeper we dug, it became clear that she was more anxious about how her son's behavior made *her* look than what Carson was struggling with internally. Beneath her knee-jerk defense to blame her son, Tammy was really afraid of her personal responsibility in the situation. But she couldn't yet recognize how to change her own behavior. Week after week, she expressed her frustration with how "bad" Carson was. Not his behavior, but Carson himself. He was a bad kid, and Tammy couldn't imagine what she had done to deserve such a tragic lot in life.

Tammy isn't a bad mom. She didn't need my lectures. She didn't need my judgments. She needed my unconditional kindness and curiosity. When I hear, *I am bad* or *They are bad*, it's a cue to dig a little deeper, which is the first step to deconstructing patterns and breaking cycles.

I asked her to face her fear: "What would it mean to you that he's a bad kid?"

"It would mean I'm a bad mother. And a bad father, you know . . . since his father died, and I have to be both." Tammy was seeking my help for her child, but I suspected that Tammy had some unresolved issues from her own childhood. I probed deeper and asked her, "When you were a child, what happened to you when you were bad?"

"What happened to you when . . ." is a valuable question that helps you reflect on your past and connect it to your present. It is a tool you can use when you notice repetitive themes of being bad and feeling like a failure arising in your day-to-day life. In Tammy's case, it unlocked a lot of useful information on not just her past but also about her approach to parenting Carson.

Tammy scoffed and rolled her eyes at the question. She explained how much worse she'd had it compared to Carson. She had been beaten regularly by her parents as a child when she misbehaved. No one had cared about her feelings or how she was doing. No one had ever told her she was a good girl or that she was smart, pretty, or worthy. All she heard was she "wasn't trying hard enough," she'd "never amount to anything," and that "no one was proud" of her. She had invested far more time into caring for Carson's emotions than anyone ever had for hers. Didn't that count?

Saying this out loud unlocked something in Tammy. It was like she heard herself for the first time—and saw that little girl for what she'd been. Helpless. Innocent. Deserving of so much more compassion and support than she'd received. Cupping her face in her hands, Tammy spent several minutes swinging between sobs and screams as she released decades of repressed pain, grief, anger, and sadness.

She also began, for the first time, to face the pain she was causing Carson by continuing the legacy of physical violence—even if there was "less" of it in her parenting style than she'd experienced growing up. There had to be a different way to communicate with her child, she realized. For the first time, Tammy was able to make a connection between her childhood and how she was parenting Carson, and only then could she start to admit how her behavior was contributing to his distress. But she had to do this in a self-accepting way. Shame led her here, but compassion and personal responsibility would bring her home to her Authentic Self.

You may experience a catharsis when you're excavating your wounds and life stories. At other times, it won't be felt strongly in your body. There's no right or wrong way to go about your healing process. Your mission is to grow beyond the limiting beliefs that you may cling to as fact. When you're doing inner child work, your priority is to trust the process and remain curious about your inner critic.

Recognize the Pattern

The words your parents said to you become the words you say about yourself and the words you speak into your children. If those words are routinely negative or demeaning, you'll start to believe this "inner critic"—and ignore the equally valid (though unsaid) good things about yourself and those around you. That's how we pass down negative parenting practices across generations.

Look, the inner critic in each of us starts from a protective place. Your inner critic has one primary mission, which is to defend you from becoming "bad." Yet it has a bizarre way of accomplishing this goal. It judges and polices your behavior, with the hope that all the resulting shame will prevent you from making bad decisions. It also shouts over any positive messages you might receive, drowning them out and making them unintelligible.

Look at Tammy, whose inner critic screamed into a megaphone 24/7. Her own parents had been consistently critical and judgmental of her, and in adulthood she had developed a loud, bossy, and demanding inner (and outer) critic. Tammy heard her inner critic loud and clear: *You have always been a screwup. Now you need to show those teachers that you are a good mom, even though you're a single parent. You clearly suck at parenting because your kid is a disaster. Cut out this crap now, or else maybe you'll lose Carson, too.*

The inner critic goes for the jugular, because it thinks shame is necessary to motivate you to be on your best behavior. It's similar to how shame-based, traditional parenting strategies "work" by judging and criticizing a child into obedience and "goodness." When you aren't aware of how the inner critic acts out this agenda, you are at risk of projecting those feelings onto an easy target: your children. This is how patterns are perpetuated and cycles persist.

Tammy had reached an important phase of the therapeutic process. She could see these patterns of shame, criticism, and dysfunction for the first time. But what should she *do* about them?

I explained to her that it was time for her to stop blaming everyone (and everything) for her own actions and behaviors. She needed to understand how she was trained to be emotionally avoidant and militant about expectations. She needed to recognize how this impacted her as a child and now as a parent. Through these important realizations, Tammy could begin to uncover how her behavior was impacting her son. Easier said than done! But that's what we'll continue to learn about in this book.

When you parent yourself first, you grieve what you weren't given in your youth. Your grief allows you to understand it, feel it, and grow around—and ultimately beyond—it. But feeling these feelings, and recognizing that inner critic for what it is (namely, not the full story), is an important first step. In childhood, we all have material, emotional, developmental, and relational needs, and it's healthy to rely on your parents to ensure those needs are met. For some, having needs came with strings attached. Many of my clients had parents who provided the bare minimum of food, clothing, and shelter but denied other important needs like connection and emotional security.

When you consider how part of your childhood negatively impacted you today, you may recall statements like *You're so ungrate-*

ful, I made so many sacrifices for you. Many grew up feeling indebted to their parents and family of origin and, as a result, struggle to do the necessary internal work to understand and let go. Yet psychological freedom is born from your willingness to understand the truth of your past, whatever that may be.

For better or for worse, we are all a product of our upbringing. Some of you may have had obvious dysfunctional upbringings; others may have been less obviously damaging. Regardless, there are probably things you'd like to change in how you parent your kids versus how you were raised. But as we've seen, that's easier said than done. We've all (myself included) engaged in parenting behaviors that we promised ourselves we'd never do, such as

- Yelling, criticizing, or hovering.

- Spanking, shaming, or controlling.

- Choosing a favorite.

- Being a martyr and then complaining that no one helps you.

- Blowing up in the face of conflict—or sweeping it under the rug.

You may feel guilty or disloyal for considering the possibility that aspects of your childhood may not have served you. Many of my clients believe that if they speak poorly about certain parts of their upbringing, it means they weren't grateful for *anything* their parents sacrificed or provided for them. This narrative—that children should spend a lifetime repaying their "debt" to their parents by remaining loyal to the family system and never challenging patterns of dysfunction—is particularly problematic. Is parenting convenient? Not really. Does parenting involve sacrifices? Yes, of course. That doesn't mean that children should feel indebted to their parents' sacrifice for the rest of their lives.

Regardless of who you were as a child and what patterns you're playing out now as a parent, the first step to breaking repetitive, unhelpful family cycles is to L.E.A.N. into them with curiosity.

How to Finally Break the Cycle

Naomi was a young mother of five children who began therapy after experiencing severe exhaustion and depression following the birth of her fifth child. In our first session together, Naomi expressed her fears that I would contact Child Protective Services to remove her children.

"When I get frustrated at my kids, I hold it all in as long as I can . . . and then I just snap," said Naomi. She felt incredible guilt about this, especially because she saw echoes of her parents' alcohol- and drug-fueled outbursts in her own behavior. "I'm not using drugs—I would never do that to a kid. But my anger terrifies me because it reminds me of my *parents'* anger. It's not okay, but I don't know how to stop my outbursts in the moment." I quickly learned that she had been burned by an oppressive, punitive child welfare system throughout her life. She rightfully trusted no one.

Naomi wanted to be a cycle breaker, to parent differently than she had been parented. Yet the intergenerational legacy of trauma, pain, and dysfunction was entrenched on both the maternal and paternal sides of her family, and she was drowning without a lifeline. Therapy hadn't been helpful for her in the past, and she was understandably doubtful that I could support her.

Clients like Naomi—who see that they react negatively to everyday parenting stressors but can't seem to change their responses in the moment—inspired me to put together a framework to heal the repetitive patterns that prevent you from being the parent you desire to be. I call this the L.E.A.N. Method, and by exercising the four steps reliably and consistently, you will begin to recognize and shift the way you respond to stress.

L.E.A.N. is a process that teaches you how to dissect your vulnerabilities and understand them from a fresh perspective. Simply put, it allows you to notice the automatic, ingrained reactions when you encounter a stressful parenting situation, like a kid who says no to a bath or a squabble between siblings. Rather than responding with anger or frustration (just as you have so many times before), L.E.A.N. interrupts the reaction. What if, instead of a raised voice or a spanking, there was another way? That's the promise of this work.

L.E.A.N. stands for:

Locate Your Safe Space

Explore the Pattern Without Judgment

Be Aware of Your Triggers

Choose a New Behavior or Action

We'll get into the details of each step in the following pages. But the results I've seen with my clients have been nothing short of life-changing.

Prior to working the steps of the L.E.A.N. Method, Naomi reacted to stress in predictable ways. First, by becoming anxious, perseverating, catastrophizing, yelling, screaming, and then spanking. Then she'd panic and crumble beneath the weight of her own judgment and shame. The L.E.A.N. Method helped her to see herself in a new, more nuanced light. Insight leads to action, and action leads to change. For Naomi to stop the cycle of reacting in anger and then wallowing in guilt, she first needed to understand the root and nature of her anger and develop more awareness about what purpose the guilt serves for her. She needed to unlearn self-rejection and adopt more self-reflection.

L: Locate Your Safe Space

Before you can successfully deconstruct any familial pattern or do this tough inner work, you must first feel safe. When I say "Locate your safe space," I'm not necessarily talking about a physical space—though it can be that! A safe space can also refer to your headspace, and it can take the form of a group of like-minded parents, individual therapy, a supportive partner, a close friend, or even your journal. As you start to grapple with your past and your present, you must establish a safety net that can catch you if you struggle to deal with what you uncover. (And believe me, almost all of us struggle with this at one time or another.) Feeling detached, stuck, disconnected, hesitant, doubtful, and judgmental of yourself are cues that you need to reestablish safety before moving forward with this important work.

If you find yourself checking out when doing this work, take a moment to regain a sense of safety through getting grounded in your body. Sit in a comfortable position and feel your feet on the ground. Pay attention to your immediate surroundings. Name one thing you can hear, one thing you can see, one thing you can taste, one thing you can touch, and one thing you can smell. This five senses exercise is a simple and accessible way to get you back into the present moment during any stress you may experience—but it is especially helpful when you're creating the time and space for deconstructing your relational and family history.

Locating a safe space helps to provide the emotional guardrails you need as you open these portals to your past. To set yourself up for success, follow these guidelines:

- Identify a physical location where you will do this reflective work. Choose a space that inspires you, and commit yourself to it.

- Do this work with someone you trust, like a close friend, your therapist, or a small group of like-minded parents. Surround yourself with people who are curious and not judgmental.

- Create a ritual to set the mood and tone for your reflective work. Try a meditative walk during which you practice noticing your thoughts and sensations without judgment. Sink your bare feet into the earth and envision your heart and mind expanding. Or sit in stillness for five minutes as you mentally scan your body for tension.

As you open your heart to the work of the L.E.A.N. Method, keep in mind that it is important to honor your need for a break and not push yourself too deep, too fast. I've found many clients—especially those with anxiety—are at higher risk for overthinking in the name of healing, so they're constantly digging for the under-lying meaning behind all their behaviors. I love that they want to commit to the process, but constant self-reflection is not what I'm suggesting. I'm inviting you to honor a consistent day, time, and place that you will designate to do this work. In the same way you may put therapy into your schedule, make the L.E.A.N. Method part of your weekly routine. If something triggering happens and you feel it needs attention, make a note to process it during the specific time you've set aside to reflect.

E: Explore the Pattern Without Judgment

When it comes to cycle breaking, exploring the patterns that hold you back is the step that you may instinctively resist. Many of my clients want me to tell them how to stop yelling at or punishing their kids. They want to know how to get their kids to listen the first time, every time. They want a recipe to stop fighting with their partners. They want to land their ship on a private, glorious island where all is calm and serene without braving the treacherous waters they must cross to get there. Let's use the L.E.A.N. Method to unlock the root of repetitive dysfunction in your life while simultaneously committing to living with more compassion and curiosity.

Are there repetitive themes in your life?

In our work together, Naomi regularly discussed themes of distrust, avoidance, inadequacy, and loneliness. Due to her parents' struggles with drugs and alcohol, she'd felt a consistent lack of support throughout her childhood. The echoes of guilt (*Why couldn't I help them?*), shame (*Didn't they love me enough to stop?*), and blame (*Why did they do this to me?*) reverberated into her own parenting journey with her five kids. Internally, her world was chaotic, yet she wore the people-pleaser mask so elegantly that no one could tell she was actually suffocating inside.

"I don't want anyone to know I'm struggling," she explained, "because if I struggle, like my parents struggled—or, god forbid, if I ask for help—I worry someone will notice and take my kids away." Facing her fears would require embracing vulnerability, so it was much safer for her to pretend that she had it all together—and that no one would really come to her aid when she asked.

When you map out the underlying themes of your repetitive, unconscious actions, you start to see a web of interconnected story-lines that allow you to make sense of why you persistently make choices that don't serve you or why you repeatedly find yourself stuck in similar dynamics or situations. Naomi noticed that she consistently martyred herself, denied her need for help, then exploded at her kids because she became too burned out to function well.

To truly disrupt these cycles, you need to start mapping out the larger themes of your internal life that ultimately drive those specific behaviors. Guilt-tripping herself every time she yelled wasn't changing Naomi's behavior. Instead, she started watching what triggered her anxiety. It was only then that she recognized her pattern: Avoiding little conflicts throughout the day with her kids and her husband ultimately led to her feeling unheard, which was something that had felt so terrifyingly unsafe for her as a child in the dysfunctional foster care system. Then she'd explode with the pent-up anger of the day—often about something that seemed small.

Naomi's patterns were understandable, even if they didn't serve her. She needed grace, not guilt. When she was growing up, conflict was incredibly scary for Naomi, and it often resulted in her being placed with a new family. She learned to be quiet to avoid future rejection. However, when the self-minimization became too much, she'd yell in desperate need for support, only to receive swift punishment. See the pattern repeating itself in her adult life?

As you reflect on *your* life, you will notice that many of the repetitive patterns you struggle with today were present in some way in your past. There are several common themes to be on the lookout for as you examine your behavior.

Theme	Wounded Inner Child Narrative
Shame	I should know better.
Inadequacy	I'm a failure. I'm bad. I'm no good.
Rejection	Nobody wants me. I'm too much. I don't fit in.
Distrust	I'm not safe. I'm powerless. I'm helpless.
Avoidance	I'm better off alone.

Think about the underlying themes behind the patterns you desire to break. These themes tell the story of how you perceive yourself and others and how you believe others perceive you. Remember that wounded inner child we learned about in the previous chapter? It's screaming for attention inside of these themes. By boosting your awareness of how these themes show up in your relationships, you'll be one step closer to more intentional interactions with everyone in your life.

Once you link the themes to your wounded inner child narrative, take a moment to pause and reflect even more deeply:

When I think about [theme], I think about/I am reminded of/I remember_____.

For example, "When I think about shame, I'm reminded of my parents scolding me for bad behavior. I felt like I couldn't get anything right."

There is no right or wrong here. Go at your own pace. Don't push yourself. This work is not urgent. Slow and steady will get you what you need.

How can you rewrite the stories you tell yourself?

If you grew up in routinely unpleasant or difficult circumstances—with parents who lacked self-awareness, took little accountability for their impact, and were not attuned to your thoughts, feelings, and needs—you had a higher likelihood of developing a story about who you were and what you deserved that didn't reflect reality. We call this your wounded inner child narrative; it's the voice that makes sweeping conclusions about you and your worth out of fear and self-preservation rather than facts. But once you realize this voice is opinion—not fact—you can rewrite the stories you tell yourself about yourself.

Prior to starting our work together, Naomi concluded that no one—not even her children—truly wanted her around. Was life really worth all this pain?

"I just bring everybody down with my negative energy," she said. "I'm constantly yelling; they're always crying. They'd probably be better off without me."

If you have a wounded inner child, these negative thoughts and false perceptions persist into adulthood. You may conclude, *Nobody loves me*, because you've associated love with pain, and to avoid pain, you resist love. You may cling to *I'm such a failure*, because you've been burned by enough criticisms from others that it's easier to beat them to the punch with your own negative inner dialogue.

In a healthy, functional upbringing—one where parents are self-aware and attuned to the child's thoughts, feelings, and needs—the child often develops an inner child narrative that allows them to feel safe, seen, heard, and understood. This allows you to approach relationships with confidence and trust. You feel connected and supported, and you generally have a positive outlook on life.

While you cannot change the wound itself, you can change how you relate to it. Let these examples inspire you to dig deep within your soul.

Wounded Inner Child Narrative	Whole Inner Child Narrative
I should know better.	I'm a work in progress, and I can learn from this.
I'm a failure. I'm bad. I'm no good.	Mistakes aren't fatal, and I can repair this.
Nobody wants me. I'm too much. I don't fit in.	I'm loved and enough as I am. I won't be for everyone, and that's okay.
I'm not safe. I'm powerless. I'm helpless.	My safety matters, and others are looking out for me.
I'm better off alone.	It's healthy to rely on the support of others, and I can ask for help.

Naomi used this same process to rewrite the story she told herself. Rather than thinking she was a worthless mother, she told herself that mothering was hard and that she didn't have to be perfect. "Everything—even all my snapping and reactiveness—can be repaired," she said to me, after we'd been working together for a while. "And apologies aren't fake, like I had assumed they were since no one ever apologized to *me* when I was a child. I'm actually changing my behavior, and my kids are beginning to notice."

By the time Naomi finished our work together, she was able to consistently offer *herself* comfort in times of stress—in effect, she became the soothing, regulating source of parental comfort she'd never had as a child. And that work on herself paid dividends when it came to her own parenting. She blossomed into a much more compassionate mother toward her children, all of whom thrived under her newfound trust and connection.

How do these patterns persist across generations?

As my therapist and mentor, Dr. Nabil Hanna, says:

What you resist, persists.
What gets repressed, gets expressed.
If you don't talk it out, you act it out.

We cannot limit our life meaning to our personal lived experiences. We're not just individuals; we're part of a complex, intergenerational family system that includes those who came before us as well as those who follow. Family systems theorists argue that relational patterns are passed from generation to generation, which means that the problems your ancestors faced potentially influence your mind's inner workings on an unconscious level. Epigenetic theorists contend that trauma can alter genetic expression. Our cultural and societal experiences also shape not only what we experience but how we experience them.

This means that when you're exploring whatever pattern you feel stuck in, it's important to be curious about the big picture. Have you seen that pattern play out with other family members? If you're struggling with feeling embarrassed by your children's behavior, did you have a parent who was often embarrassed by yours? Did they have a parent who felt embarrassed by *them*?

Perhaps you have a history of physical trauma and abuse like Naomi, and as a result your body is instinctively wired to overreact to any perceived threat to your safety by exploding in rage and then cowering in fear. Naomi was convinced her reactivity meant she was a terrible mother. Helping her recognize that early childhood trauma and significant environmental disruptions are believed to shape a person's health outcomes gave important context and meaning to her narrative, creating more space for inner gentleness and self-compassion.

We all adopt patterns as a means for survival. Some of those patterns are functional—they help us learn to love and care for one another, to feel supported, and to provide a solid base for growth and connection. Dysfunctional family patterns, on the other hand, get in the way of development and our ability to have healthy relationships. Both functional and dysfunctional patterns lay the groundwork for how you'll interact with your own children.

There are any number of dysfunctional patterns and habitual patterns that are passed down from generation to generation, some more obviously detrimental than others—punishment that exceeds the misbehavior (getting locked out of the house, soap in the mouth); physical control (hitting, slapping); or emotional, physical, or financial neglect. Any of these patterns can carry over into the way you parent your children. If you react to something your children do—without thinking about why—your patterns may be asserting themselves. Your job is not to judge the patterns but to get curious and seek to understand them.

Taking the time to examine your parents' behavior to trace how that shows up in your life is something that will help you on your journey. Again, this is not to put blame on your parents but to shine a light on what they were going through. For example, if they were embroiled in an addiction of any kind, like Naomi's parents were, that could have dramatically interfered with their ability to be the parent you most needed. While Naomi herself didn't struggle with addiction, the reverberations of her upbringing by two parents who wrestled with substance abuse were still being felt well into her adulthood.

Physical or emotional violence (or the threat of violence) can also be passed from generation to generation. Corporal punishment is very common and an almost expected form of discipline and control in some families. Yelling, blaming, and shaming may have been common in your childhood. Often, what is "normal" and accepted in your family becomes the way you behave when you have a family of your own. You might not even know there's another way.

Generational patterns can crop up around so-called good parental behavior, too. We think of attention from our parents as a positive behavior trait. But if a parent is overinvolved—the proverbial helicopter parent—their intrusive or protective instincts can negatively impact the child's opportunity to develop autonomy, independence, self-confidence, and self-control. You need to give children the chance to stretch their wings and, yes, even make mistakes, especially while they're young. If they don't, they risk making much bigger, higher-stakes errors when they're older . . . and they might not have the emotional skills to deal with failure.

It is beyond the scope of this book to explore the range of dysfunctional or problematic family patterns that can occur. Every family is different, and challenges and dysfunction can play out differently in each home. What about you? What patterns do you recognize in your own family system? Take an inventory of your life experiences by asking these questions:

- What happened to me then?

- How does what happened show up for me today?

Don't get caught up with recalling specific incidents from your past if they don't come easily to you. Most of our memories are felt inside our body, even if our brain cannot recall details. In future chapters, I will teach you how to listen to the wisdom of your body. For now, if you're struggling to take inventory of your personal life experiences, you can reverse the line of questioning:

- What themes are present in my life right now?
- Do those themes feel familiar or connected to anything from my childhood experiences?

Patterns will repeat themselves until you make an intentional effort to stop them. Cyclical patterns are hard to unwind, because they are deeply ingrained in the fabric of your entire being. In fact, your nervous system seeks out familiar, predictable patterns, even if those patterns do not serve you. The familiar is comfortable, no matter if it hinders safety or logic.

That was certainly the case with Naomi. The more aware she became of her tendency to avoid her repressed shame by acting out her anger, the angrier she became with herself. "I could tolerate myself more when I wasn't aware of what I was doing. Now that I am more aware, I feel even more pressure and responsibility to stop, and some days, I just can't," she told me. Her inner child had been carrying decades' worth of pain . . . and she had been carrying the burden alone. She resented her parents for being unavailable to her most basic needs and uncovered some hidden resentment toward her partner for his lack of emotional availability. To tackle her chronic loneliness, she had to learn to be vulnerable and start saying what she needed. She had to grieve the reality that she was an emotionally orphaned child and then let her parents off the hook for not showing up in any reliable way. Shifting her mindset was her avenue for deep healing.

You may have strong negative reactions as you examine the patterns you're trying to break. These emotions are important, and it's vital for you to feel them so you can release them. Allowing yourself to experience anger, resentment, pain, and shame is an important part of your personal healing journey. You can love, value, and honor your parents while still feeling like something was missing in your relationship and how they parented you. You can have fond childhood memories and still feel like your needs weren't adequately acknowledged or met.

While you can't go back in time and change your birth family or how you were parented, with awareness you can move forward and improve your connection with your children. Keep in mind, however, not every cycle is meant to be broken in this lifetime. Inevitably, there will be something that you pass along to your children for them to examine and work through in their lifetime.

Perhaps you've broken the family legacy of physical abuse and coercive control with your children. Great! They won't have to face adulthood with the psychological remnants of abuse hardwired into their bodies. But maybe you're still working on breaking the cycles of perfectionism, self-sabotage, or being a workaholic. That's okay. You have limitations as a cycle breaker, and your job is not to hand your children a perfectly curated life free from all suffering. Your job is to teach them how to manage the inevitable sufferings and challenges associated with the human condition.

ASK YOURSELF

- What dysfunctional patterns was I surrounded by growing up?

- In what ways do I see those patterns playing out in my life today?

- What's the connection between the themes of my wounded inner child narrative and the patterns I wish to change?

- What type of situation/problem is most likely to cause me to reenact a pattern?

- When I get triggered or feel reactive, what's going on in my body? If my body could speak, what would it say?

A: Be Aware of Your Triggers

The next step in the L.E.A.N. Method is to pinpoint when and how you are physically reenacting patterns in your family dynamic and relationship with your child. Your aim is to build more awareness of what triggers you, which will enable you to break cyclical patterns more effectively.

Let me start off by saying that becoming triggered is not a sign of weakness or incompetence as a parent—even if you feel overreactive and out of control. There's nothing wrong with you, and it doesn't mean you're a bad parent. All parents get triggered by their children.

But this is also true: Children are not intentionally triggering you. They are not manipulating you into getting what they want. Your kids are not responsible for your reactions. When you're triggered by your child (or by anyone else, for that matter), your reaction reveals something about *you*, not about them.

Why are our kids in particular so darn triggering? Well, children challenge the ways you've learned to survive your relationships. They teach you how to love, honor, and respect the parts of yourself that you may have learned to reject, deny, or abandon by learning to love those same qualities within your children. They hold up a mirror to our ingrained reactions and our automatic responses. We don't always like what that mirror shows us.

About six months into our work together, Naomi asked for help with her four-year-old child, Harlow. Naomi described Harlow as spirited, spunky, and strong-willed. Harlow never accepted no for an answer, constantly pushed her parents' boundaries, and was physically aggressive with her siblings. She struggled to make friends in school. Even at four years old, Harlow was stepping into the role of the "black sheep" of the family.

Naomi wasn't the only one triggered by Harlow's behavior—everybody seemed to be. The preschool was threatening expulsion, and her siblings hated having to dodge the toys she impulsively threw. But by using the same L.E.A.N. tools we'd been working on to examine her background, Naomi was able to make sense of why Harlow's behavior was particularly frustrating and triggering for Naomi as a mother.

Through our work together, Naomi had already recognized a false narrative that had defined much of her early life: *I'm not smart enough to handle this. This is all my fault.* Remember, she had been raised by parents struggling with drug addiction and alcoholism. Naomi had internalized a lot of guilt and blame, and she knew that her immediate response to this negative inner dialogue was to freeze—as if she had just seen a ghost. This was her body's way of alerting her to pay close attention.

Naomi realized that whenever she felt unsafe in her own body—when she felt stress and started to hear those negative beliefs intruding into her thoughts again—she would shut down. And that was exactly what she had found herself doing when Harlow acted out. Rather than comforting her child (whose disruptive behavior was an obvious sign of distress), Naomi would instead do the opposite. She'd retreat. Naomi felt her daughter's helplessness, and her conditioned response was to get small, become invisible, and avoid being in the line of fire.

This behavior had served Naomi well when she was a child. It had allowed her to survive significant childhood trauma. But it was no longer relevant for her as an adult, as a woman, or as a mother. Harlow was not a physical threat, although Naomi's body was wired to respond as if she were. Harlow needed the exact opposite of distance: she needed her mom's comfort.

Harlow sensed Naomi's disconnection, which only amplified her demanding, aggressive, and emotionally dysregulated demeanor. She could tell when her mother was going "offline" and would do everything in her power to bring her back. A parent's absence—be it physical, emotional, or psychological—is deeply felt within a child's being, and they are hardwired to do whatever it takes to reengage with their protector, the parent.

By building awareness around how Harlow triggered her physically, Naomi was able to recognize how she unintentionally contributed to the dynamic with her daughter that resulted in so much stress and suffering for everyone. By connecting the dots between her current reactions with the *impact* of her past experiences, Naomi was able to rewrite the wounded narrative that she was to blame. She released the need to be "fully healed" to have a healing relationship with her children. She honored the fact that complications in her upbringing did not fully prepare her for responding to Harlow in the way she needed, but parenthood afforded her infinite opportunities to learn, grow, and evolve right alongside her children.

Coping with Your Triggers

The next time a reactive pattern is triggered, take a moment to pause. Breathe. Feel your feet on the floor. Relax your shoulders. And then:

- Name it: *I feel* _____. State the emotion as simply as you can. This inspires empathy within you.

- Frame it: *I feel* _____, *because*_____.(For example: *I feel hurt, because I'm not being heard.*) Make the connection between your trigger and the emotion it elicits. Expand on this as much as you feel is necessary and appropriate for the moment. This inspires gentleness within you.

- Claim it: *I'm responsible for how I interpret my feelings and for getting my needs met.* Notice the role you play in perpetuating the repetitive dynamics you're hoping to change. This inspires courage within you.

Name, Frame, Claim is a powerful exercise that you can do in any triggering moment or after the moment has passed. Because it takes practice to be able to moderate your triggered reactions in the moment, most of my clients start this process by reflecting on their triggers after the fact. The more you L.E.A.N. into what bothers you, the more intuitive it will feel to shift your behavior in the moment.

N: Choose a New Behavior or Action

Imagine you had twenty suitcases, each one filled to the brim. In the L-E-A of L.E.A.N., you're essentially removing all the stuff, organizing it, and determining what you want to do with it. The final step is N, where you actively follow through with your decision. Choosing a new behavior is the courageous step you'll take to start seeing meaningful change in yourself and within your family dynamic.

Developing new patterns of behavior requires time and effort. The more you can consistently identify and unravel dysfunctional or problematic patterns, the more you will find yourself inspired to intentionally make new choices.

The more Naomi allowed herself to recognize the impact of her emotional retreat at even the slightest of conflict with Harlow, the more comfortable she became with changing her own behavior. When she stopped expecting Harlow not to trigger her internal urge to shut down, she began viewing Harlow's behaviors with more compassion. Rather than feeding her inner critic (*You're just not the right parent for this child!*), she gave herself more compassion: "Harlow is tough to read, but I won't give up trying to understand her, even when I get it wrong." Over time, Naomi found herself offering more gentle embraces, her physical presence, and more affection during Harlow's meltdowns. She closed her eyes, got grounded in her body, and became the safe space for Harlow that Naomi always needed as a little girl.

· · · · · ·

THE L.E.A.N. METHOD IS AN INTROSPECTIVE DEEP DIVE INTO THE family dynamics, patterns, and unspoken rules that have led you to where you are today. With heightened awareness of how the past has shaped you, as well as your commitment to no judgment and more compassion, you can dramatically change how you show up for your children in the present. And as you'll see in the next chapter, this will ultimately set you free—free to be a better parent and a happier version of yourself.

CHAPTER 3

• • • • • •

Self-Awareness
Sets You Free

L AURA, A MIDDLE-AGED MOM OF TWO, SMILED THROUGH HER
tears as she expressed her deeply held worry that her children
were suffering from extreme anxiety.

"They are not like other children," said Laura intensely. "Everything is a very big deal to them. The tiniest change, me stepping
away for just a second, even doing things they absolutely love . . .
these are such nightmare experiences for them. They truly cannot
cope with life."

I hadn't met her children, but it was clear that *Laura* was the
one with anxiety. Like many of my clients, her focus was on her
children, and she wasn't yet aware of her own needs.

When parents insist that their child has a specific problem, I
often find that it is an issue that the parents also struggle with. If
the child struggles with aggression, the parents may engage in patterns of outward or passive aggression. If the child struggles with
anxiety or depression, there may be patterns of mood disturbances
in one or both of the parents. If the child struggles with eating, a
parent may be stuck in diet culture or there may be a family

history of sensory-processing challenges. And on and on. The issue with your children likely starts with you, so if there is something concerning you about your child's well-being, go inward, reflect, and ask yourself, *Is this really about my child? Or is it something I'm projecting onto my child that's actually about me?*

According to Laura, her eight-year-old daughter had obsessive-compulsive disorder, tics, and anxious ruminations about death. Her five-year-old son absolutely refused to go anywhere or be with anyone if Mom was not present. Based on what she was saying, I was concerned that the children were suffering. However, in my subsequent assessments, I didn't observe anything related to these issues. In fact, I found them to be well-adjusted children who enjoyed playing with their mom. Based on Laura's reports, I was expecting socially impaired children, but what I saw were developmentally unremarkable, perfectly average, securely attached, and kind kids. After several child-parent play therapy sessions, I concluded that the children didn't need to be in treatment.

Laura had unconsciously made her personal fears and anxieties her children's issues. She did this not out of malice but rather through a lack of self-awareness. She misinterpreted typical childhood behaviors, like her daughter twirling her hair on her finger and her dramatic emotions, as deeply serious mental health concerns. On their own, these behaviors are often nothing more than coping mechanisms to deal with boredom, hunger, exhaustion, or childhood itself. For Laura, facing her own internal distress head-on was too psychologically overwhelming, and she did what many parents do: she focused her efforts on "helping" her children.

After all, helping someone else is a lot safer, psychologically, than helping yourself. But in order to really be an effective parent, you need to first help yourself. And to do that, you need to cultivate a sense of awareness of your own strengths—and shortcomings.

Self-Awareness and Effective Parenting

We don't intentionally disconnect from our children when things become more stressful. When we react to our children's stress, we are demonstrating *our* learned behaviors. How you respond to stress reflects how you learned to feel safe in relationships—particularly in vulnerable, difficult, or challenging moments.

If you had a parent who

- Frequently screamed at you: you might have responded by shutting down and avoiding the pain of the encounter. You may notice yourself repeating this shut-down-and-shut-out pattern with your child.

- Poked and criticized you: you might have responded by becoming defensive and anxious. You may notice yourself reenacting this escalation pattern with your child.

- Raged at you then went radio silent: you might have responded by anxiously clinging to get reassurance that you weren't being abandoned or rejected. You may notice yourself walking on eggshells around your child to not feel that same anxiety.

- Was abusive but was your only source of security and safety: you may have felt confused by having to seek comfort from the source of your fear. You may notice yourself reenacting this internal tug-of-war when you feel flooded by your child's needs and behaviors, trapped between wanting to be their safe haven and feeling like the person who is harming them the most.

Your reaction to your child is typically not connected to what is happening in the present. It is most often a reaction to what has happened to you in the past. Your ability to engage in self-reflection in the moment helps you to recognize the way your wounded inner child narrative impacts how you show up for your children in the present.

As you learned in chapter 1, the deepest needs of the inner child's experience are to feel seen, heard, understood, and safe. By enhancing your self-awareness during stressful, challenging moments, you pave the road for meeting these deep and important needs for yourself and your child.

Occasionally, my oldest child will reject my hugs, push me away, and tell me he doesn't want to be bothered by me. Ouch. When this happens, my wounded inner child narrative is revealed. My heart races, my throat clenches, and my body does everything in its power to escape the threat. All I hear is, *You're not enough* and *You disgust me.* Without self-reflection, I would be much more likely to react viscerally and defensively. *Who do you think you are? I am your mother, and you better respect me.*

The shame and sadness of these inner child wounds can feel intolerable, and so the unaware parent makes them the child's burden to bear. With self-reflection, however, you can start to see things more clearly. You might, for example, notice that your child's rejection feels like a punishment. Perhaps your parents defended against their own emotional distress by punishing you. Having this realization enables you to be a more effective parent . . . because it gives you a choice in how you react.

You can choose not to repeat the cycle. Rather than blaming your child, you can sit with the uncomfortable feeling of being punished and provide yourself grace, love, compassion, and nurturance.

This journey is a lifelong process that has breakthroughs and setbacks, but over time, self-reflection helps deliver patience, consistency, and the harmonious mindset you need to parent in a healing way. The more you reflect on yourself, the more you become aware of why you are the way you are—and open the portal of wonder into why your child is the way *they* are.

Self-reflection actively encourages you to dig for the deeper meaning behind your child's behaviors, so you can appreciate your child for who they are at their core. At the end of the day, we all want to feel valued, seen, like we belong, and that we matter. This doesn't mean that we let our children rule the roost. It means that we accept the psychological and relational responsibility that comes with the privilege of raising children: we must commit to knowing ourselves so we can help our children come to know themselves.

Parenting Is a Relationship

Most parenting books consider the parent-child dynamic as operating in one direction—from parent to child. Your implied job is to "fix" your kid. Tantrums? Do these three things. Not listening? Take this "easy" approach. Toileting troubles? Here are the dos and don'ts.

But parenting isn't a one-directional relationship; it's a two-way street. Without clear guidance on what it means to be in a parenting relationship with your children, quick-fix tips about "improving" their behavior will have a temporary effect at best. Things may look nicer or run smoother for a moment, but the core issue is not being appropriately addressed.

True relationships involve give-and-take—and that give-and-take here isn't just between you and your child. As we've already seen, our relationship (or lack thereof) with our *own* parents has a profound impact on how we parent our children. This book will help you start to understand what it was like to be in a relationship with *your* parents when you were a child. This knowledge will in turn help you to forge a better relationship with your child.

Historically, the child-parent relationship has received minimal spotlight or acknowledgment. The traditional parenting paradigm teaches us that children should be seen but not heard, and a child who acts out must be punished. Children's opinions and ideas are not as valuable as an adult's, so their thoughts and beliefs are considered largely irrelevant. When children speak out against climate change or gun violence, they are often mocked by adults in power. They think that children couldn't possibly conceive of the gravity of such problems—nor could they offer valuable solutions. In this paradigm, children speaking back to a person in a position of authority is the worst offense, and they will need to be put in their place. *It's for your safety*, they are told. *You need to learn how to be in the world. The world won't cater to you.* Perhaps children should simply focus on being children: having fun, feeling carefree, and being completely "protected" (i.e., cut off) from adult matters.

For many, childhood is an oppressive period to survive, and real power is gained in adulthood. When you raise power-hungry and power-starved children by using the child-parent relationship to dominate and control them, as they reach adulthood you create an epidemic of authoritarian-driven individuals who—without self-reflection—will reenact their need for power by suppressing and controlling the most vulnerable . . . and there is no one more vulnerable than our children.

This historical bias against children—known as childism—has adversely influenced parents' awareness of their impact on a child's developing mind and soul. It has infected the inherent beauty that exists in the child-parent relationship. I am not suggesting that we throw caution to the wind and let our children run free à la *Lord of the Flies*. I am suggesting that the condescension that pervades all our beliefs about children exists unconsciously because of how our parents were in relationship with us. It is, therefore, your work to become aware of how your parents spoke *to* you and *about* you when you were a child. By exploring this relationship dynamic, you will gain a deeper awareness of what you bring to the child-parent relationships in your home.

As a child, I heard far too frequently how much I embarrassed my mother. My voice, my presence, my bigness—both in personality and the shape of my hips—was always "too much." This eroded my self-esteem, prompting me to adapt a mask of perfection to manage the internalized contempt I harbored for myself. I promised that I'd never project the shame of embarrassment onto my children. That was until my son, who was four years old at the time, behaved in such a way that I felt absolutely mortified, and my unconscious bias came pouring out of me.

We were at a roadside café, and a young disabled man came in with his caretaker. My inquisitive child had several questions about the young man's condition. Without knowing about his situation, I responded as best as I could to satisfy my son's curiosity. As the young man slowly headed toward the restroom, my child jumped up from his chair and began screaming at the top of his lungs: "No, he's scary! Don't let him take me away!" This startled the young man, who turned around and walked back to his table.

I felt awful. Not only did I feel like the worst mom ever, I felt like I was raising an evil, non-empathic, narcissistic child. The patrons in the restaurant were shocked and stared at me, waiting for my next move. "What is wrong with you?!" I whispered to him in that belittling way that every parent uses when their child embarrasses them in public. I apologized to the young man and his caretaker on behalf of my child. I felt my son needed to be punished, and making him feel the shame and badness I felt inside of me was the only way to ensure that this horrific moment would never happen again.

That day, in a classic reactive moment, my threatened inner child hijacked my system; the mature inner adult was nowhere to be found. I wish I hadn't reacted that way, but I've also learned that guilt-tripping gets you nowhere while self-reflection leads to healing. My expectations for his behavior were absurdly high, and it was up to me to notice and change this. My childist—and childish—behaviors showed that even I, a staunch advocate for respecting a child's developmental needs, had more self-reflection work to do.

Afterward, I spoke with my son about what happened and apologized: "I'm sorry I reacted the way I did. You needed my support, and I refused to help you. That wasn't okay." I told myself, *It's not his job to alleviate my fears of being a public embarrassment. It's his job to push me to face this fear, heal the wound, and find more inner peace.* Cycles are broken because each challenging moment reveals exactly what needs to be corrected, healed, and transformed.

When you reflect on your reactions and recognize that they come from within you, you can then be curious about what is going on with your child (rather than simply reacting to their behavior). Self-reflection gets you to a place where you realize that your kid isn't acting out because you're a bad parent. Their behavior is just where they are in the now, and they need support, structure, and guidance.

Had I been in a reflective headspace in the moment, perhaps I would have offered him support: "I know you're scared, but that man is not trying to scare you. He just wants to use the restroom." I also could have offered him guidance: "Let's learn more about physical disabilities together so next time you can offer empathy, love, and kindness." Getting to this reflective, nonjudgmental, supportive place requires slowing down in the moment.

Slowing Down Is Essential

Perhaps the biggest hurdle for engaging in self-reflection is our fast-paced environment. We live in a go, go, go world, and our hectic lives are driven by the clock—we must be at work at a certain time, or we have a meeting or appointment that we can't be late for. Children, on the other hand, live in the here and now. They aren't bound by the social construct of time that we eventually learn to live by. They often react to chronic rushing by resisting, becoming anxious or overwhelmed, or experiencing dysregulation. Our knee-jerk reaction is to blame them for not keeping up. But we're wrong. They don't need to keep up; we need to slow down.

Self-reflection is a practice of slowing down and tuning in. Every time you're triggered, it's an opportunity for you to ask yourself, *What is this about for me?* By asking this question, you are reprogramming what no longer serves you. Self-reflection upgrades your soul's psychological hardware. It helps you recognize that parenting is not the urgent task it's made out to be. Parenting is like bearing witness to the development of a tree. It's a slow, meticulous unfolding as the seedling sprouts, grows its first branches, continues to stretch into the sky, and eventually becomes a majestic home for some of nature's sweetest creations. Each child is their own unique plant species, and parents are the gardeners who thoughtfully examine the conditions that enable each plant to thrive and to reach their highest and best potential.

Over the course of my career in private practice, nonprofit community health clinics, and the mommy and me program I created for my community, I've been fortunate enough to observe thousands of babies, young children, and their parents. I'm always struck by how simple children are. I don't mean that in a pejorative way; I mean that in the most admiring way possible. The simplicity of a child's essence is something all parents can strive to mimic and embody.

Children fully explore objects, faces, and new settings. Sometimes their play is active and engaged with other peers; sometimes they seek the comfort and closeness of their parents. When they fall, often they don't focus on falling as much as they work to get back up and try again. If hurt, they let themselves feel the hurt, and they're open to your comforting embrace. Sure enough, once the difficult moment has passed, they're ready for the next.

They are not driven by deadlines and clocks. They are driven by their inherent desire to experience, sense, and feel. They don't have an agenda for what they should experience but are totally open to the moment as it is with no preconceived ideas. Dare I say that we can learn a lot from our little ones.

We Need to Pay Attention

Alysha, a mother of two children ages six and eight and pregnant with her third, sought therapy because she was stuck in a vicious cycle of "mom rage," as she put it. Mumbling almost inaudibly, she began our work together by admitting, "I'm a monster, and I'm damaging my kids. I need to stop, but I don't know how. I just keep yelling at them. Inside, I tell myself to stop, but I don't. It's almost like it feels good to just unleash on them. Of course, I feel terrible after, but that doesn't stop me from doing it again. I'll go home after this session and keep doing it and will only feel a little bad about it. I hate this."

Alysha was deeply lacking when it came to community support and emotional connections. Being married to a media spokesperson meant frequent relocations, interfering with her and her children's ability to feel rooted with a supportive network. When her spouse was home, she continued to be the default parent while he remained uninvolved in their family life. He provided financially for the family, and she served the family, unfortunately at the expense of her own needs. The classic stay-at-home mom, she was self-sacrificing, endlessly obliging, and silently suffering. Her spouse wasn't a bad father; she sang his praises when he had the energy to make an effort by occasionally cooking meals or attending the girls' soccer games. However, resentment brewed as she found herself stuck in a pattern of suppressing her loneliness until it boiled into the rage she couldn't suppress. This happened daily—sometimes multiple times per day—and hearing her kids say, "Why are you always so mad? I just wish you were happier," was the wake-up call she needed.

Alysha's parents didn't help her understand her internal world and make sense of emotions like anger, disappointment, or shame. Her childhood was average and happy enough, but the guidance she received for understanding her emotions and managing their impact was minimal. Instead, she was raised in an environment where she feared upsetting her parents, so she did everything "right." She was the quintessential good girl, stricken by perfectionism and overwhelmed by isolation.

The problem with being the "good" child is that your good behavior is not seen as a survival tactic. Parents mistakenly believe that you don't need emotional support because you're doing fine on your own. This lack of focus on the "good" child is especially true if there is a quintessential black sheep in your family. Parents are often drawn to support the children who are acting *out*—the externalizers—while largely ignoring the children who are acting *in*—the internalizers. In those family systems, parents are preoccupied with the obvious needs of the troubled child, unconsciously placing a hidden demand on the good child to maintain their good-ness and not further distress the family. If you wore the good child mask, you probably learned to internalize your fear, anger, rage, and shame to "save face" and lighten the family's load. If you're reactive like Alysha, the weight of your sacrifice may finally be catching up to you.

Alysha was stuck. She wanted to yell less, hated the fact that she constantly rejected her children's attempts to connect with her, and resented how annoyed she felt with them. She was tired of feeling like such a bad mom, yet she clung to guilt, shame, and self-punishment. How much can you expect from someone who is des-perate for—yet cut off from—the necessary support systems to survive the early years of parenthood?

Many clients and mothers in my groups are like Alysha. They are trapped inside their own minds and exhausted by how de-manding and difficult it is to make changes. My solution to this universal "stuck" feeling that we all experience from time to time was inspired by one of my favorite childhood stories, *We're Going on a Bear Hunt*. The book says, *We can't get over it. We can't go under it. We've got to go through it.* I developed the M.O.V.E. Method to teach you to move through your unconscious thoughts and feelings and transform your reactivity into intentional responsiveness. This process actively teaches you how to attune to your underlying needs, as well as the needs of your child in the moment.

The M.O.V.E. Method

The M.O.V.E. Method helps you to listen to yourself better and thus your child. Whereas the L.E.A.N. Method is a self-reflection tool, the M.O.V.E. Method is an in-the-moment tool to get you grounded more quickly. There are four action steps:

- Monitor Your Triggers
- Observe Your Thoughts
- Vary Your Perspective
- Enact Change

When you're just getting started, the M.O.V.E. Method may feel a little awkward, but it's worth the effort. It teaches you to slow down in a heated, challenging, or difficult moment so you can activate the self-reflection process and break your habitual patterns in real time.

Monitor Your Triggers: "What's Happening in My Body?"

Alysha began to realize that the moment before she exploded at her children, her heart began to race, her palms became sweaty, and she felt a heaviness in her chest. Teaching her to slow down and monitor her physical response to stress helped her to realize that these physical responses were her body's cue to slow down and listen inward. Rather than trying to shut down her children's noise so she could feel more regulated, she found it was far more powerful to make sense of the internal noise her body was alerting her to. In one week of this practice, Alysha cut in half the number of times she exploded at her kids, and over time, she ultimately reached a level of patience that she felt good about.

Listening to the wisdom of your body—like Alysha's racing heart and other physical symptoms—can give clues about what you need to regulate. Many of my clients—myself included—were not taught the skill of slowing down, listening to their bodies, recognizing physical sensations, and productively moving through stress. You may have been conditioned to look to your parents for wisdom and guidance without ever learning how to look within, let alone trust what your internal guides were communicating to you.

When you start to feel like you're beginning to get angry or are losing control, try to pause and S.I.T.:

- Slow down.
- Internally sense.
- Talk to the feeling.

This is a daily practice. Like yoga or running, if you only do it occasionally, you won't get the full benefits. It takes consistency to start a new habit, and the more comfortable you become with sitting with your own uncomfortable feelings, the easier it will be for you to S.I.T. with your child's vulnerabilities as well. To get started, I suggest that you engage in S.I.T. for five minutes daily until it becomes an automatic practice for you.

Slow down

This is perhaps the hardest part of this practice, as well as the most essential. Place your hand on your heart while breathing slowly and deliberately. Give your mind and your body a chance to settle down and get still. Once you feel settled, think about the reactive pattern or trigger you want to work on within yourself.

Internally sense these three body cues

- What emotion comes up for you?
- Where do you feel it in your body?
- Does it have any particular sensation?

Alysha noticed that yelling elicited anxiety and fear, both of which she experienced as a heavy elephant sitting on her chest. She also noted a flickering sensation around her heart, throat, and stomach.

For some people, slowing down and intuitively sensing their true emotions and physical experiences can feel overwhelming, especially if they've spent a lifetime building a dam around their vulnerabilities. If this happens to you, you can ground yourself by placing your hand over the part of your body that feels the loudest, heaviest, or most unpleasant. Then breathe deeply into that space. For Alysha, that meant placing her hand over her heart and sending her breath there. Consider this your body's way of communicating something important with you and expecting a response. Much like hunger pains, the body will scream louder until you finally answer the call.

To answer, say, "Feeling, I hear you. I'm not ignoring you. I want to understand you." If you feel angry at the feeling, frustrated with it, or eager to make it go away, then you need more time to sit with it without judgment or agenda. If you want to get the emotion to work with you—rather than against you—you need to practice honoring it, however it shows up. When you honor the emotion, it usually softens and becomes open to change.

Alysha knew she felt curious and open to her sensation when she was able to say effortlessly, "Anxiety, I hear you. Fear, I'm not ignoring you. I'm not afraid of you. I want to understand you."

Talk to the feeling

Ask the following questions, but do not force any answers—let them come to you.

- "Feeling, what's your biggest worry or fear?"

- "Feeling, how are you trying to protect me?"

- "Feeling, what are you trying to teach me?"

If you do not get a response, that's okay. Sometimes the emotion or sensation is not ready, so be prepared to accept that from time to time. When you do get a response, listen with the intention to understand and to honor, not to fix or to change. Most likely these questions will lead you to deep insight into your subconscious mind.

When Alysha asked anxiety what its biggest fear was, she told me what she learned: "It's afraid that I'm failing and I'm not a good enough mom." She inquired further about anxiety's attempt to protect her. The message she received was, "If I'm not hard on you, then you'll keep being an asshole. Don't you see? I'm protecting you from messing up your daughter."

Alysha was moved by what anxiety wanted to teach her. Anxiety said, "I want you to still feel good, even when you're messing up." Every time Alysha overreacted to her children, the spirit of anxiety visited her to help her expand in self-compassion, kindness, and accountability. Repeated emotions and sensations are your invitation to grow and develop your capacities for self-compassion and grace. The more Alysha committed to this practice, the easier it became for her to monitor her triggers in the moment with her kids: she connected her racing heart and heavy chest to feeling anxious and scared. She needed reassurance that she was good even if she wasn't perfect. She started telling herself that everything could be repaired, and she finally learned not to sweat every little misstep.

Becoming more intimately involved with your internal experience in this way—and treating it with the respect, compassion, and curiosity it deserves—gives you an edge when it comes to raising your children. The more you learn to sit with what makes you uncomfortable, the more organic it becomes for you to help your child learn to do the same.

Observe Your Thoughts: "What's My Automatic Thought in This Moment?"

Just like you can teach your body new ways to respond to stress, you can teach your mind new ways to interpret whatever stress you encounter. Stress responses are how you've learned to cope with the pain of life. For example, a parent who overdramatizes a situation when nothing serious has occurred will usually teach their child to do the same.

These stress thoughts also feed your wounded inner child narrative. Let's say as a child you concluded that you were on your own. You believed that everyone you cared for always deserted you. It didn't matter how good you were or how lovable you attempted to be. Now, as an adult, you find yourself engaging in black-and-white stress thoughts. When your children reject you, you think, *My kids don't want anything to do with me.* Without self-awareness, you may repeat this belief in your mind, which simultaneously conditions your body to brace for impact.

The following chart lists some of the most common stress thoughts. Once you identify your common stress thought patterns, try becoming more aware of them throughout the day—but resist the urge to judge them as being right or wrong. Recognize them as an indication that you're feeling stressed about something and you're trying to cope with the stress. When you think, *Gosh, I'm feeling stressed*, your body reacts differently compared with, *You suck, you promised you wouldn't lose your temper and there you go again!*

Stress Thought	What It Is	Example
Highlight the Negative	An automatic focus on something negative while ignoring the positive, especially when there are plenty of positives to attend to or acknowledge.	You have a wonderful day with your child, but because bedtime was challenging, your whole day is ruined.
Overdramatizing	Magnifying a situation so intensely that you imagine the worst-case scenario has happened or will happen, despite there being little to no evidence for it.	You worry that a single fight with your partner will lead to divorce.
Black and White	Responding to stress with absolutes like "always" and "never."	You are always failing your kids. Your kids never listen to you.
What If-ing	Asking "What if" to predict the future by projecting your worries outward.	*What if my child does drugs? What if I've messed them up? What if they don't like being around me?*

Stress Thought	What It Is	Example
Martyrdom	Expecting your self-sacrifice to be rewarded and acknowledged and then harboring resentment when it isn't. This is an especially common pattern in women.	You are tapped out but refuse to ask for help. You convince yourself that you should just do it all because everyone else seems to. You run yourself ragged before you ask anyone to notice your needs.

Becoming a careful observer of your stress thoughts and the resultant behavior opens you up to the opportunity to transform your old way of thinking to a new perspective. Your goal is not to eliminate this habit but to identify what is happening in the moment. With this insight, you can then shift your perspective to a service thought.

Vary Your Perspective: "Is There Another Way to See This?"

Once you understand how your body and your mind react to stress, the next step is to ask yourself, *Is there another way to see this situation?* Research suggests that being able to reframe our unhelpful stress thoughts to a more supportive perspective will help reduce anxiety. Varying your perspective is key to healing your wounded inner child narratives and breaking cycles that keep you feeling stuck.

There are many perspectives from which you can unpack any stressful encounter. Your job is to see the situation through as many lenses as you can. For example, if you're quarreling with your child, use these three lenses to understand the situation more deeply:

- How do you view the situation?
- How might your child view the situation?
- How might a fly on the wall view the situation?

A service thought—unlike a stress thought—gives you a more nuanced, solution-oriented way of understanding a problem. Think about ways you can actively shift any stress thought into a service thought.

Stress Thought	Initial Perspective	Service Thought
Highlight the Negative	*This whole night was ruined because it took him forever to fall asleep.*	*He needed me a little more tonight. It was frustrating, but we had a really fun day. Maybe he wasn't ready for it to end.*
Overdramatizing	*My child has a fever. They are probably going to get really sick. What if they start having seizures like the child next door?*	*My child has a fever. I'm feeling worried about how to handle this. I'm going to reach out to the pediatrician for guidance.*

Stress Thought	Initial Perspective	Service Thought
Black and White	*My child never shares. He is always so possessive on the playground.*	*My child is still learning how to share. He hasn't quite mastered this skill yet.*
What If-ing	*My child just told me to go away. What if they grow up to not like being around me?*	*Something must be happening inside for my child. I'm also noticing my fear of rejection. I need to attend to both, but separately.*
Martyrdom	"Look how much I do for you. No one appreciates me."	*I keep giving with the expectation that others will give back to me. Instead, I need to focus on taking what I need so I can sustain this.*

To better track your stress thoughts and to discover ways to transform them, use your journal to make a note of different assumptions and beliefs you catch yourself thinking throughout the day. Then, see if you can determine what type of stress thought it is (it's okay to create your own names based on whatever is the most comfortable). Finally, imagine alternative ways you can view the situation. If you're really stuck, work with your therapist or a trusted friend in your social circle for more guidance and support.

When you can see your situation in a different light, the door opens for you to not only reframe the situation in your mind but to also make changes in how you respond to the situation.

Enact Change: "How Do I Want to Respond Now?"

Once you have a new perspective on the stressful situation, you can ask yourself, *How do I want to respond now?* This is an empowering position. Rather than your default reaction triggering dysregulation and unconscious stress thoughts, you can now thoughtfully examine the choices you have.

Kerry, a middle-aged mom, felt seriously challenged by her six-year-old daughter's behavior. Tiffany frequently berated her mom with insults you'd expect from an angsty adolescent.

"She says things to me like, 'Shut up you sh*tface,' and 'I don't have to listen to you,'" Kerry reported. In response Kerry would understandably shut down, allowing defeat and helplessness to take over her entire being. Then Tiffany, hypersensitive to feeling rejected, escalated even more when adults retreated from her. They were trapped in a vicious cycle.

Kerry believed she was being abused by her child. But as I showed her through our work together, she was actually projecting her own wounded inner child narrative onto Tiffany. Kerry's own father had often verbally accosted her as a child, getting angry and dressing her down for even minor infractions. As a result, Kerry tried to be "perfect" as a child, even as her resentment had grown. She learned to minimize her emotions. To survive, she had to be as small as possible. Now that she was a mother herself, Kerry was playing the only parent role she knew: she was repeating her part in the cycle. She wanted her daughter to be "perfect," and when she wasn't, Tiffany lashed out and Kerry played dead to survive the pain. Therapy was not only about helping Tiffany find more acceptable ways to express herself; it was also about helping Kerry make her wounded inner child whole. Here's what the M.O.V.E. Method accomplished for Kerry in our work together:

- **Monitor Her Triggers:** When Tiffany went on one of her rampages, Kerry's body went limp and lifeless. She felt defeated and afraid.

- **Observe Her Thoughts:** Kerry automatically thought, *I don't deserve this. She should treat me with respect. She always acts out when I ask her to cooperate. There's nothing I can do.*

- **Vary Her Perspective:** *I'm not my father. Perfection isn't necessary. My child is still learning to cooperate. And I'm still learning how to show up for her when I'm triggered.*

- **Enact Change:** Kerry learned to support Tiffany's emotions while still holding clear boundaries around her behaviors: "You are allowed to feel angry and upset. I'm not okay with you screaming at me. How can I help you calm your body so we can talk about what's bothering you?" As Kerry made these changes consistently, Tiffany's behavior also improved. She found more productive ways to get her needs met, and they built more relational security together.

Like Kerry, you can gain the skills to take a closer look at the patterns of behavior that drive the way you interact with your children. Once you establish the habit of recognizing your triggers, tuning in to your automatic inner voice, acknowledging your emotional reactions without judgment, and treating yourself with compassion, you are on your way to breaking cycles and discovering a healing way to be with your children.

CHAPTER 4

• • • • • •

The Beauty of
Boundaries

MBER—A MOTHER OF FIVE CHILDREN AND A CHRONIC PEOPLE pleaser—was asked to bring her friend's kids to and from school for a few weeks while her friend went on vacation. Amber wanted to help her friend, but she was overloaded and on the brink of burnout. But like any good people pleaser, Amber reluctantly agreed, although in her heart she knew she would resent her friend for it.

"I feel like she's asking me because I must be the only person who can help her," said Amber. "But I'm so exhausted and I really don't think I have it in me to do this."

Amber had grown up in a family environment where telling an adult (or anyone, for that matter) no was a punishable crime. She had learned to always say yes with a smile, even if she was seething in rage. She bottled it all up, worked hard in school, and climbed out of a life that seemed destined for self-destruction. When I met her, things seemed to be going great—she had a loving marriage, beautiful kids, and a wide circle of friends who appreciated her. Who wouldn't appreciate Amber? If anyone ever needed anything—a last-minute volunteer to step in at school, a neighbor to water your lawn—Amber would be there. She was reliable, beloved . . . and quietly seething.

Amber feared saying no in any context would have catastrophic consequences. So she never did, and she got busier and more resentful at every turn. By the time her friend came to her with the seemingly innocent carpool request, she was at a breaking point.

How did she get there? Amber had moved a lot as a kid, she explained to me, and she'd had limited opportunities to make long-term friendships. In her experience, that meant that all friendships were fragile. If a relationship broke down, it would be her fault. Plagued with loneliness and longing for meaningful friendships, she concluded that being a good friend meant always agreeing to others' requests, even if doing so meant making herself uncomfortable. She became the yes-woman in her circle of adult friends, but she had secretly vowed never to ask anyone to support *her* in any material or substantial way. Her relationships were becoming increasingly one-sided, and she was ready for a much-needed upgrade.

Amber was struggling with communicating her boundaries. When I suggested that she let her friend know that she wasn't available to do carpool for several weeks, given that she already had so much caretaking on her plate already, she began to panic. She noticed her racing heart, her sweaty palms, and her desire to shift her position, signaling that sitting with discomfort was an awkward but important exercise. She observed that her mind was polluted with extremes and what-ifs: *What if she never wants to talk to me again because I backed out? What if she can't go on her vacation and it's all my fault?*

I challenged her to vary her perspective on these thoughts. Her feeling of anxiety was real and informed by a past where it was futile to say what she needed. But her thoughts on this specific situation were not valid. Eventually she settled on trusting that if this friend were a good friend, she would appreciate Amber speaking up and would not end the friendship just because Amber was honest about her personal limitations. Enacting change and trying something new means taking a risk. With some encouragement, Amber chose herself.

Amber told her friend clearly, compassionately, and respectfully: "I know I agreed to do the morning and after-school carpool while you were on vacation, but unfortunately, I don't have the capacity to do it now. I know it might disappoint you to hear this. I really value our friendship, and I hope that you can understand where I'm coming from." Amber was surprised when her friend responded affirmatively and lovingly. Not only did she confirm that she had other people she could ask, but she thanked Amber for reminding her to be more mindful of others' circumstances before asking such a huge favor of them. This was a turning point for Amber: she had been honest about what she needed, and it had been received without any sign of condemnation.

Like Amber, if you put in the practice, you will also learn that better boundaries lead to deeper connections. Parenting yourself first is about carefully tending to your inner needs, healing what feels broken inside, and growing around the wounds that keep you imprisoned in the past. Boundaries are how you bridge the gap between how you were conditioned to think and behave and the desires your healing work has revealed to you. To take your healing work to the next level, you cannot be afraid to state your needs clearly, compassionately, and respectfully. And you must learn to release your fear of disappointing others.

This chapter will not teach you how to sever contact with any boundary pushers in your life. I recognize that there are circumstances where that's necessary. This chapter will support you in your more functional relationships, but if you are no contact with family members or feel you must go no contact, please discuss your goals and needs with a licensed mental health professional.

What Is a Boundary?

A big misconception about boundaries is that they are intended to control another person's behavior. Nope. If you are creating them to control another person—friend, family member, partner, or child—then your boundaries won't be successful. A boundary that seeks to control another isn't a healthy boundary; it's setting yourself up for codependency. Perhaps, for example, you're tired of your mom's constant criticisms of how you're not living up to her expectations. You decide to stop calling her and give the bare minimum when she calls you. This is not a boundary. You're giving her the cold shoulder and a light version of the silent treatment. Eventually, she'll notice, and she'll try to get you back into your normal dynamic—where you're the canvas for her projections of insecurity. Pretty soon, you'll fulfill your original role: the unwilling container for *her* unprocessed shame and blame, all of which has now seeped into your identity. The cycle begins again.

Boundaries, by contrast, are clear statements about what you will and will not tolerate and how your behavior will change if someone violates your limits. When you set a boundary with someone you care about, imagine that you're drawing a bridge between the two of you. While you may stand on opposite sides, the boundary says, "This is how I'm willing to stay connected with you." Healthy boundaries allow you to feel safe in relationship with others. They aren't intended to change others or make other people "better" for you; rather, a healthy boundary will change how *you* show up in the relationship.

Boundaries express your needs and your personal limits.

Rather than giving Mom the cold shoulder and appearing disinterested when interacting with her, you could let her know, "Mom, I'm not okay with all the critiquing of my life choices. It hurts me to think that you're disappointed with how I'm living my life. I'm happy with where I'm at, and when I need your guidance, I will ask you." This approach requires significant vulnerability. It's so much easier to bottle it up, ignore the problem entirely, and pretend that you'll deal with it later. However, the latter approach won't lead you to a better relationship. Healthy relationships aren't afraid to have hard conversations. Telling someone you love that they're hurting you isn't always easy, especially if they're not used to you being assertive. But when you approach relationships this way, you learn how to have healthy, reparative relationships with others.

The first time you set a boundary, be prepared for pushback. In the previous example, your mom may put herself at the center of the discussion: "You think this is bad? You should have grown up with Nana. I had it way worse. At least I care about you. She didn't care about how I turned out." She's trying to pull you back into the dynamic you unconsciously agreed to many decades ago, whether that's a caretaking role in which you apologize and bow to your queen, a fighting role in which you compete against each other for the title of "The Biggest Sufferer," or anything in between. Don't take the bait. Train yourself to see the reaction for what it is: a shame response from someone tormented by emotional immaturity.

How People Respond to Boundaries

How someone reacts to your boundary says more about them than it does about you. I encourage you to trust in the division of responsibility for boundary setting—you set them, and they react to them. When you set a boundary from a place of self-worth and feel compassion and respect for the other person, you are not responsible for how they react. However, when my clients begin their boundary work, they worry:

- They will be angry with me.
- They will hate me.
- Maybe I'm a terrible person.
- They won't like me anymore.
- They're going to think I'm difficult.
- What's wrong with me? Why can't I just go along with it?
- What if I'm hurting my kids by having a boundary with this person who's hurting me?
- Maybe they're right . . . I'm the problem.

If you've spent your life being conditioned to carry the weight of someone else's emotional immaturity, it makes sense that you would continue to feel responsible for their behavior. Unfortunately, you have zero control over how other people will receive your boundary. Your only job is to clearly state what you need compassionately and respectfully, so that you can feel safe, authentic, and connected to the other person rather than insecure, fake, and resentful.

Boundary reactors tend to express their shame by minimizing your needs and personal limits. They use defense mechanisms like name-calling, attacking, dismissing, and rejecting your claims to try to avoid accountability for their impact on you. Most people who do this aren't necessarily intentionally trying to harm you (unless they are true narcissists). Their behavior is unconsciously driven by their desire to avoid discomfort. But that doesn't mean you need to tolerate being on the receiving end of someone's emotional immaturity. You can cultivate compassion for them while simultaneously detaching from any expectations that they will change. This may also enable you to be clearer and more consistent with the boundaries you choose to uphold.

You know someone is pushing your boundaries when they scoff or mock you with statements like:

- You're no fun anymore.
- All this boundary stuff is stupid. You need to let it go.
- You think you're above us now, don't you?
- Stop acting like I'm the problem. Maybe you should look in the mirror.
- If you don't like it, then leave.
- Stop acting like that. I'm not doing anything wrong.
- After all I've done for you, and this is how you repay me?
- What's wrong with you?
- Why are you trying to ruin our good time?
- Get over it.
- No one can take a joke anymore, jeez!

You don't have to tolerate this behavior. But to send a clear message, you will need to follow through with a direct consequence. Using the earlier example, you can try telling your mom that it hurts when she criticizes you and that you will seek her guidance when you need it. Be prepared for her to push back. She might try to gain your pity by sharing her sob story about how hard it was for her growing up, a subtle but meaningful way boundary reactors avoid the responsibility of pushing your limits without much regard for you. Do not try to reason with your mom or convince her that she is doing the same thing to you that her mother did to her. (Unless she's in individual therapy, she won't see the parallel, and your efforts will be wasted.) Instead, reiterate your boundary and send a clear message: "Mom, I love you, and this is not up for discussion. Excuse me." Then walk away. She may roll her eyes with a sigh of disgust. But this is how she's releasing *her* shame. You don't have to pick up that shame! When you disengage from the argument and create physical distance, you can start to cultivate your own emotional safety. That's the beauty of boundaries.

Boundaries Have a Learning Curve

People may not respect your boundaries immediately, especially if you eventually cave in to their demands or apologize for how your boundaries have affected them emotionally. (All that teaches them is that they get to keep pushing back at your boundaries for longer!) Give *yourself* time to learn how to confidently state your boundaries, and give *others* time to learn how to not take those boundaries so personally. The people in your life who love you and care about you don't want to hurt you.

It will take time for others to understand that they must respect your boundaries. When someone who has never faced boundaries in a relationship is faced with them for the first time, they're going to mess up. It's natural, and it's okay. You don't have to cut off communication with someone entirely because they messed up a few times. If someone crosses a line, you can reiterate your boundary—in the same way that when your children make mistakes you continue to reiterate the same message until they get it. We give our children opportunities to learn because we love them and we want to be in a relationship with them. We also want to teach them how to be in a relationship with us. When it comes to other relationships in our lives, because we love those people and want to make those relationships work, we've got to put in the effort of having uncomfortable conversations so we can build a bridge of safe connections between us.

Continue giving the people you love opportunities to practice learning how to respect your personal needs and limitations. You'll soon recognize the boundary pushers who won't make any effort for real change because they'll routinely humiliate you, degrade you, put you down for having boundaries, or resort to the emotionally immature responses described earlier. If this continues to be a problem and they take no accountability or make any attempt to change, you may determine that you've put more work in this relationship than you're willing to. You may decide to end the relationship. If you get to that place, then at least you know you tried. They may not understand, but in your heart, you can feel good about your efforts. You can disconnect, grieve the loss, and surround yourself with relationships that have a healthy give-and-take.

How to Set a Boundary

Learning how to set and hold boundaries is a way of life, which means the more you practice it, the more confident you will become. Boundary work is much more fulfilling when you're doing it with others who are on a similar journey, but don't wait for them to get started on your own healing path.

1. **Do not apologize for someone's reaction to your boundaries.** Let them learn to be with their own discomfort.

2. Be accountable for your own dysfunctional behavior. If you yell, tease, or are passive-aggressive when you communicate a boundary, it's going to be difficult for them to hear you and respect that limitation. If you do communicate out of anger, make a point to call yourself out and take steps to resolve it. Accountability is an essential part of healthy boundaries. This is important modeling for your children and will normalize that owning our mistakes helps relationships feel safe and more connected.

3. Do not engage in fights. Disagreements and respectful conflicts are acceptable. But when things get nasty, make a point to disengage and focus on regulating yourself (and protecting your children, if applicable). If excessive immature fighting is a chronic problem, especially within your intimate relationships, discuss this with a licensed mental health professional for a clear path forward.

4. Avoid giving long, drawn-out explanations. Many of us feel we must give too much information when we're setting a boundary, especially about topics we've already litigated time and time again. Such as: "Dad, I've already told you, I'm not comfortable with you making comments about the children's weight. When you did that to me as a kid, it made me feel self-conscious. So, I'm asking you nicely not to damage them with such remarks." Rather than attempting to convince someone that their behavior is harmful for you, just be simple and clear: "Dad, I'm not okay with comments about the children's weight. Kids, let's go outside and play." Then leave.

5. Establish a boundary quickly. Particularly with long-term relationships, you soon know when the conversation starts to veer into uncomfortable or unsafe territory. If you wait too long, anger, resentment, and/or your wounds may begin to take over, which won't allow you to communicate your boundaries in a clear, compassionate, and respectful way.

6. **Do not beg or plead with someone to respect your boundaries.** If they aren't willing to find a way to work with you, then they do not value your relationship (most likely because they're still learning how to value themselves). This may be tough to hear, especially if you're struggling with a significant relationship, like with a parent or a spouse. But you are not someone's punching bag. You deserve just as much respect and honor as you give to those around you.

7. **No obligations.** Your time is your most precious resource, and none of us knows exactly how much time we are allotted in this lifetime. Spend it how you desire and with whom you desire. If you feel obligated to see someone, reflect on that sense of obligation. Where is it coming from for you? Is it a personal wound? Or is it a relational wound that needs repairing? Get clear on this.

8. **Role-play your boundaries with someone you trust.** This practice will help you learn to use your words in more stressful moments. This is particularly true for anyone with a pattern toward people pleasing, who may find saying no or initiating any kind of disagreement stressful and difficult. Rehearsing can help you become more confident with your boundary-setting skills.

9. **Live your life according to what makes you feel good about yourself.** When you feel good about what you're

doing, you'll spend less time worrying about whether others approve of you. You'll stop looking for approval externally and navigate the world knowing that you're not only enough as you are but have so much goodness to offer the world around you. You'll encourage others to do the same for themselves. This is not selfish, as you may have been conditioned to believe. This is self-honoring work that is necessary to approach your relationships in more healed ways.

How Outside Pressure Impacts Your Boundaries

Crystal, a stay-at-home mom, is devoted to parenting in a supportive, available way for her children. But every year around the holidays, she finds herself dreading family gatherings. She adores her family, but she doesn't love the judgment she receives for parenting differently from everybody else.

"They're always commenting on the choices I make," says Crystal. "Like, they think I'm being too controlling because I want to get them to bed on time. But they don't have to deal with the meltdowns the next day. I do."

Crystal is careful about communicating boundaries with her kids in a clear, consistent, and connected way while also taking the time to be warm, loving, and playful. Her family is less intentional about how they interact with their children. Yelling, insults, and punishments are the norm. Her family also loves drama, but Crystal is desperately trying to escape her past and find more inner peace and calm. She often feels mandated to participate in the family drama and accept their criticisms without objection.

Crystal hates spending her time like this, but every year she caves to the pressure and agrees to attend. Instead of being a joyful experience, each gathering leaves her feeling salty and resentful.

She needs confidence with unapologetically asserting her needs and setting some clear boundaries. But this, of course, is easier said than done.

Every year, bedtime for the little ones is a constant source of friction. Although her family members don't see a problem with keeping their children up late, Crystal wants her kids on a predictable sleep schedule (for everyone's sanity). When she told her family that her young children, ages three, five, and six, struggle with staying up late and she'd like to open presents at the beginning of their gathering rather than the end, she felt pressure from her family members.

"Why would you rob them of this great tradition?" her mother said. "We've always opened gifts at the end of the party!" Crystal was worried this would escalate into a larger issue, and she hated to be the "difficult" one. Guilt-tripped, she caved—and sure enough, her children didn't handle the late evening well. The next day, she was left to care for emotionally dysregulated and sleep-deprived kids. She sighed as she recounted it to me: "Why don't I just listen to myself?!"

Crystal, like many of my clients, has been programmed to prioritize the needs of others at the expense of her own. When you're anxious to please, fearful of disappointing others, or conflict-avoidant, you learn to make yourself uncomfortable to allow others to feel more comfortable. You learn to sacrifice yourself out of obligation rather than out of generosity, love, and a sincere desire to serve. Family gatherings at any time of the year often highlight that healthy boundaries are an area of growth for most of us.

Had Crystal set a compassionate boundary, she may have felt a little better the next day: "I know it's disappointing that we'll have to leave by 9:00 p.m., but if you're open to moving the gift-opening tradition a little earlier, we'd love to participate." Even if her family pushes back with more criticism and guilt, part of Crystal's boundary work relies on her releasing all expectations that they will change their behavior to meet her needs. People usually make changes when it benefits them. If her family was to continue to pressure her, she could simply end the conversation with "We've discussed this. Let's find something else to talk about now." Don't get me wrong—I'm not discounting how incredibly hard it is to maintain composure and poise when confronting someone in this way. But until you start insisting that your needs are as important as everyone else's, others won't know to prioritize you in the way that you truly desire.

Why Boundary Work Is Hard

My first encounter with boundary work was when my therapist, Dr. Hanna, asked me, long before I ever had children, "What will you do to protect your children from the dysfunction of your family?" Oof.

With growth comes pain, and what I discovered in my own journey was that boundaries disrupt the order that you had previously (and unconsciously) established with another person. When things get shaken up, the natural instinct is to fall back on old patterns. This is why setting boundaries feels the hardest with the people we've known the longest: our relational patterns are set, and the system reacts to change by trying to return to what we know. Do you ever feel like your teenage self when you're back in your childhood home with your parents and siblings? Then you know what I mean. With those kinds of long-standing relationships, everyone prefers to assume familiar routines and roles.

Many of us were raised in the traditional parenting paradigm. Spanking and other punishments were the norm, our parents did not apologize to us, children were seen but not heard, and we were expected to do exactly as we were told. But now, as parents ourselves, we've decided to parent differently. Instead of spanking and other punishments, we're teaching our children about their emotions and setting limits in a clear, consistent, and connected way. We apologize when we make a mistake, and we see our children as valuable contributors to the family.

This decision to parent differently from how we were raised threatens the status quo of our family of origin. When you're not physically together, their remarks aren't as bothersome, and you can focus on your day-to-day life and forget about their opinions. When you're physically together, you may not be seen as a full-grown, autonomous adult. You may still be seen as a child and are expected to follow suit with the family's preestablished order: *Do as you're told.*

Bringing new ideas, beliefs, and boundaries to the system is a big no-no. You are seen as being "out of line," because you're not punishing your kids and instead are helping them process their problems. You are a disruptor, but in a positive way. However, the system itself is aggravated by your audacity to question your family's way of doing things and find your own way through parenthood. Who do you think you are?

You might be hit with critical comments: "You're spoiling your children!" "You think you're better than us." "This style of parenting is terrible—you'll see." "Your kid is a brat, and it's all because of you." They aren't retaliating because they believe these things about you. They're retaliating because on a deep, unconscious level, they want to feel validated in their own decisions, even if that means attacking you. They want to conserve the past and resist change. And this is why boundary setting can sometimes feel so daunting and repetitive.

How to S.E.T. a Boundary

I've come up with an easy-to-remember guideline to help you S.E.T. a boundary. You'll know that you need to S.E.T. a boundary if

- You feel saying no would not be acceptable.
- You feel you're saying yes out of obligation or a need to please.
- You're feeling pressured to do something you don't want to do, don't have time to do, or are unable to do.
- You're scared that someone might continue to behave in ways that hurt you if you don't S.E.T. a boundary.

How you word your boundaries can vary across topics, family style, and cultural backgrounds, and so rather than providing scripts that might not work for everyone, I've developed some guidelines that can help you feel confident, clear, and connected in your boundary-setting style.

S: State what you need clearly with any necessary limits. This can be done simply by starting your boundary with "I need," "I'd prefer," "I'm not okay with," or "This doesn't work for me."

E: Express compassion. Boundary work is more effective when you lead from your heart and express an understanding of where the other person may be coming from: "I hear you," "I appreciate you," "I know this is important to you."

<u>T</u>: **Treat with respect.** Your delivery matters, so be mindful of your tone, attitude, and energy when you set your boundary. A hint of defensiveness can invite someone to push back.

Consider this a framework for creating a boundary that builds a bridge and not a wall. The S.E.T. framework can play out in a number of different ways in many common scenarios.

Jenny said that since they had their second child, her partner's life hasn't changed as drastically as hers. Resentment took over as she silently kept score of all the ways his needs were prioritized and all the days she went without any real time for herself. When he casually mentioned a three-day golf trip after just returning home from a two-week-long work conference, she could have taken her anger out passive-aggressively. Instead, she chose to set a clear, compassionate, and respectful boundary: "It doesn't work for me to have you gone for another few days after you were away for two weeks. I need more support." They found a way to make sure that both of their needs were considered.

Gina was distraught that her partner continued to yell at their children despite their regular conversations about self-regulation. She was beginning to doubt if their partnership would work. David was a trauma survivor and was actively working on shouting less, but it wasn't always working—and Gina was getting fed up. She needed to set clear boundaries around his behavior, which was having a negative effect on her and their children. Gina repeated this boundary consistently: "It's hard for me to hear you yelling at the kids, so I'm going to ask you to please stop. I can take over and give you a moment to cool off." At first, David's shame wounds consumed him as he pushed back on her need for more emotional stability in the home. With time, he learned to accept her boundary as a peace offering, and they both learned how to effectively support each other, even when they weren't at their best.

My husband struggles with my direct, no-nonsense, East Coast Italian style of communication. Apparently, I'm not the most generous with my compliments and am more likely to notice what he's doing wrong rather than what he's doing right. No surprises there, given how little positive feedback I heard about myself in my own home growing up. In a vulnerable moment, he set a boundary with me: "I don't like it when you speak down to me. I need you to notice my efforts more and find a better way to share any criticisms you have of me. Remember, I'm doing my best."

Ugh. Talk about a gut punch. It hurt to hear this. I wanted to fight back: "You're asking me to do something that is completely unnatural for me!" But I knew that was coming from a place of inadequacy. I felt like a pretty crappy wife. Especially because he had to tell me this . . . an embarrassing number of times. Eventually, I had to swallow my pride and make an effort to honor his boundary. Like anyone, he deserves emotional safety, and I'm capable of learning new things.

How to H.O.L.D. a Boundary

Boundary reactors are people who respond negatively to your boundary but ultimately back off. Boundary pushers, on the other hand, not only react negatively to your boundary, but they will continue to push back on your limits until you relent. You don't have to give in to boundary pushers. If your boundaries are challenged, you can maintain them gracefully and assertively. Here's how to H.O.L.D. a boundary even under pressure.

H: Honor their feelings. How they feel is how they feel. "I hear you" and "I can understand where you're coming from" are powerful statements to disarm a boundary pusher.

O: Offer an out. Let the boundary pusher know that there will be a consequence if they continue to violate your boundaries. This consequence may be that you'll leave or you'll ask them to leave:

"If you're going to drink like this for our entire visit, I'm going to have to ask you to please leave."

"She said she's not open to a hug. Please give her some time to warm up to you, or else we'll have to get going."

"Again, we don't use stigmatizing language like that, especially in front of the kids. If it happens again, we'll have to end the visit."

L: Limit dysfunctional behavior. Honoring emotions does not mean excusing misbehavior. If someone continues to overreact in ways that make you feel uncomfortable, be explicit about what they're doing that's a problem for you and let them know a better way to connect.

"I can see you're heated. I'm not okay with all this yelling. Please stop, or we will have to get going."

"I hear that you're disappointed we must go. I get it. I'm not okay with feeling guilt-tripped about it. Please stop so we can enjoy the rest of the night."

"I love you. But I'm not okay with where this conversation is going. So, I'm going to end it. We can try to talk about this another time."

D: Don't take responsibility for their reaction. Their reaction says much more about their state of mind than it does yours. You can't get anyone to stop a behavior unless they are willing to do it themselves. Holding the boundary with crystal-clear intentions is important for keeping the bridge of connection open between you and someone else.

Relationships that are healthy or that have the capacity for health will eventually learn to accept your boundary. Those people will stop feeling offended by your needs and will learn to make room for you, especially when your requests are reasonable.

· · · · · ·

IF THE BOUNDARIES WERE BLURRED IN YOUR UPBRINGING, THIS work will feel foreign at first, but it will ultimately have a positive impact on everyone in your life . . . especially your children. The more you S.E.T. and H.O.L.D. your boundaries confidently, clearly, compassionately, and respectfully, the more support they will have with building healthy bridges of connection in their future relationships.

If you feel obligated to stay connected to someone, that's a good sign that you either need stronger boundaries or you've outgrown the relationship. Just because someone is a blood relative doesn't mean that you owe them your time. Others may not always be on the same healing wavelength as you, and one thing I've learned on my boundary journey is that not all relationships are built for a lifetime. If you're not happy with the way others are treating you, continue healing your inner critic so you can change how you relate to you. From this more centered, grounded, and aligned place, you can build beautiful bridges of connection with relationships that have an equal balance of give-and-take.

Empower yourself to assert your needs with confidence, compassion, and respect (for everyone involved, yourself included).

Your boundaries do not need to come with an explanation; "This is what I need" or "Please respect my request" is sufficient.

By adapting the S.E.T. and H.O.L.D. frameworks, you can avoid the guilt-shame rabbit hole that keeps you stuck in failure and in-adequacy. It's a crucial step for interrupting this and other dys-functional patterns, and I bet that you'll discover, as many clients have, that most people are not as opposed to your boundaries as you've imagined they would be. Although they may be unfamiliar with certain boundaries, or triggered at times by your requests, most people in your life love you and want you to feel honored and loved by them. Your boundaries are the bridge to teaching them exactly how to do that.

PART TWO

· · · · · ·

Caring for the Child in Front of You

CHAPTER 5

· · · · · ·

Cultivating the Connection Garden

I N PART ONE, YOU LEARNED HOW TO UNDERSTAND AND ATTEND to the needs of the child within you. Now, you are going to do that same work with—and for—the child in front of you.

Bentley was a five-year-old ray of sunshine who struggled with destructive, intense, all-consuming meltdowns. According to her parents, Lindsay and Ryan, she was defiant, bossy, and overly emotional "for attention." When I spoke with Ryan, he recounted the frustration he and his wife felt about the situation.

"Nothing is ever easy with Bentley," he said. "It's a miracle if we get out the door in the morning without a total breakdown. Our house is pure chaos most of the time. We are pretty sick of it."

Lindsay and Ryan had done everything in their parenting tool kit to get Bentley to change, including punishments, consequences, removing privileges, time-outs, and spanking. Nothing was curbing her behavior. And their relationship—the one between Bentley and her parents—was really suffering.

Bentley's challenging behaviors had sucked up all the joy, spontaneity, creativity, and playfulness out of parenting. Bentley acted out, her parents felt triggered and isolated by her behavior, and then they blamed Bentley for their family's troubles. When parents and children struggle to bond like this, I call it a Connection Desert—both parties are parched for love and attention, but they're lost and thirsty, without a map. They need to be reoriented and refocused on what really matters: one another.

Why We Struggle with Connection

You know you grew up in a Connection Desert if you were told repeatedly to stop acting out for attention, felt an underlying sense of loneliness, were expected to figure things out on your own, were neglected, were consistently belittled for desiring something, or were subjected to constant criticisms and rejections. Perhaps you felt like connection was something that only happened in movies or TV shows, but the reality of your family life appeared starkly empty and detached.

In the Connection Desert, children are left to navigate the harsh terrain alone, without the guidance and support of attentive parents. The lack of emotional nourishment leaves them feeling emotionally abandoned and unseen, activating the inner child wounding process and perpetuating limiting beliefs that they are not lovable, not wanted, and not enough.

A Connection Desert becomes a breeding ground for transactional relationships. Children may learn that their worth is tied to their accomplishments and how well they comply with their parents' demands. Sadly, conditional affection becomes an oasis in this thirsty land, as was the case for my adult client Anita.

Anita struggled to process her resentment toward her parents, because they had done their best and she didn't recall them behaving in any seriously traumatizing ways. Despite this, she remembered her childhood as lonely, full of pressure to "be good," to not make mistakes, and to make her parents proud. She felt their love the most when she was responsible and serving *their* ideas of who she needed to be. But when she faltered (or when she dared to assert her own ideas of what she should do or who she should be), they were quick to withhold praise and affection until she found her way back into their good graces. If children like Anita have to wear a mask to get their need for connection met, they will.

"When my parents were separating, my grades started to drop," Anita remembers. "But it was like, no one was tuned in. My dad came down super hard on me and told me I couldn't stay on the basketball team if I didn't get my grades up. He refused to understand that I'd already lost so much, and if I lost the team, I lost my friends. As long as I looked good on paper, it didn't matter to him what I was really feeling inside. I know he just wanted the best for me, but I needed his love and support, not his reprimands."

The Connection Desert is also a breeding ground for repeating dysfunctional or problematic family patterns. Despite her challenging behavioral issues, Bentley could not be blamed for the family's distress. There were myriad factors, including both parents' feelings of isolation as they struggled to balance work and family life. There was a chronic sense of loneliness between them, amplified by the fact that they both came from Connection Deserts of their own. Bentley witnessed Lindsay and Ryan's daily fights over the smallest of conflicts. From her perspective, she was simply mimicking what was being modeled for her, because any source of connection—even when it was out of anger and contempt—was better than no connection at all.

A child who is acting out is screaming with their body, *Help me! Connect with me! I can't do this alone!* This is a shift from traditional models that label "attention-seeking" behavior as bad and encourage parents to ignore the behavior. We push children deeper into the Connection Desert by ignoring their calls for support. Longing for the emotional connection they need to flourish can lead them to look for it in self-sabotaging ways.

Lindsay was great at self-sabotage. Having grown up in a Connection Desert, she learned early on that being a good girl who never burdened anybody was vital for her survival, so she pushed others away and became hyper-independent. When she became a parent, she worried about burdening Ryan by asking for too much support—so she didn't ask, further isolating her from the emotional connection she craved. Lindsay was the mom who always brought the home-baked cookies on snack day. She insisted that her older daughter (Bentley's sister), Juniper, always looked perfectly dressed (just like Lindsay herself). But between work, parenting, and keeping up the facade of flawlessness, Lindsay was always busy and felt, she told me, "like I'm drowning." But she never thought to ask for help.

This pattern continued as Juniper grew up. Desperate to ensure her daughter would never be a burden in the classroom, Lindsay maintained the same absurdly high expectations and performance demands for Juniper as she had for herself. And Juniper tried the best she could to keep up. But what I saw (and Lindsay struggled to realize) was that this quest for perfection was sabotaging Juniper's self-esteem. By passing along the Good Kid mask to her daughter, Lindsay was perpetuating this cycle for another generation.

What Lindsay needed was a sense of attunement with others, a more deeply felt connection to those in her life. Yet she struggled. She only knew how to create distance and remoteness—a new generation of the Connection Desert—despite at some level understanding that this psychological environment did not serve her growing up, and it wouldn't serve Juniper, either. What I helped Lindsay do—though a lot of hard work and introspection on her part—was to help her start planting the seeds for a lush, thriving Connection Garden where the child-parent bond thrives and flourishes.

The Value of True Connection

The Connection Garden feels vastly different from the Connection Desert. In this metaphor, you are the gardener and your children are the plants. Your job is to meticulously tend to each of your growing plants' differing soil, water, and sunlight needs and adjust accordingly based on what you observe.

Bentley had a voracious appetite for connection. She was starved for that safe feeling you get when someone really *gets* you. Instead, she battled with constant rejection and distance from her parents, triggering her to act out in disruptive, aggressive ways, perpetuating a cycle in which she couldn't get her needs met. As both parents became more reliable, consistent, and predictable with meeting her connection needs in times of stress, Bentley began to seek connection in less distressing ways. Instead of screaming and hitting, she started asking for a hug. Instead of being too busy to pause, Lindsay and Ryan gave her what she needed.

We cannot expect our children to thrive in environments that they're not built for, nor can we force them to adapt beyond their abilities. We must be willing to make whatever adjustments are necessary to support their optimal development. Some children grow like weeds. Plop them in the sun, give them water, and once they take root, they will flourish with minimal upkeep. Some children grow more like sensitive orchids, requiring very specific conditions and an intense amount of patience for them to bloom. Light allows everything in nature to fulfill its life's purpose; without light, life does not exist. Connection is the source of light for your child's overall well-being. The more you shine the light of connection, the deeper and stronger their roots anchor in their Connection Garden.

Connection is the driving force behind the soul of humanity. It's a biological and psychological imperative. When we can predictably rely on feeling safe and connected, we can more easily weather the inevitable storms of life. Unfortunately, if you grew up in a Connection Desert, your methods of asking for and receiving connection may be all out of whack.

If you grew up in a home that utilized traditional parenting methods—such as spanking and other punishments, shame, or isolation—you may have been raised to believe that certain behaviors "earned" connection, while others were punished with disconnection. Withholding connection is a power move that serves the parents' superiority complex and undermines the child's innate drive to seek comfort and reassurance. When such manipulative tactics are used reliably and consistently, they have the potential to negatively impact the relational intimacy that is meant to be shared between a child and their parent.

We live in a society that is deprived of meaningful, profound connections and chronically dismissive of a child's vital need for connection. Simply put, we need one another. Not only to survive but to thrive. Building an emotional bond makes this human experience worth it. Without it, it's like trying to live without sunlight.

Connection Is Not a Transaction

Five-year-old Tori, a sweet little soul, was in a play therapy session with her dad, Matthew, enjoying a game of Chutes and Ladders. When Tori hit the mammoth chute and slid down to practically the beginning of the game, she became frustrated and Matthew's voice turned sharp: "If you can't handle losing, then I'm done playing with you." Tori's frustration became a ferocious roar as she flung the board and its pieces in all directions. Matthew threw up his hands in surrender, looking over at me.

"This is what I always deal with!" he said, exasperated.

Beyond the surface of the tantrum, Tori wasn't only navigating winning or losing. Her developmentally appropriate black-and-white thinking had taken over all logic and reason. Winning equals good, losing equals bad. It's not losing itself that torments children; it's feeling like they're flawed and inherently wrong that cuts like a knife. In that heated moment, when Matthew pulled back a hint of connection, he poured fuel onto the blaze, echoing her belief that she's a bad, awful kid.

Beyond her frustration, Tori's board-game-flipping fiasco was her plea to stay connected, especially in moments of vulnerability. Matthew, being the cycle breaker that he was, rewrote the moment. He looked into Tori's eyes and admitted, "I think I went overboard. I get why you felt frustrated with that super long chute. It caught you off guard, and it made you feel crummy inside." In that moment, you could feel the shift. Tori's heart softened, and she nodded in agreement. Together, they picked up the mess and regained connection.

In the quiet moments that followed, Matthew's thoughts turned inward as he was flooded by memories of his own past of feeling loved only when he played by the rules and was the obedient, pleasing child. In that reflection, he felt the weight of transactional love like a boulder on his soul and realized how suffocating those expectations had been.

As they squeezed kinetic sand together, Matthew chose a new path. He decided to break the chain that shackled him by bringing more intentional awareness to the cycle of transactional love. With that decision, he was rewriting not only his story but Tori's as well.

Why We're Stingy with Our Love

Children growing up in this transactional dynamic are often riddled with confusion because it's never clear what causes a parent to withdraw their affection, making them unable to prepare for the emotional debit. It's a soul-crushing game that can warp an entire life.

My client Shaina was expected as a child to anticipate her parents' needs—for example, by always serving tea and snacks to her parents' friends when they visited their home. But when she didn't match their expectations (as she failed to once, when she was distracted on a social visit), humiliation rained down. Shaina's parents called her selfish and "unfit for the role of a future wife," simply because she did not think to offer refreshments to the guests in a timely manner. Shaina was fifteen years old.

Transactional love is not intentionally intended to hurt a child but to teach them how to win the adult's favor. There's a lingering idea that holding a crying baby too much will spoil them or that saying no just to teach a lesson will somehow save a child from feeling entitled. Let me be clear: it doesn't. What withholding connection does is leave a child hurting and hungry for the stamp of their parent's approval.

Under the facade of transactional love, children learn to get their core relational needs of feeling safe, seen, heard, and understood met by mimicking what they believe is expected of them. They look for validation outside of themselves because their confidence has been earned through pleasing others, rather than being felt within. When you shift your mindset to uphold connection above anything else, your child learns that they don't need to prove anything to be cherished. They feel it in their core, and it becomes the compass they use to navigate different relationships throughout their lives.

Love is a force that shapes us all. We're wired to connect and to weave those threads of belonging. But when love turns into a transaction—"I'll love you if . . ."—it tells the desperate-for-love inner child that they're only good enough if they mold themselves into what *you* desire them to be. They slip into a Masked Self, seeking approval at every turn, even if it means losing their true essence.

I was around ten years old when I realized that my mother's behavior wasn't going to change. I started to accept that some mornings I'd have to quietly slip out of the house to avoid being smacked or verbally abused. I started to take note of her moods and learned when to be quiet at dinner and try to do exactly what she said without any fuss. I started isolating myself in my room, revamping a tiny walk-in closet into my own personal sanctuary, which became a much-needed retreat space as I began plotting my way out. I was suffocating under the mask. I hated who I was expected to be and feared who I was becoming—a mirror image of her self-hatred, shame, and despair. I had given up on feeling love and connection.

When we tie intimacy and closeness to good behavior and achievements, kids miss a vital lesson. They don't learn they're valuable just for *being*; their value gets shaped by what they're *doing*. Transactional love wires kids to constantly seek their worth outside, when all along, it's been woven within.

These transactions go beyond parenting. It's reflected in a capitalist system that has taught us our worth hinges on what we *do*, not who we *are*. You were trained to stand and sit on command, recite daily allegiances, and move when bells rang. You were ordered to keep your mouth shut, your eyes on your own paper, and not to share your ideas with one another because that would be cheating. You were told to stay in your lane, without being informed that the lane was already paved for you, based on factors that were completely outside your control—like the color of your skin, the amount of money in your bank account, the language that you spoke, the religion you were indoctrinated into, your gender identity, your sexual orientation, the size of your physical frame, your physical abilities, and whether you were conventionally attractive. You were rewarded for doing whatever it took to climb to the top. If you fumbled, it was a character flaw, not a systems flaw.

Now we work eight to ten hours per day for nearly all our lives and barely have time to enjoy this precious, beautiful human experience we've all been gifted. Our children spend less unstructured time outdoors and more time getting their homework done. They're overscheduled with activities and volunteer hours in order to make their college résumés "competitive." They must go to a good school, so they can get a good job, so they can feel bad about wanting (or needing) a vacation. If any of us live long enough to retire, many of us are either too sick, too tired, or too strapped for cash to enjoy whatever time we have left. But we do it anyway because what other choice do we have but to survive?

Transactional love exploits the human need for connection like your labor is exploited for someone else's personal gain. When you use emotional security as a bargaining chip to get your child to comply with you, you're perpetuating the capitalist agenda of loyalty over livelihood. You're telling your child, "Do what I need you to do, and maybe you'll thrive. But slip up, and I'll snatch away the very thing you depend on: emotional sustenance, connection, belonging." We can do better than this.

The Cost of Transactional Love

If you grew up in a house where your worth seemed tied to your actions or your parents' mood, those inner child wounds might emerge from time to time. It's common to see your child's behavior as "bad," much like your own parents did, especially when you hit those rocky moments. You might find yourself reacting by pushing your kids away, cutting off that emotional tie, resorting to punishment or control, or scrambling to win back their favor. I know it's tempting to go down the guilt-and-shame rabbit hole when you reenact the pattern that you're desperate to change . . . but that won't fix it. The fix comes from a shift in perspective.

EXERCISE: YOUR CONNECTION NEEDS

Take a few moments to reflect on your connection needs when you were growing up.

- Did you grow up in a Connection Garden, a Connection Desert, or somewhere in between?

- How do your past experiences shape the relational environment you're creating for your children today?

- If you grew up in a Connection Garden or Connection Desert, what Stars (positive people/experiences/memories) can you take with you as you nurture your kids' gardens?

- What Shadows (negative people/experiences/memories) creep up for you when you need more connection or you sense your children's desire to connect?

End this reflective practice by thanking yourself for your courage and vulnerability.

The Six Seeds of Connection

In the Connection Garden you're growing with each of your children, you're tending to a garden of love, and each seed is a vital ingredient for their full growth potential. When you plant and care for the following six seeds, you can expect your children to feel nourished and supported by you.

- Attunement

- Curiosity

- Co-regulation

- Playfulness

- Reflection

- Repair

These powerful Connection Seeds are the driving force behind your child embodying joy, trust, and a solid sense of personal identity. When you make attunement, curiosity, co-regulation, playfulness, reflection, and repair priorities with your kids during the ordinary, everyday moments, they will eventually do the work by themselves. This means that you're not responsible for making your child do well at school—that is their responsibility. Your job is to attune to any underlying needs that may be interfering with their schoolwork, support their regulation, be curious and playful (rather than judgmental), reflect on what wounds this situation may be triggering for you, and repair any missteps along the way.

Seed 1: Attunement

My eight-year-old client Jack came into his session bouncing off the walls. He struggled to choose an activity as his parents talked over him and for him. When I invited his mom and dad to slow down, close their eyes, and focus on being in the present moment together, Jack almost instantly regulated. He began gently rocking a baby doll, sparking our interest and curiosity. His mom acknowledged that they didn't rock and hold him much anymore. Jack turned to them and said, "I know. But I still need it." He left the session much more regulated because he seemed to get this vital need for attunement met. His parents left feeling more confident in knowing how to meet their child's intimacy needs.

Attunement helps you decode the meaning behind the stormy moments you share with your kids. Instead of punishing your child's tantrums or disrespectful clapbacks, you can be much more effective if you read between the lines and wonder what they're trying to say with their behavior. If the behavior could speak words, what would it tell you? Listening to your child with this style of intention builds intimacy and trust, something kids crave like a cozy blanket on a chilly day. If you want to see your children light up, make an intentional effort to offer them your time, presence, and affection. With practice, you will become a great listener, and any hard outer edges you may have will begin to soften. By tuning in to your child's emotional waves, you'll show them that they can come to you with whatever's weighing on them. No judgment, just love.

In a play therapy session, I invited seven-year-old Joey to let his imagination flow with one of my favorite drama therapy exercises—create a six-frame comic book–inspired story about a hero of his choosing, one that ultimately reflects how a child sees themselves in the world around them. Joey struggled and erased every attempt before throwing the crayons and ripping the paper. Jackie, his mom, jumped in and said, "That's him being defiant. That's what I deal with all the time!"

This was a classic moment of misattunement. Jackie wanted Joey to be a good boy and follow the instructions, and she assumed he was not complying with the pressure of an obviously challenging task. Children need adults to tune in to them so kids can tap into their true essence. By labeling him as "defiant" or "unruly," she was putting him in a box before we heard his story.

To our surprise, Joey sheepishly admitted, "I'm not trying to be defiant. It's just that I want to make it perfect because what's the point if it's bad?" The truth was revealed. Joey's refusal was a swirl of anxiety, tangled with the pressure to perform, that tied him in a knot. He needed more than the open-ended directions I had given him. He needed a path—a map—to navigate his inner world. He had already walked through the rough terrains of being bullied by peers and lived in the shadow of his big brother's bright light. When we nudged him to unveil himself in what I thought would be a simple, fun art exercise, he needed the reassurance that he would be free from judgment.

Instead of focusing on his defiant behaviors, we focused on his internal need for safety and connection. Jackie looked into her son's eyes and said, "Of course you want it to be perfect. The world around you feels so messy, and you're trying to make it feel a little more together. Maybe the hero's journey is being okay with things not being perfect."

Then, something magical happened—his shoulders eased, the anxiety reduced, and suddenly Joey was alive with a vibrant spark in his eyes. Over crayons on an ordinary Monday, Jackie did the dance of attunement, ultimately meeting his needs—to feel safe, to be seen, to be heard, and, above all, to be understood.

This crazy, beautiful life we're blessed to experience is wild.

We wake up, hit the ground running, get the kids breakfast, go off to school and work, orchestrate a litany of after-school hustles, finish homework, eat dinner, take a bath, and crash our heads on the pillows for some bedtime stories for them and favorite streaming service for us. Then, the sun comes up, and it's the same ride all over again.

Most of the parents I've spoken with are caught in this loop, and it's easy to miss the simple moments that matter most. So, while I understand that not every moment can be a connection moment, if you can carve out a little pocket of time for meaningful connection every day, you'll hand your child a treasure they'll carry forever. They'll grow to know that when things were tough, you were there for them. You listened. You held them close.

If you have connection wounds from your own past, you can heal them by how you choose to show up in challenging moments with your kids. Try deciphering their messages. "You're the worst parent ever!" might be saying, "I feel like the worst kid." "Get away from me now!" might be saying, "I need you to trust me more." "I hate you!" might be saying, "I'm so mad and upset." The more you tune in to their call, the more supportive you can be. Instead of coming into these moments ready to lay down the law, what might happen if you come with the energy to understand and help?

The more you make yourself available to support your children through the challenging moments they'll encounter, the more they'll internalize your sturdy, consistent leadership. When you're the support they crave, you're doing more than soothing their troubles. You're teaching them the words to describe the mess that's brewing inside them. You're showing them how to navigate complicated emotions with grace and compassion. If you're feeling stuck with the "teaching" aspect of parenting, you may have some unresolved wounds around feeling left to figure things out on your own. It's possible that you have not yet internalized the voice of a compassionate, secure, emotionally resilient leader. If this is the case, that's okay. Revisit Part One with this in mind so you can grow beyond the limitations of your past and embody the parent you desire to be.

Seed 2: Curiosity

The curiosity you have for your children fortifies the connection you share. Learning to observe your child's inner state without judgment is a skill that has been discussed by many experts on child development and children's mental health, including Maria Montessori, Magda Gerber, Alicia Lieberman, and Patricia Van Horn. It is a practice I carry with me in my personal life with my own children, as well as something I teach in the mommy and me groups I lead. By boosting your observation acumen, you become a more skillful detective and gain a much better read of your child's inner world and thus demystify behaviors that would otherwise leave you scratching your head.

Go to a room in your home with your child where it is safe to play and move freely, according to your child's specific developmental stage. Ideally, the room will have natural light and no electronic distractions (or have them turned off). Age-appropriate toys should be available. Set up the environment so that your child does not need to rely on you. If you're observing a not-yet-mobile infant, you can lay them on their back for this exercise, especially if they'd need a lot of support on their bellies. If you're observing a toddler, you'll want to make sure the room is completely childproofed, so you don't have to police their actions. If you're observing a school-aged child, set out tools that spark their creativity and imagination, like an art kit, Play-Doh, or dolls/action figures.

Your only job is to sit back in your chair, breathe, and maintain your presence. Put away any distractions for a few minutes and take the time to be curious about your child's emotions, what they're thinking, how they solve problems, and what they're interested in. If you get lost at any point, simply bring your attention to where their eyes are looking, which will tell you what they're curious about, and what their hands are busy with, which will show you what they're working on.

Resist the urge to direct their attention or try to teach them the "right" way to do something. Offer support only when it's necessary (e.g., when kids become physical with each other). Otherwise, challenge yourself to sit back and let the moment play out. Observation is a chance for you to learn to tolerate your child's struggles, as well as an opportunity for your child to learn how to tolerate their own frustrations without risking someone disconnecting from them.

In these precious moments together, you will notice that the rhythm of the room slows down, the air becomes more peaceful, and you can breathe more deeply. Allow the back of the chair to support you, rather than maintaining tension in your back and shoulders to stay upright. The mothers in my classes say this exercise feels almost meditative. Believe me when I tell you that there are days when, in a room full of fourteen mothers and fourteen toddlers, you can hear a pin drop. It's an incredible strategy for tuning in and deeply connecting with the here and now.

As you watch your child, ask yourself: *What do I notice happening inside my child's mind?* Practice noticing your child without judgment. If you find yourself thinking, *Why doesn't my child play like other kids?*, this implies your child is doing something wrong, and the thought is judgmental. When that pops into your mental landscape, shift the way you're noticing your child: *My child seems invested in staring at the ceiling today. I wonder what they're noticing up there.*

In addition to observing your child, ask yourself: *Where am I*

119

emotionally right now? Do I feel grounded, present, relaxed? Stressed, annoyed, tired? Is there any tension in my body that I can release? Is my mind wandering away to my never-ending checklist?

If you're struggling to stay present in the moment, don't judge yourself. Instead, bring your attention back to the room. If you catch yourself judging your child for any reason, you can turn that energy inward and be curious about yourself. For example: *I wonder why it bothers me that my child isn't playing like others do? Did I learn somewhere that it's important to keep up? What happened when I couldn't keep up?*

This style of observation is a basic mindfulness practice that invites you to slow down and be more present with your children. It is the opposite of the current culture of overloading your children with constant entertainment, correction, stimulation, and activities. Although it is a joy to enter the fantasy land of a child's imagination, you do not need to be your child's primary playmate. Nor do you need to be always entertaining and engaging them—an overwhelming pressure that haunts nearly every parent I know. Perhaps most significantly, this exercise can simply be a chance to feel enamored with your child's joy and zest for life.

Think of this practice as an additional way to engage and play with your child that has a meditative, relaxing effect for both of you. This style of play isn't the only form of play I suggest you share with your child, but this is an avenue for self-reflection and deeper understanding of your child's internal world. By resisting the urge to fix, control, change, or provide educational directives (e.g., "What color is this?") while they play, you send vital messages: *I trust that you are competent. I'm curious about how you see things. I'm invested in knowing more about you.* By keeping yourself quiet during this exercise, you give your mind and body the time they need to get centered, focused, and regulated. It also means your child won't have to manage any of your unintended disruptions as they explore the world around them.

The earlier you introduce this way of interacting with your child and the more faithfully you practice it, the more independent and confident your child will feel in their play as they get older. You will rely less on screens as virtual babysitters while you're making dinner, because your children will know how to sustain attention and direct their own interests without relying on a screen to do the work for them. Additionally, if you have more than one child, these sit-back-and-watch moments become excellent practice for your children to learn important social skills like playing fair, turn taking, sharing, collaboration, and respectful communication.

Seed 3: Co-regulation

At an infant mental health training that I attended in 2019, Dr. Bruce Perry, a world-renowned leader in trauma and the developing brain, said, "A dysregulated parent cannot regulate a dysregulated child." He went on to say, "Only a regulated parent can regulate a dysregulated child. And a dysregulated parent will dysregulate a regulated child."

Parents often believe it is their duty to get their child to stop screaming or flailing, and they do so without any real awareness of how *their* nervous system impacts their child. Research tells us that what's happening beneath the surface is half the battle when it comes to supporting our children through big moments. During the safety talk on an airplane, they remind us to put on our own oxygen mask first before assisting others. This is something we must commit to as parents; otherwise, you will not be helpful if you're not feeling grounded and safe in your body.

Finding an internal physical calm is something I've spent the past twenty years cultivating for myself, as this was not modeled, encouraged, or taught to me growing up. For instance, I had an incredibly stressful day at my job, and I carried it home with me. I tried to shake it off and redirect my energy to being present for my kids, but I found myself ruminating about the problem at work and some potential crisis we were facing. It didn't take more than two minutes for my children's energy to adjust to mine, and soon they were flooded with the tears I was trying to hold in. As I held them while they bawled their eyes out, I felt the itch to tell them to cut it out so we could move forward with our nighttime routine. My impatience and avoidance felt familiar. As a child, I was often enveloped in my mother's intensely repressed loneliness, and her response was to rage at us and then retreat to her room as if nothing had happened.

Not only did my kids need me to get more grounded in my body, I needed to do so as well. In my efforts to co-regulate with my children, Dr. Perry's theory that a parent's regulation is key when it comes to building deep connections was proven to be true. I used Name, Frame, Claim to sort through my emotional distress: *I'm feeling depleted, because I haven't taken the time I need to fill myself back up. I'm responsible for how I interpret my emotions and get my needs met.*

I needed to feel connected and grounded. Then I got curious: *Could this be what my children need?* Sometimes what you need is reflected by what your children need. I came home more distracted than usual, which they immediately sensed. It had been a long day, and they were needing the security of a regulated reconnection.

While I'm experiencing this soulful excavation, I'm rocking my kids back and forth while rubbing their backs and softly kissing the tops of their heads. One child is curled in my lap; the other is pushing me away so he can bang on a door. I invite the door banger back for deep-pressure hugs, and shortly after he melts into my lap.

I brought my mind back to the here and now and asked: *What would feel good right now?* Singing was the answer. You may have a different response, based on your situation. You may want to continue rocking and holding, breathe, take a walk, or get a drink of water together. There is no perfect way to co-regulate with you and your child, so commit to being fully in the present moment and allowing it to unfold organically.

I decided to softly sing about the feelings my kids were having to the tune of "Twinkle, Twinkle, Little Star": *You are oh so very sad. Very sad and very mad. Why don't grown-ups listen more? Have to pound pound on the door. You are oh so very sad. Very sad and very mad.*

Both boys were perfectly still as I sang. The wails of the more dysregulated child transformed to soft whimpers until he finally caught his breath and released a soothing exhale. They wiped their tears and gave me a hug. They each got a book and asked to snuggle and read before they peacefully drifted off to sleep. I supported the children in front of me, but let's not forget the child within. My inner child, who longed to feel comforted by her grown-ups in big, confusing moments but instead felt blamed and rejected, felt cared for in this process, too. I left the experience feeling replenished rather than drained. This is the power of getting grounded in your mind, body, and soul first, as an effective way to soothe your child's distress.

The most effective way to get grounded in your body and soothe yourself is to feel your feet firmly planted on the ground. I like to imagine that I have electronic prongs on my feet, the floor beneath me has two sockets, and I'm "plugging" myself in. Put one hand on your belly and another hand over your heart. Breathe in slowly for four counts while you visualize your breath coming in through your nose, down your throat, flowing past your heart, and expanding your belly. Keep your attention on the visual or on the soothing sensation of your breath (either is fine) while you hold your breath for three slow counts. Then exhale for seven counts while you fully empty your lungs, continuing to focus your attention on the visual of the breath leaving your body or on the warming sensation as your breath leaves your body.

If you become easily overstimulated with too much auditory input, try earplugs or headphones to dampen excess noise so you can more easily self-soothe. Or you may find that listening to relaxing music may be helpful to contain your energy and get you in the right headspace to support your kids.

Your children may continue to scream, yell, or push back while you do this, but I encourage you to trust that they are learning by watching you self-regulate rather than overreact. This isn't performative; you simply need to adapt this approach to suit your unique style and then put in the work to make this second nature for you. For some, this will be easy to implement. For others, it may take time. Be patient with yourself, and take the time you need to grow into this.

Seed 4: Playfulness

Sascha presented as an intensely shy and passive tween. She didn't make eye contact or verbally engage with me, despite my admittedly overzealous attempts to connect with her. Her mother, Katya, was concerned about Sascha's wild imagination. It was as if Sascha lived in her own world and had completely abandoned the "real world," and this had Katya worried.

Sascha used a dollhouse to tell her story through play. She constructed a home complete with a bedroom, a living room, a kitchen, and a bathroom. Inside lived one child, and no one else. She moved the child from room to room, in a life that was simple, ritualistic, but lonely, with a tone that felt serious, flat, and sad.

Then she used wooden blocks to construct a fantastic castle just outside the house. Her eyes lit up as she constructed a moat, tall towers, and grand steps leading to the enormous castle doors. She had a sparkle in her smile when she told me that this was where Princess Carmella lived. She constructed a side-by-side look into her reality—lonely, isolated, boring—and her ideal fantasy—opulent, majestic, important—to show me that it wasn't the fantasy world she was stuck in. It was the "real world" that had her trapped.

Prior to beginning our work together, Sascha had worked with many different providers who demeaned her imagination. If she changed her name or gave "false details" about who she was, she was ignored or corrected to discourage her from living inside her fantasy. This only seemed to force her further into isolation and to disconnect more. Through her play, she consistently mentioned feeling misunderstood and that something was wrong with who she innately was. Play gave her a voice to communicate, and it was up to the adults to listen.

I decided to join her world and be curious about what it symbolizes. Could Sascha be trying to tell us that she felt lonely and stuck in her home, confined to banal routines and unable to express her real gifts? She saw herself as a hero of sorts, someone who came to inspire others to be kind and stand up for those who were different. As our sessions continued, these became weekly themes, and so instead of trying to get her to quit the "fantasy world," we focused on building upon the strengths that her imagination conjured up for her, like knowing her personal boundaries, feeling confident to express her needs in her own way, and believing deeply that she was a good, amazing human. Even Katya got on board, no longer afraid of where Sascha's imagination might take her and willing to join the ride for the first time. This opened up a world of more joyful, pleasurable moments together (something they had lost for many years).

Cultivating more playfulness as an adult is a powerful way to build intimacy with your child, and it is healing for your soul, too. Most adults I know have forgotten how to play, take themselves far too seriously, and generally feel overwhelmed with an incredible amount of responsibility, all of which dampen the playful energy that exists within all of us. However, playfulness, spontaneity, and creativity are the antidote to anxiety and nature's best anxiety reliever. Many of my clients find they can express themselves—and understand their children better—when they increase playfulness in their daily lives.

If you dislike the idea of being playful with your children, you may have some unresolved wounds around vulnerability and intimacy, so be sure to explore this using the tools from Part One. When we engage in play, whether it's symbolic play like as in Sascha's case, or if you're simply setting a playful tone in the morning by being silly and affectionate, you're embodying vulnerability and connection. Playing with children is not about entertaining them but about connecting with them. Through daily playfulness, you share in a back-and-forth conversation that exists completely in the present moment. When you see that playfulness is the way *in* to your child's soul, you'll stop unintentionally pushing them *out*.

To make playfulness a bit more accessible for you, try something new tomorrow. Start your day off slowly with your children by gently scratching their backs to wake them up. Give them snuggles every time you pass by their chair as you make breakfast and get lunches ready. Pretend to be robots, monsters, superheroes, and villains while you get dressed and ready to go. If you've got a big kid, they need play with you, too. Don't harp on their homework or grades so much. Instead, make a fool out of yourself by attempting to use their cool new lingo. Listen to their favorite music with them. I bet taking any of these steps will make play feel less intimidating and may allow everyone in your family to feel lighter.

Seed 5: Reflection

Imagine that you're ready to snap, because your child asked you a question that you've already answered ten times in the past hour. In moments like this, if you can reflect, you won't likely project. Use the N.E.A.T. Method to soothe your impulses and help you get unstuck emotionally. With practice, you'll learn to observe your internal state from the perspective of a fly on the wall. When you can watch your own mind in action, you'll have much more physical and emotional control over yourself.

N: What are you needing? Perhaps you need some physical space or a break in your conversation with your kid.

E: What are you feeling emotionally? Maybe you feel stretched thin and tired of repeating yourself.

A: How are you acting? Perhaps you're rolling your eyes; exhaling in an exaggerated, irritated way; or giving off a "get away from me" vibe.

T: What are you thinking? Maybe you're thinking something must be wrong with your kid, because there's no way they need to hear the same answer ten times in a row if they are "normal."

The magic that comes next is up to you. Many parents often find themselves easing up on their children after this brief self-reflection exercise. This does not mean that they are "soft" and let their children walk all over them, but they do lead from a place of compassion and grace. They can make room for the fact that yes, it's annoying to be asked the same question ten times in a row, but at the same time the young mind requires repetition and nurturance to absorb what it's learning. The power of self-reflection allows you to hold two truths in mind at the same time, and not feel the pressure to make one idea the winner and the other the loser. Instead, you learn the art of accepting what is, without the need to change it.

This may sound good in theory, but you may be wondering, how do I get my child to stop asking me the same question repeatedly? Before you feed this need for control, can you reflect on your need to get them to stop? Is there an underlying wound here for you? Children often repeat questions not only because they're trying to learn but because they're interested in connecting. It may be useful to notice if you're trying to control your child's style of connecting with you and if so, what is that about for you? What are you trying to protect yourself from experiencing?

My client Dana was struggling with this very issue with her son, Jacob. "He's just not reading that I'm over it!" she announced as she curled up in the corner of my couch. Dana knew it wasn't her son's responsibility to be attuned and responsive to her, yet she needed that from him. Beneath her anxious exterior lived a litany of memories of emotional neglect and abandonment by her mother, who did her best but who also couldn't concern herself with Dana's underlying thoughts, feelings, and needs. Dana was unconsciously trying to protect herself from feeling unnoticed and uncared for, and she spent years projecting this onto her child, making it his problem to manage.

What was Dana really <u>needing</u>? She needed to grieve the loss of feeling seen, heard, understood, and safe in her childhood. She also needed more concrete support.

What was Dana feeling <u>emotionally</u>? She was feeling burned out by how she was expected to show up and had very little social or emotional support to sustain herself.

How was Dana <u>acting</u>? She was pushing her son away and seemed visibly irritated by his presence.

What was Dana <u>thinking</u>? She felt it wasn't fair that others weren't as consumed with her needs as she was with theirs.

Dana committed to using N.E.A.T. in her daily interactions with her family. Although nothing else in her life had changed—the stressors and her lack of social support remained the same—she started coming to sessions with a glow in her eyes. Her energy felt lighter, her skin glistened more, she was more regulated, and for the first time, she didn't seem so crushed by anxiety. Most important she started to feel like less of a rage monster and began enjoying her child more.

Trust that your capacity to reflect is a strong pathway toward deeper connection with your child. The more reflective you become in everyday moments, the more self-awareness you build over time. The more self-awareness you have, the easier it is for you to attune to your child's underlying needs and be curious about their perspective of the world around them.

Seed 6: Repair

Repair is the final seed you must sow for a meaningful, lifelong connection with your children. When you unintentionally cause harm, it's important to say sorry without flipping your apology and blaming your behavior on your child. For example, "I'm sorry I frightened you, but if you just listened the first time I asked, then maybe I wouldn't have yelled" is an insincere apology. It redirects the blame onto your child, rather than owning your part in the conflict you're facing together. "I'm sorry I frightened you when I yelled" is a healthy apology.

Too many parents have told me that apologizing to their

children is frivolous and that they never received anything of the sort from their own parents. They also like to point out that kids don't remember, so why should we constantly say sorry? Avoiding repair teaches your children that the impact doesn't matter if their intentions are benign. Your intentions can be purer than the day is long, but if you do something that causes harm to your child— even if you think it "shouldn't" cause harm—you're still on the hook for an apology. A genuine apology says to your child: *I care about you. You're important to me. I believe in us. I love you.* Receiving a message like this following a rupture warms the relationship and allows you and your child to move forward with less resentment and shame.

If you're waiting for an apology from your own parents, you may be waiting a long time. You cannot waste time trying to mend parts of your past that you were not responsible for. Parents are always responsible for their own behavior, and they were also responsible for how their behavior affected you. If they refuse to accept accountability and maturely move forward, please know that you can do better. Release your need for an apology from your parents to whatever spiritual entity speaks the most to you so you can break this cycle and do things differently with your own kids.

All parents mess up. There is no such thing as a perfect parent who is consistently poised, always says the right words, and never makes any mistakes. Good enough parenting is getting it "right" 33 percent of the time and scrambling through the rest of it. Take an inventory of events in which you apologize but repeat the same pattern. This repetition is an indicator that there is an unresolved inner child wound that needs your attention for you to make a meaningful shift in your actions.

Imagine you're like me and are not a morning person. You have to get up and get everyone going, but every day, you stay in bed as long as possible, and then you're anxious about getting out the door on time. So, you scream at your kids to get them to hurry up, and everyone's stress levels are at an eight before you're out the door.

This scenario (and similar parenting issues) deserves an authentic apology and a commitment to personal growth. Repairing with an authentic apology contains the following elements:

- Say it from a heartfelt place: "I'm sorry."

- Take accountability for your part: "I yelled out of frustration because I overslept and struggle with moving quickly in the morning."

- State what you'll do differently: "I'm going to get better prepared the night before and go to bed earlier so I can manage the mornings more gracefully."

- Commit to the steps necessary to do it differently: Get an accountability partner. Use the tools from Part One to work through any psychological barriers associated with repetitive patterns that don't serve you.

- Invite your children to reflect on their part (if necessary) and help them problem-solve new ideas: "How can you be more efficient in the morning, so we spend less time negotiating and more time enjoying each other?"

I've walked countless parents through the repair process, and every so often someone will ask: "I feel like I'm constantly apologizing and then turning around and doing the same thing. When does my apology become an empty promise?"

This is the voice of the overactive inner critic. The inner critic needs you to stay in a chronic guilt and shame state so it can keep you alert to all your failures and ensure that you don't mess up again. Check your expectations of yourself. It takes an immense amount of effort to change behavior, and your apology—when coming from a place of authentic connection and love—is not an empty promise. It is an act of hope and a shining light in the darkness. If you continue to apologize for the same mistake and you're struggling to embody the changes you desire, remember that it's not about how many times you fall off the horse; it's about how many times you're willing to get back on and keep going.

Guilt for your behavior is normal and healthy. But the shame that has you spiraling means you're missing self-compassion and you're being far too hard on yourself. Compassion is a key ingredient to neutralizing shame. All great parents mess up from time to time. Parents who own their mistakes and focus more of their energy on their wins with their kids ultimately feel more confident in who they are as parents.

Sowing the Seeds

Something incredibly inspiring happens when you commit to cultivating attunement, curiosity, co-regulation, playfulness, reflection, and repair into your daily interactions with your child. You spark joy within their soul and truly delight in their loving, powerful essence. You nurture trust and relational security, a vital component of all healthy interpersonal dynamics. You respect your child's autonomy and give them the opportunity to show you just how capable they are. You protect your child's self-esteem and confidence and help to guide (not shape) their soul's calling in life. Finally, you honor your child's individual identity, giving them the gift of becoming who they are. Not who you need them to be or who you expect them to be. But who they innately know they are.

When planted and appropriately tended to, these seeds not only nourish your child's spirit, but you will find that they feed the littlest, most vulnerable version of you, who perhaps needed more authentic connection but didn't know how to find it. Parenting from this connected place is like returning home to the core of what it means to be human. I'm confident that you will find peace in this approach to being in relationship with your children.

None of this happens overnight. In fact, you'll continue to sow these seeds throughout childhood and adolescence. You will need to prune away shame and shower your seedlings with compassion. You will need to combat the bugs that will try to eat away at your sweet little sprouts with your curiosity, conviction, and well-timed guidance. Let your love (not your disappointment) shine through your eyes and your voice. Let your care (not your disdain) pulse through your heart and your hands. May your soulful drive for connection be the thing your child recalls the most when they examine the stamp you left on them.

CHAPTER 6

• • • • • •

Demystifying Your Child's Behavior

E VERY BEHAVIOR IS ATTACHED TO A FEELING, AND ALL FEEL-
ings are attached to a need. Children use outward behavior to
communicate what's happening internally. They may not have the
vocabulary or awareness to express what is going on with them in
a moment of upset, worry, or fear, so their *behavior* becomes a
guiding light for you to understand what they need. Your job is to
react less to the behavior and respond more to the underlying need.

My nearly three-year-old client Ella pleaded, "Just one more
hug for my baby, and then I'll go." As she repeated this multiple
times, her mother, Deena, grew more and more impatient: "She
does this all the time. She doesn't want to leave, and so she draws
it out. It's exhausting and I don't know what to do."

Deena had other children to attend to, and Ella demanded so
much from her. Typically, Deena invested a lot of time, effort, and
energy into stopping Ella's behavior, by telling her no, grabbing her
hand, and forcibly removing her from a situation. This never ended
well. Ella would resist, push back, get physical, and persevere

with more insistence on what she wanted. Deena consistently missed what Ella was trying to convey.

With careful observation and more attunement, Deena figured out that transitions were hard for Ella, and she didn't want the special time to end. When Deena conveyed this to Ella, her body posture softened and a frown appeared on her sweet, angelic face. She was masking her sadness with rigidity and perseveration, a sentiment that Deena recognized as something she did herself when she felt stressed and trapped. Unmasking Ella's sadness was not the final step Deena needed to take to support her child in this moment (and other everyday moments that resembled this interaction). Beneath the sadness lay a delicate need. The question was, what exactly did she need, and how could Deena help her get this need met?

Parents are often so distracted by their children's behavior that decoding a need feels like a complicated puzzle that they're not confident they can solve. At my suggestion that a child may need something from the parent, they often protest, "My kid has everything. What more could they possibly need from me?" I can empathize with defensiveness like this, especially if a parent's needs—be they physical and/or emotional—were neglected in their childhood. You may have grown up in such an emotional desert that any attention paid to your children feels like a significant upgrade. *My kids should be grateful for what they get!*

But it's not developmentally supportive to leave kids completely on their own to figure out what they need. Children can't get their needs met without the support and guidance of a trusted grown-up. They will try, but they usually aren't very efficient or effective in meeting their own needs without your help.

When you adopt a needs-based framework for decoding your child's behavior, you will foster more closeness, attunement, and connection with your child. You'll be a better guide for your child to understand how their needs influence their emotions and behaviors, so they can be equipped to express their needs constructively—rather than destructively—as they continue to grow and mature. A needs-based lens equips you to help your child thrive in childhood, adolescence, and well into adulthood. If needs are met consistently, reliably, and predictably throughout childhood, children grow up to be adults who feel confident about meeting their own needs—while trusting that others are reliable sources of comfort as well.

This goes against some established cultural and social narratives. Often in Western society there are shame and failure attached to needing the support of others, a core belief that gets embedded in the new mother right from the start. This is *her* baby, and therefore *she* must do everything cheerfully and without complaint.

To heal from these social wounds, we require a needs surplus. If we returned to our roots of being interdependent human beings who rely on support, safety, and comfort in our relationships, we wouldn't only survive . . . we'd thrive. We'd be better attuned to getting our own needs met as well as helping our children with theirs. Consider this a call to action to keep up your important work of responding to your own underlying needs, so you can support your child in getting their needs met.

IT'S OKAY TO NEED

People with a history of trauma or neglect, or people who had narcissistic or highly critical parents, will often feel as if there is something inherently shameful about needing or desiring *anything*. If this is you, be aware of any triggers that arise when your child needs your support. If their needing you makes you frustrated, use Name, Frame, Claim to quickly decode what's happening internally for you in the moment:

> Name it: *I feel annoyed by my kid's constant neediness. My throat feels tight, and my chest feels heavy.*

> Frame it: *I remember dealing with problems on my own as a kid. I was made to feel stupid if I was struggling or needed help, so I generally try to avoid needing others. Now I recognize that I'm conditioned to avoid my kid's needs as well.*

> Claim it: *I'm responsible for how I interpret my feelings and getting my needs met. My child needing me is not a punishment for my failures or a test of my goodness; rather, it's simply my child not being mature or skilled enough to meet their own needs just yet. I need to ground my body with some breaths and then get curious about my kid to gain some clarity about this specific moment.*

Parenting with the Ladder of Needs

The Ladder of Needs is a framework for understanding what's happening beneath your child's behavior. It's not a checklist but a fluid map that helps you get to the heart of the matter in any given moment with your child. Rather than focusing on your child's deficits, you can pour intentional energy into helping them reach their true potential by guiding their needs. With your support, your children can learn how to climb up and down their Ladder of Needs to gain mastery of themselves and their relationships.

LADDER OF NEEDS

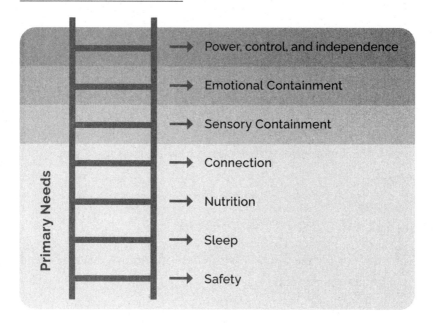

From the bottom up, the first four rungs of the ladder represent your child's most vital, essential needs of safety, sleep, nutrition, and connection. The top three rungs are the "higher" level of needs of sensory containment, emotional containment, and power, control, and independence. The four primary needs on the lower rungs must be addressed consistently and reliably; otherwise, any sensory distress, emotional distress, or power-related needs your child has will be exacerbated—and thus cause more friction—in the child-parent dynamic.

The ladder can serve as a flowchart of sorts when you are faced with a child who is upset or acting out of the ordinary, and you're unsure what is motivating their behavior. Starting at the bottom of the ladder, ask yourself: *What does my child need right now? Does my child feel physically unsafe? Is my child tired? When was the last time my child ate?*

From this more attuned listening state, you can confidently respond accordingly. Don't waste precious energy stressing about getting it wrong, because that will make you want to give up or send you into a guilt and shame spiral, especially if you overreact to your own internal distress. Instead, focus your attention on trying to decode the need. It doesn't matter how long it takes. Your child does not need you to do it quickly or get it right every single time. In fact, your child is built for you to be imperfect because your imperfection helps them learn how to exist in an imperfect world.

Rung One: Safety = The Protector

The need for physical safety is the bare-minimum essential need your child requires. Kids need to know that their physical integrity will be protected at all costs. Without a sense of safety, they are notably more distressed, struggle to retain valuable lessons, and maintain a chronic hypervigilance of their surroundings. When children feel safe and protected, they learn to trust that others are there to help and support them. When they feel rejected, dismissed, or ridiculed for their pain—especially by their parents—they can make sweeping conclusions that no one cares.

When the fundamental need for safety is activated, children are wired to look for protection. The most protective thing you can do for your child when they feel physically hurt is to acknowledge what you see in a non-dismissive way.

Dismissing the hurt: "Oh, wipe it off. You're fine. Stop being such a baby!"
Protecting the hurt: "You fell, and your knee is bleeding. Ouch, that hurts. Let's get you cleaned up."

When your child's need for safety is triggered, your job is to become the Protector. First, acknowledge the hurt, and then help your child feel better. Do whatever is necessary to ensure that your child's safety is prioritized. Band-Aids, ice packs, hugs, and kisses are great ways to acknowledge your child's physical suffering without overdramatizing it or completely rejecting it. When you are the Protector, you give your child the confidence that you care for their physical well-being, which allows your child to focus on other important things in their lives. After you help your child through a scary or frightening moment, help them get back up with a try-again attitude. Teach them to become familiar with and use the phrase "Let's try it again," which will build resilience and grit to face life's challenges with confidence and courage.

You may not have had someone in your corner when you were a child, and the role of Protector may feel unfamiliar, but you can turn that around with your child. Maybe you didn't have parents who acknowledged your physical hurts in a kind, compassionate, caring way. Perhaps your parents were the reason why you felt physically unsafe, and you had no choice but to live in those stressful conditions. Your pain could have been acknowledged inconsistently. It's possible you were raised to be "tough" and not show any signs of vulnerability or "weakness," especially if you're a man who was raised with stereotypical male expectations. If you have an inner child wound when it comes to feeling safe and needing a protector, prioritize showing up for yourself in a protective, nurturing way. If your back hurts, don't ignore it. If something feels off in your body, go see the appropriate doctor and get some support. Resist the urge to rush your pain along or avoid it altogether. By internalizing the Protector you always needed, you can learn to become the Protector of your child.

Rung Two: Sleep = The Soother

My client Tania had lost all patience with her six-year-old daughter's tantrums. The tantrums would occur multiple times per week and had caused significant disruptions to their family. Everyone was walking on eggshells around the child, terrified of detonating the bomb of her explosive emotions. Turns out, she was sleep-deprived—and when sleep is off, everything is off.

Getting enough sleep is critically important for a child's development and well-being. Not only is sleep vital to our nervous system's general regulation, but adequate sleep is critical to prevent type 2 diabetes, obesity, poor mental health, injuries, attention issues, and behavior problems. According to recent studies, today's children are the most chronically sleep-deprived children of any generation of kids. In fact, the Centers for Disease Control and Prevention reports that one third of today's children are not getting the sleep they need. Specifically, six out of ten middle schoolers and seven out of ten high schoolers are not getting adequate sleep.

GETTING A GOOD NIGHT'S SLEEP

According to the Mayo Clinic, the hours of adequate sleep can be determined by age group:

- Infants four to twelve months old: twelve to sixteen hours, including naps
- Children one to two years old: eleven to fourteen hours, including naps
- Children three to five years old: ten to thirteen hours, including naps

- Children six to twelve years old: nine to twelve hours
- Teens thirteen to eighteen years old: eight to ten hours
- Adults: seven or more hours

The benefits of sleep are huge—improved mood, attention, and behavior, not to mention brain development and overall growth. Sleep needs to be a high priority for every member of your family, and I strongly advise that you create healthy sleep habits for yourself and your children. Unfortunately, the disruption of circadian rhythm by the blue light emitted by electronics has contributed to poor sleep habits in many children. You can combat this phenomenon by limiting screens before bed. I recommend turning off screens two hours prior to bedtime, but this may vary home to home. Find what works for you.

When it comes to setting up your child for sleep success, stick to the basics with a simple, repetitive routine that remains constant through the week, including weekends. The four Bs—Bath, Brush, Books, and Bed—work well for most families. Have a consistent wake-up time and bedtime and stick to them. Remove all electronic devices from your child's room. Encourage lots of activity during the day so your child is ready to rest in the evening. For support with the nuances of infant and toddler sleep, I recommend Heather Turgeon and Julie Wright's book *The Happy Sleeper*, as well as their book for tweens and teens, *Generation Sleepless*.

If your children resist naptime or bedtime, tell them, "You don't have to fall asleep, but you do need to close your eyes." This boundary gives your child some control and almost always helps them fall asleep faster. If your child gets out of bed because they're distracted by toys, remove the toys from their room, and ensure that their bedroom is primarily for sleep, not play.

Rung Three: Nutrition = The Provider

Allie was my tenderhearted three-year-old client who struggled with explosive meltdowns when her mom, Lisa, told her no or gave her a direction. One could easily assume that she was a strong-willed little tot who was poised for pushing her parents' buttons. But after deep investigation, it was clear to me that Allie was hangry, and she couldn't regulate until her nutritional needs were satisfied.

We all need food and water to survive. Many big emotions, tantrums, and emotional dysregulation—in people of all ages—are due to feeling hungry or being dehydrated. Lisa hesitated to give Allie snacks because she worried that she would begin to associate explosive meltdowns with obtaining food. This is a behavioral lens for understanding Allie's motivation. But a needs-based lens gives us a more nuanced understanding of Allie's internal experience.

Our bodies need food for fuel, and when we're running out of fuel, the body detects that as a threat. Some children have an exaggerated threat response like Allie, who had a difficult trauma history that included foster care and adoption. Even if the response itself is not exaggerated, when the body demands food, that's all your brain can think about. If the hypothalamus is working hard to motivate you to find some food, the neocortex—which powers our ability to use logic and reason—might not be as sharp, especially for children whose brains aren't fully developed until twenty-five or thirty years old.

Lisa had to let go of the idea that she was reinforcing bad behavior by feeding her child. Her primary job was to be the Provider. Food is not a reward for good behavior, and it doesn't have to be earned. Food is vital to our survival. If your child's big feelings and big behaviors are due to being hungry, then they need to be fed. Period. You can discuss the challenging behavior and come up with a better plan for how they can express their hunger needs once you've provided some sustenance. Help your children make the connections between what they needed, how they were feeling, and how they were acting. Here's what that looked like with Allie:

BK: "How do your brain and belly feel now that you've had something to eat?" Here, she is invited to reflect on her current feeling.

A: "Much better!"

BK: "What were you feeling before you had your snack?" She is being challenged to think about how she was feeling in the previous moment.

A: [playfully growls] "Mad! My belly hurt."

BK: "What did the big, mad feelings make your body do?" Now she has to connect her feelings to her behavior, building more self-awareness and emotional intelligence.

A: "It made me hit, throw, kick, and bite! I couldn't stop it!"

BK: "What's a different way you can let us know that you're hungry next time?" This is your opportunity to teach constructive ways to get their needs met.

A: "When my belly hurts, I can tell Mommy." We helped her come up with this plan. It was also Lisa's responsibility to watch Allie's physical hunger cues, like holding her belly and pacing in circles. The better Lisa became at listening to

Allie's hunger cues, the more skilled Allie became at listening and communicating them.

Rung Four: Connection = The Comforter

Elijah was the clown of his kindergarten class, always goofing off and defying his teacher's requests. His anger often turned violent, and he was on the verge of expulsion. His parents, Ezra and Hannah, were undoubtedly concerned. They had tried rewards, punishments, consequences, removing privileges, time-outs, ignoring . . . and nothing seemed to work. After a few sessions of working together, Ezra threw up his hands in frustration: "He's doing all of this for attention!" There's a common misconception that if you ignore a child who is acting out for attention that they will stop. But as discussed, children's need for attention is an essential survival need, and therefore, removing attention only further activates whatever survival tactics they can access. When they're attention-seeking, they're actually connection-seeking. Children need parents who respond to connection-seeking behaviors by becoming the Comforter.

Elijah was on high alert most of the day. Yet none of these challenges presented when his parents gave him their time, presence, and affection. When he sensed their distraction (e.g., scrolling on their phones, checking emails), he reacted in the way humans are wired to react when we feel threatened: get big, get loud, and physicalize the fear within to get attention and support.

The Six Seeds of Connection solved Elijah's chronic dysregulation. The more Ezra and Hannah poured attunement, curiosity, co-regulation, playfulness, self-reflection, and repair into him, the more Elijah came to trust their leadership. He grew more confident in himself and faced fewer problems at school and with peers, and the entire family felt happier.

Rung Five: Sensory Distress = The Sensory Container

Rose described Landon as having been an energetic baby in utero, and not much had changed. He was one of the first babies in his mommy and me class to crawl, which gave Rose some anxiety. He loved to examine other babies' faces and hair—and by examine, I mean poke, prod, and pull. Rose would try to contain him, but soon he'd be back into his peers' bubble space (i.e., personal space) with even more intense interest and curiosity.

Landon always had an adorable smile on his face, one that made you wonder what mischief he was about to get into. He always kept one eye on the door and would dart the moment he could. He'd also get "hands on" a lot—a phrase I use for when little ones hit. He'd pass a peer and impulsively get "hands on," or he'd snatch a toy from a peer, bop them with it, and then run away, peering back over his shoulder, seeming to invite them to a game of chase.

His impulsivity worried Rose. She was afraid to have an "aggressive" child and was beginning to feel isolated from her fellow mom friends, who became more protective of their children when Landon was around. Meanwhile, Landon seemed happy as a clam, not a care in the world, just living his sweet little life oblivious to the impact his physical actions had on others. For a child under two years old, this is developmentally expected. Still, I wondered if underlying sensory-based needs were motivating his behavior.

As a licensed marriage and family therapist, it is beyond the scope of my practice to describe the intricacies and nuances of our sensory nervous system. Nor am I trained in diagnosing or treating sensory-processing disorders, conditions that affect how the brain interprets sensory-based stimuli. If you're looking for an in-depth analysis on this subject, consider Dr. Mona Delahooke's *Brain-Body Parenting* and Carol Stock Kranowitz's *The Out-of-Sync Child*. However, I'd like to explain the very basics of your children's sensory needs and help you learn how to become a Sensory Container for your child when these needs present themselves.

The world around us is incredibly stimulating. I can barely enjoy a cup of joe at my local coffee shop without being distracted by the hustle and bustle of doors opening and closing, fire trucks blaring their sirens, espresso machines clinking and clanking, and conversations from other patrons—and I'm a full-grown adult with appropriately integrated sensory systems. A child's brain is still learning how to process all the rich information that comes with living in an engrossing, enticing world.

Receiving and interpreting the physical world around us is called sensory processing, and every animal—including humans—is always processing its senses. When you go outside, your body recognizes whether it's cold or warm and then communicates to your brain whether you need a jacket. Essentially, your senses are working slightly ahead of your brain's interpretation abilities, with the mission to help you navigate the world in a physically safe and regulating way. When your senses believe that something feels unsafe or dysregulating, they will alert your brain to react. Some people are afraid of heights, and when they stand at the top of a building and look over the edge, their sensory system gets overwhelmed and panics. Saying they're afraid of heights technically means that their vestibular nerve is overactive in how it communicates threat.

Sensory distress is often misidentified and labeled as bad behavior. Landon was already being misperceived as a troublemaker due to his "physical aggression" and impulsive tendencies. When Landon impulsively struck another child on the back of his head, it wasn't because he was trying to hurt his playmate. Rather, he was struggling with proprioception, the understanding of where his body stopped and his buddy's head began. His brain-body system was eager to feel integrated, and impulsive hitting would persist until this was mastered.

148

To help him get this need met without bopping his friends, we gave Landon slow squeezes down his arms and legs while reiterating the boundary to keep his hands to himself. The effect was immediate. Not only did he appear less physically tense in his body, but the spontaneous smacks reduced dramatically and eventually were eliminated.

The child who feels overwhelmed and overstimulated in their body is saying, *Give me a physical container to put all these sensations!* At home, Rose committed to being the Sensory Container that Landon needed. Sometimes she'd give him "pillow presses," where he would lay down on his belly and she gently pressed a pillow onto his back for ten presses at a time. She also wrapped him up like a burrito, gave him big bear hugs throughout the day, and gave him heavy work, where he helped load the washing machine and transfer wet clothes to the dryer. Occasionally, she asked him to help her make the room bigger by pushing on the walls (kids love this one). Activities like this, ones that demand the body exert itself in big, dynamic ways, feed the proprioception nerve and give your child's body the important feedback it needs to regulate and feel grounded.

It is beyond the scope of this book to provide a detailed analysis of all the facets of sensory-processing-related issues. If you believe your child has a sensory-processing concern, I strongly suggest you seek support from a pediatric occupational therapist to learn more about your child's unique sensory profile so you can best support them.

Rung Six: Emotional Distress = The Emotional Container

Paulie and Shannon called me in a panic because they had no idea how to manage their seven-year-old son's emotional outbursts, and they were desperate for support. Ollie was a particular child who struggled when his expectations did not match reality. If he expected to watch an additional show in the morning before school but had already watched the agreed-upon twenty minutes, he would explode into an angry fury that often resulted in striking and hurting his father. On the outside looking in, there was no real "reason" for Ollie's temper.

As a careful and curious observer of children, I know that physical retaliation usually carries a deeper message. The child has something important to say, and physical aggression is their best way of saying it. This is not to suggest that we should simply excuse a child who hits. But instead of writing off the child as being disobedient and unruly, we can recognize that they have a deeply important need that has gone unmet. As the keeper of a child's needs, it's the parent's responsibility to try to discern the true meaning behind the child's behavior. Perhaps Ollie needed a more consistent Emotional Container: someone who was neutral and nonreactive to his emotional distress, someone who could help bring ease to his body and mind.

Ollie seemed angry, tense, and anxious . . . and unable to contain it all by himself. When he became agitated over something seemingly innocuous—like a toy figurine not standing in the exact way that he expected it to—Paulie was quick to shut down Ollie's reaction by over-rationalizing the moment, dismissing Ollie's frustration, and trying to get him to see how ridiculous he was behaving. He was trivializing Ollie's reaction, which often resulted in a fight or a blatant refusal to interact with Dad. Paulie escalated further, doubling down on his point that Ollie's behavior was unjustified. Paulie announced that his son was trying to manipulate him to get his way: "He knows how to get a rise out of me. This is exactly what he wants."

Many parents I work with are like Paulie, so wrapped up in their own emotions that they struggle to understand that children aren't trying to manipulate them to get what they want. They're not triggering you to annoy you. Instead, you may be triggered because it's hard to manage challenging behaviors. Maybe you did not have emotionally mature enough grown-ups in your youth who were available to help you work through your messy, complicated feelings in a contained and supportive way. Perhaps your parents left you to yourself: "No one wants to be around you when you're acting this way." Perhaps they stifled your tears: "Nobody likes a crybaby." Perhaps they beat the emotions out of you: "I'll give you something to cry about." If you didn't get the repeated message that your emotions were okay, feelings didn't last forever, and someone would help you through it, then it's quite likely you'll find yourself triggered in some way to survive the pain.

We must learn to separate our children's pain from our own. As a mother, I know how distressing it feels to see my children struggling emotionally. It takes every ounce of power I have not to reenact my familiar patterns of avoiding, shutting out, and shutting down to survive. Growing up in an emotionally obtuse, immature, and tumultuous environment left me completely unprepared for adulthood, where pain is inevitable. Because I didn't have a felt sense of someone holding my hurts with me, I had no compass for asking others to support me. Your child's behavior evokes whatever you learned to repress, ignore, dismiss, or deny in your youth, and your emotional response has to do with your unresolved shame.

Children under the age of fifteen rarely have a hidden agenda with their parents. They are products of the environment that their family, society, and culture have created for them. While that may sound blunt and perhaps harsh, it's a hopeful message. While you don't have much control over the social and cultural messaging, you are the captain of your family's ship. As much as your kids may want to steer the ship, they don't have control of the overarching family dynamic. When you sense that your child is in emotional distress, it's time to take hold of the helm and steer them toward emotional awareness and intelligence. They are looking to feel emotionally safe, an internal state of resonance where in the height of vulnerability they are not overwhelmed.

Children need to borrow your emotional intelligence so they can make sense of what they are feeling and experiencing. Being your child's Emotional Container gives them the gift of learning how to be with their own pain and hurt. When your child is experiencing these raw emotions, holding the emotions with them feels like trying to hold sand. If you grip and squeeze the sand, it slips through your fingers. When you cup the sand and hold it delicately and patiently, the sand settles safely into the container you've constructed.

If you're struggling to be your child's Emotional Container, your first job is to continue investing the time, effort, and energy into building your own emotional resources, all of which are laid out for you in Part One. It's a sign of advanced emotional intelligence when you can be present with your emotions, regardless of how powerful they may feel inside, and sit patiently with them as the storm eventually passes. All human beings will experience big, difficult emotions. It is part of the soul contract that we all take when we agree to this wild, precious human life.

Feelings need to be felt, not fixed. I noticed that Paulie consistently tried to minimize Ollie's emotions as irrelevant, which appeared to amplify Ollie's anxiety. In another session, Ollie appeared on edge as he complained that his schoolteacher put too much pressure on him. Before I could model emotional containment, Paulie rebutted, "Well, that's his job, son. You're going to have to put up with it. I don't know what to tell you." It was clear to me that he felt awkward knowing his son was in an uncomfortable, inescapable environment, and this was his best way of trying to defuse Ollie's pain. Ollie reacted: "Fine, it's not like you really care anyway!"

Ollie needed to hear, "You shared something important, and I made you feel like I didn't care. I'm sorry about that. I'm listening now. School feels like a heavy weight on your chest. Is that right?" This opened the door for a more healing connection after a series of miscommunications that left them both feeling pretty crummy. Eventually, Ollie's anger bubble deflated, and Paulie gained confidence in his skill set to show up in a powerful way for his son. When children get the repeated experience of feeling seen and heard in an emotionally difficult circumstance, they integrate the emotional containment you're providing for them, which ultimately becomes the baseline for their general regulation as they grow and mature.

In emotionally distressing situations, your child needs to know that you see them, hear them, and understand them. Doing so consistently helps your child more courageously deal with the inevitable pains of this human experience. Resist the urge to make the feelings stop, and instead focus on ways to support them on the emotional roller coaster.

If you don't understand why your child is feeling so emotionally overwhelmed, try to maintain a neutral state of mind and be curious about the *process* of feeling itself. Try not to get caught up in the *content* of what your child shares. Instead, help your child make sense of what they're actively experiencing.

You can walk your child through the process of feeling by posing these questions:

- What are you feeling? or, If your [*body part*] could speak, what would it say?

- Where are you feeling [it] in your body?

- What does [it] feel like? Heavy as a rock or light as a feather? Still like a statue or fluttering like a butterfly? Hot like fire or cold like ice? Stiff as a board or loose like a wet noodle?

- What does [it] make your body want to do?

- What is another way you can express [*this emotion*]?

The key to being an effective Emotional Container is to avoid rationalizing away your children's emotions and instead empathize, support, and help them move *through* each feeling. You can help your child shift their impulsive reactions and problematic behaviors once you've reestablished safety in their emotional world (more on that in chapter 9). By tending to this sensitive need, you will also give your child the gift of emotional resilience and confidence.

Rung Seven: Power and Freedom-Seeking = The Collaborator

Kinsley was a powerhouse five-year-old. To say that she was an intensely independent, march-to-the-beat-of-her-own-drum type of child was a total understatement. She was quirky, confident, and savvy. When her parents told her she couldn't do something, she constructed and executed plans to get her way regardless. It felt like there was no stopping her. By the time her parents, Lydia and Connor, called me for therapeutic support, they were beside themselves: "This girl is out of control. She doesn't listen to a word we say. She's ruining our entire family."

We all have a need for power and freedom. This is especially true for children, because when they sense that they are being controlled—even subtly—they are much more likely to resist and react in ways that aren't functional. When Lydia or Connor asked Kinsley to do something, they rarely (if ever) asked for her opinion on the matter. Kinsley's noncompliance by asking for more time was seen as disobedience, for which she was punished. Their mentality was to break her will, which only appeared to embolden her resistance.

Developmentally, human beings are internally motivated to feel capable and competent. Think of an infant who, with great determination and persistence, repeatedly practices rocking on hands and knees until they can finally propel themselves forward, much to their delight and satisfaction. There is an internal push toward autonomy and independence that begins to develop around eighteen months old. When this need is nurtured, honored, and supported, the child emerges at around three years old with a healthy sense of willfulness. They build on their innate will as they discover self-esteem, their purpose, and their personal identity. This drive evolves as children turn away from their parents' influence and start to look toward their peers, engaging in more risks and thus more opportunities for growth, maturity, and autonomy.

Rather than respecting this need for power, control, autonomy, and independence in our children, most of us spend a great deal of energy unintentionally disempowering and stifling their quest for freedom and individuation by controlling virtually every aspect of their lives. Wear this, go here, do that, sit down, get up, and let's go. We are in the driver's seat for much of their lives, especially in the early years, and we forget that nobody learns to drive by sitting in the back seat. Many parents are challenged when children try to take the wheel much earlier than they anticipate, struggle to trust the process, and have trouble letting go of their need for control.

Parents often begin using control-based interventions to assert their will over their children at about eighteen months. This may be triggered in response to the stress of having a demanding, power-hungry young child or it may reflect a historical attitude that children are somehow silly, incompetent beings who are here to learn from us. It is not often thought that adults can learn from the pure love of a child, their openness to new ideas, unquenchable thirst for knowledge, never-ending creativity and inspiration, and unadulterated joy. Instead of seeing the child-parent dynamic as a symbiotic relationship that gives and takes from each other and thus requires mutual respect for one's individual autonomy, we're generally conditioned to see children as parasites who take and take and take, forcing us to double down on their inherently sinful and greedy nature so we can teach them how to be a "good" person.

We do this in subtle and not-so-subtle ways. We threaten to take away their prized possessions if they don't do what we say. We punish them by yelling at them, spanking them, or subjecting them to public humiliation. We tell them they can't make their own decisions, and if they question our authority, we'll hammer down on the four cardinal words said by every controlling parent: *Because I said so.* We tell them they are to be seen but not heard. We criticize their choices and find opportunities to remind them of how embarrassing they are and what disappointments they are. We manipulate the bond we share by offering them conditional love and acceptance based on their embodying the fantasy that we've crafted in our minds about who they are. Children raised in such environments internalize that their need for power is shameful and bad, cultivating a disempowered state of self-doubt and uncertainty that leads them to abandon the Authentic Self and adopt the Masked Self. Children who do this appear to be "good" kids on the outside, but it's often hard to tell what they're really feeling on the inside.

It is common for parents to feel uncomfortable supporting their child's need for power, control, and autonomy, and to do so is viewed as letting children be responsible for running the show without any adult guidance. We are subtly conditioned to believe that if we grant children control over their own lives, then they will grow up to be entitled, self-centered narcissists and we would be weak, lazy, and ineffective parents. The truth is that children deserve to feel empowered in their decision-making process, and this comes about when we can be the Collaborator.

Lydia and Connor perceived themselves as the Disciplinarians rather than the Collaborators. They viewed Kinsley's intense defiance, persistent negotiating, and epic tantrums when she didn't get her way as something innately bad that they needed to fix. Rather than acknowledging Kinsley as an important part of the family team who had valuable opinions and teaching her the vital skills of working together, they focused their energy on squashing her into something more manageable. This backfired in every way possible. Kinsley was unwilling to adopt a Masked Self, which left everyone in chronic conflict, burnout, and exhaustion.

During a home visit, Kinsley became enraged when she was told she could not have any chocolate. Quickly, she darted toward the kitchen and climbed the cabinets, convinced that her mother must be hiding it. Her parents frantically tried to pull her down, only for her to escape their grip and search again. She sat in time-out for five minutes before she snuck into the kitchen again. Lydia resigned: "There is no controlling this. She's not going to stop."

Lydia was right: Kinsley was not going to magically stop. When her heart was set on something, she was determined to get it, something Lydia noticed in Kinsley's temperament right from the very start. This quality is great for a future leader but difficult to parent. When a child is hell-bent on their way, resist the urge to demand your way, and at the same time be careful about jumping completely out of the way. Demanding your way sounds like: "I'm counting to three, and if I get to three, you're going to be in big trouble." Jumping out of the way sounds like: "Screw it. If you fall, don't say I didn't warn you." Your words may vary, but the sentiment behind them is centered on controlling the child's physical actions or simply absolving yourself of any responsibility over your child. Neither of these stances are supportive. Instead, you want to find the middle ground. This is where being a Collaborator can serve your family.

1. **Shift your mindset.** Your child is not acting out only to test you. They are resisting to test *themselves*. You are collaborating on their personal growth and development just as much as they are learning to cooperate with your family flow. When children express their need for power in big, demanding, over-the-top ways, it's often because they are feeling disempowered, helpless, or out of control in certain aspects of their life. Try to understand their powerlessness and teach them more constructive ways to get their needs met.

2. **Connect with your child and honor their ideas.** You may need to take a deep breath and ground your body. Remind yourself that this is not an emergency. You will get through this together. In response to Kinsley's demand for chocolate, Lydia said, "You don't seem to like my plan. What's your idea? I'm listening." Kinsley said that it wasn't fair that Mom and Dad didn't have to ask for chocolate, so why did she? She wanted more autonomy and control over how she fed herself, which is not unreasonable for a child her age. When parents elevate chocolates and candies into prizes and rewards for good behavior, not only is it a subtle way to control the child, but it also makes those treats more alluring and exciting. Kinsley was especially attuned to feeling con-

trolled, which activated her need to resist their psychological grip with more fire and persistence.

3. **Deliver boundaries with consistency, clarity, and connection.** It is vital when you're collaborating with your child that you are clear about which behaviors are acceptable and which are not. You do not need to convey this with a shame-inducing tone. However, it is necessary that you spell things out clearly for your child. Lydia said directly, firmly, and lovingly: "That makes so much sense. It doesn't feel fair that Daddy and I have more freedom to choose when we get to eat chocolate. You want to have more charge over when chocolate is on the menu . . . and climbing the cabinets and scaling them like you're Spider-Girl is not safe, and I cannot let you do that again." Because Lydia took the time to honor her child's need for more personal control and power, Kinsley was able to accept the limit placed on her behavior.

4. **Encourage problem-solving.** It's time to unlearn the limiting idea that children must comply at all costs. Instead, invite your child to work with you. Be careful not to do all the solving if your child is at an age when they are exercising this important cognitive task. Your child builds emotional intelligence, stress resilience, and conflict competence when you step back and support their problem-solving process. Lydia said, "So you really want chocolate right now, and we are in the middle of your play therapy session. How should we solve this problem?" Kinsley came up with an agreeable plan: "What if I have one piece right now, and then after dinner I have one more piece?" Mom agreed to the plan. Making these types of accommodations within reason are especially

important for your children. It tells them that you value their input, you respect their ideas, and you'll consider their opinions when doing so is reasonable and makes sense.

Helping kids to get comfortable with negotiation and collaboration is not conventional wisdom. The traditional approach to parenting heavily relies on the power hierarchy, with the parent at the top and the child subservient to the parent's rule. This crushes your child's innately sovereign spirit and is not helpful to the relationship you're nurturing with your child. When your mission is to break a child's will, they will spend the rest of their life trying to be unbroken. When you intentionally create an environment in which working together is a cherished, reliable practice, you'll find that your child's power needs are routinely met without it necessarily being a big deal. Sure, they'll have their moments—we all do—but you'll repeatedly return to this practice of supporting their autonomy needs rather than suppressing them.

Sometimes we will not be able to accommodate a child's request to negotiate, perhaps due to timing, logistics, or the fact that their requests are not reasonable. For example, working hard on a piano lesson does not necessarily warrant a request to skip school and go to Disneyland. When you're unable to collaborate with your child, take the lead calmly, lovingly, and sensitively.

You can tell them, "I love your idea. Thanks for sharing it. But we're going to go in a different direction." Be prepared to hold the feelings this might elicit by becoming the Emotional Container for them. It's unlikely that you'll have a Brady Bunch child who says, "Oh, shucks!," snaps their fingers, and happily moves forward. (Wouldn't that be a dream?) More likely, you'll have a child who expresses their disappointment through tears, frustration, or anger. Validate and comfort your child while being clear that sometimes grown-ups follow children's ideas, and other times children follow grown-ups' ideas. The more consistently you have this balance in your relationship with your child, the more they will come to trust that you do care about their opinions, even if you can't always put them into action.

A Final Note on Needs

Having needs—and requiring them to be met in a timely enough manner—is an inescapable fact of the human experience. You may have been raised in an authoritarian household where your basic needs were provided for, but giving you anything beyond food, clothing, and shelter was thought to make you entitled and snotty. Allow me to reassure you that meeting children's needs does not create bratty children. In fact, it is quite the opposite. Neglecting their needs is likely to leave the child in a "needier" psychological state. As they grow, their emotional maturity may be stunted, and they may expect others to meet their needs for them.

As adults, we have the autonomy to get our needs met. If we are thirsty, we go get a drink of water. If we are too hot, we take off our sweater or turn up the air-conditioning. Kids are developing an understanding of their needs, and that's where parents serve a crucial role. The Ladder of Needs is a framework that enables you to bring a fresh perspective to your interactions with your child. When you see your child acting out, one of the first questions you can ask yourself is: *I wonder what they're needing right now?* Their behavior may not fully match the need that needs to be met. A crying child may be thirsty and in need of a drink; a child having a tantrum may be sad and in need of your emotional containment and support. Using the Ladder of Needs as your guide, start with Safety and continue until you can clearly identify the need, and then respond to help fulfill that need. As the interpreter of your child's needs, assess the situation before you respond. Try to determine what is lurking behind the provocative behavior. From this more attuned space, you can help your child to connect the dots between their behavior, their emotions, and their underlying need. It's okay if it takes some time to learn how to "categorize" their needs, but with practice, you'll get the hang of it. The more you make this framework a part of your daily life, the more you'll teach your kids to assert themselves and honor their needs and desires as they mature.

. . . . . .

CHAPTER 7

Calming Their Stress and Anxiety

TALLULAH AND JEANIE STRUGGLED TO BE ON THE SAME PAGE about how to raise their six-year-old child, a sensitive and strong-willed sweetheart named Rocco. In addition to constant disagreements about how to raise their feisty young child, Tallulah was facing a high-risk pregnancy and was bedridden due to potential risks for serious complications. Jeanie was underemployed and had to work extra hours to support the family. There was a lot going on, and they were struggling. Naturally, it was easy to blame Rocco's disobedience for the chaos they couldn't control.

When you find yourself pointing your finger toward your child, notice that there are always three fingers pointing back at you. Let those fingers be a reminder to go inward and be curious and compassionate, rather than critical and accusatory. Your children are a product of the environment that *you* create for them.

Rocco was reacting to the stress of his family environment with intense emotional outbursts. Kicking, biting, hitting, and throwing were becoming his norm, and his moms were desperate for answers. Like most parents I work with, their first instinct was to deny the role that stress was playing in Rocco's life. Parents naturally want to reject the notion that their children feel the strain that surrounds them! It's in our best interest to believe that our children are immune to disruption in the home. We comfort ourselves with the delusion that children are living in an idyllic fantasy, because it gives us hope that our children may not feel the weight of life's stressors the way we do. Although we like to think that we're protecting them from facing hard things in life, in reality, they're experiencing them alongside us and looking to us for direction and guidance in how to handle them. The answer is not to ignore the stress or try to shield kids from it, but to help them understand it at an age-appropriate level.

Stress and Anxiety Are Contagious

Let me assure you that it is common to feel anxious or stressed—it happens to all of us. I am not placing blame on parents by suggesting that their stress or even their mental health issues *cause* mental health issues in children—mental health is far more nuanced than that. But I ask parents to remember that when you're reactive to the stress in your life, you project your anxiety outward, influencing your children's inner voice with the noise and racket of your own. If, however, you can regulate that stress, you are more likely to teach your children to cope with life's stressors in a way that can favor mental health distress and dysfunction. You won't be able to remove all the stressors in your life, but you can learn new ways to cope that are healthy and supportive.

Modern parents are incredibly stressed. I've noticed a trend over the past several years that show that parents are becoming more and more burned out as they attempt to keep up with the grind that our hustle culture demands. Millennial mothers reportedly experience more anxiety than mothers from the Boomer generation, and 70 percent of parents say that family responsibilities are a significant source of stress in their lives. A two-generation longitudinal study of pregnant women revealed that millennial mothers are more depressed than mothers in the 1990s.

I am troubled by the lack of public acknowledgment about the causes of stress, anxiety, and depression experienced by today's parents (especially mothers)—and the fact that we are suffering from these symptoms *more* than previous generations did. Instead, we're told that we've "gained a lot more awareness of mental health," that "previous generations were less likely to talk about mental health problems," and that the only reason why it seems like modern parents are struggling more is that we're so vocal about all the problems inherent in parenthood. While this may be true, this cannot be the only reason parents feel more on edge and less secure as they try to navigate the modern challenges of raising their children.

Modern parents are expected to balance their work and family lives with ease and grace, despite how demanding parenting today is. When I was growing up, my mother's version of playing with me was handing me a dry rag and a can of Pledge. If I didn't want to clean the house all day, I needed to be out of the house, completely unsupervised. Today's mothers who work outside the home spend just as much time tending to their children as did stay-at-home mothers in the 1970s. On top of that, the expectation to give our children the best of the best opportunities permeates our lives. With social media comparisons and a significant lack of personal support, many families feel as if they're failing, they aren't capable, and something must be wrong with them.

Social media parenting influencers in particular often create anxiety. When I first started teaching, Instagram wasn't a space where people shared ideas (it was more for image sharing), and so "controversial" topics like whether to sleep-train your child were between parents and their care providers. Now, you're given hundreds of hot takes on issues that aren't that significant to child-rearing, like whether you should "lie" to your kids about Santa Claus, which often leaves parents feeling even worse.

In many ways, modern parents have been led astray from their own intuition. You are told to put all your parenting decisions in the hands of the experts and ignore what might feel true to you. In my personal and professional experiences, I have found the lack of inner listening and the overreliance on experts to have significantly increased parental stress and anxiety. (And I say this as a so-called expert!) It has also created a codependent relationship with information. Without the information, you feel an emptiness and a lack of direction. Yet with the information, the emptiness persists, because you must now rely on others to know which direction to take. I'm encouraging you to find the balance. Consider the perspective of someone who has devoted a large portion of their life to parenting and children, but also listen to your gut— you know your child better than anyone (even if it doesn't feel that way sometimes).

Cultivate Your Inner Knowing

If you're overrelying on outside sources to tell you what to do to "fix" a problem, the following steps will help to increase your inner wisdom. This practice will allow you to detach from the anxious need to solve your parenting woes instantly and will help you feel more comfortable in the not-knowing. The more confident you become with sitting with the unknown, the more self-assured and less stressed you will feel as a parent.

1. When you're stumped by something parenting-related, before you search outward for answers, go inward. Ask yourself: *What is my heart telling me?* You'll know that you are in alignment with your highest self when your head feels clear, your feet feel grounded, your breath flows easily, and you feel at peace. To get there, all you need to do is make an intentional effort to slow down and be with yourself first.

2. Once you are clear on your internal direction, feel free to search outward for additional insights and opinions. If you find a direction that contradicts what feels true to you, ask yourself: *What's leading me to follow this guidance: fear or security?* Let's say you've chosen to wait to give your child a smartphone. You may find convincing arguments online in favor of giving children early access to phones. If you decide to go against your intuition because "the experts said so," you're acting out of fear, which will throw you out of alignment and add more stress to your mental load. If you decide that a smartphone could potentially be appropriate for your child and your family, and you make this decision confidently by balancing both your inner knowing and the information you're consuming, then you're acting with security.

3. Keep the door open to reevaluate. As human beings, we are constantly evolving and changing. Why shouldn't we allow ourselves to do the same when it comes to parenting? What has felt supportive and helpful for you today may not be the case tomorrow. When that happens, tell yourself: *My inner knowing has evolved. What feels truest to me now?* Work on listening to yourself.

Different Stressors Your Child May Face

When faced with your child's challenging behavior, in addition to understanding their unmet needs and your personal triggered reaction, it's important to be attuned to the challenging circumstances they may be navigating. Not all of these will be a part of your unique family dynamic, but I encourage you to consult this list when you're curious if underlying stress may be motivating your child's behaviors and emotions. By being aware of the stressors that negatively impact your children's behaviors, you can support them in building stress resilience.

- Moving to a new home
- Starting a new school
- Birth of a new sibling
- Adding bonus children or stepchildren to the family
- Changes in childcare
- General changes and transitions
- Parental discord (even if you're fighting while they're sleeping—they're still absorbing it)
- Lack of social or community support
- Prolonged separation from a parent (e.g., a parent who often travels for work multiple days per week)
- Death/loss of someone close to the child (including pet loss)
- Parental separation or divorce (when managed intentionally and consciously, separation won't damage your child, but you will need to be mindful of how you help

your children with the grief and loss that comes with a family breakup)

- Poverty or marginalized socioeconomic status
- Racial or ethnic marginalization or discrimination
- Sex or gender marginalization or discrimination
- Religious marginalization or discrimination
- Major illnesses or hospitalizations
- Social media
- Limited privacy and lack of trust from grown-ups (i.e., parents tracking children's phones via GPS)
- Cultural expectation to always be connected
- Foster care and adoption
- Isolation and disconnection due to the pandemic
- Gun violence (the leading cause of death in children involves firearms) and the active shooter drills that 95 percent of American schoolchildren must submit to are associated with a 39 percent increase in depression, 42 percent increase in stress and anxiety, and a 23 percent increase in overall physiological health problems, including kids aged five years old through high school.
- Violence in the community
- Parental drug or alcohol abuse
- Violence toward the child (including physical, sexual, verbal, or psychological)
- Parental neglect
- Serious household dysfunction (untreated parental mental illness, parental incarceration, domestic violence)

While many of these sound like obvious stressors, even so-called minor stressors can have a big impact on tiny humans. Like many preschoolers, my eldest child struggled with transitioning into preschool. I thought nothing of it, provided him empathic support, and thought that his separation anxiety would eventually work itself out. Months passed, and it was the same struggle every night before school and at drop-off. I couldn't identify any unmet needs, but some notable stressors were present. He started school around the same time we had a lapse in childcare and after a period in which we'd changed care providers many times due to various issues. Of course he was struggling!

He was also grappling with something far less obvious. He started preschool around the four-year anniversary of a significant hospitalization he had in infancy. He repeated several times that he was scared to go to school, because "what if they take me away, and then I won't see you and I'll cry for you and you won't come, like when I was at the hospital?"

Totally caught off guard, I stayed curious with him, asking what he meant when he said "at the hospital." Surely he had no recollection of his surgery when he was eleven weeks old! He proceeded to describe the moment when I handed him to the nurse, and she rolled him to the operating room without me. He described the long narrow hallway, the bright lights, and everyone in white coats. His description was exactly how I remembered it. I was shocked. He said he woke up and "then they killed me again," another detail that surprised me, given that the surgeon said he aroused too soon and they had to administer more anesthesia to finish the surgery. Then he cried out, "And I cried and cried for you. And when you didn't come fast enough, I thought you were never coming." Heartbroken, I held him in my lap, comforted him, validated his feelings, brought clarity to his story, and helped him find a way through it. After processing this story together, we were able to put the stress (and trauma) of that experience behind us, and he has never had an issue with transitioning into school since.

Stress is largely unavoidable, and it's not a parent's job to try to prevent children from encountering stress in their lives. The parent's responsibility is to model and teach children the important steps toward stress resilience. While we want to protect children from soul-crushing adverse experiences that lead to toxic stress (i.e., abuse, violence, and so on), they need to develop stress resilience so they can better manage life's inevitable stresses. Try to be mindful of the impact that stress has on your child specifically, and then help your child to make sense of the particular stress they're facing.

How Stress Affects a Child's Behaviors and Emotions

My feisty five-year-old client Everleigh was clearly stressed out by kindergarten. With all the hitting, yelling, kicking, and shoving, every morning felt like a battle for her parents to get her out the door. Prior to our work together, her parents used traditional discipline methods to try to eliminate her misbehavior. They spanked, yelled, took away privileges, and frequently put her in time-out.

Rather than being curious about the fears she had regarding school, they assumed she was being difficult to "get her way" and then retaliated in controlling ways. Any time she expressed a disinterest in school or a hesitancy to enter the school grounds, they would dismiss her complaints: "School is necessary, so quit your whining!" It seemed clear to me that their aggressive and rejecting behavior was fanning the flames of Everleigh's stress reactions. She needed someone to support her with her stress. Instead, her load grew heavier with shame and loneliness.

Children rarely act out arbitrarily, and so I was curious about her indifference to school. Everleigh shared that she had an overly strict teacher who often yelled at the class, took away recess as a punishment, and expected the kids to be quiet and never cry. A frown grew on her face as she disclosed that, despite trying her hardest to be a good girl, she was consistently on red on the behavioral modification chart—a public shaming tool.

At home, Everleigh got the message that she was constantly failing, only to go to school and receive a similar message. Her behavioral and emotional upsets were in direct response to the start of her new school and the relentless pressure she felt from her parents to never mess up. Notably, similar issues surfaced about eighteen months earlier, when her sister was born. Everleigh was naturally more physically and emotionally dysregulated (as many children seem to be during this type of life event), and her parents came down hard on her with the belief that they had to do it now or she'd never learn. But when a child's stress is not dealt with in a supportive, nurturing way when it happens, it compounds, potentially exacerbating behavioral and emotional issues when additional stressors develop.

When children are feeling stressed, it's unlikely they are going to sit down and share with you what they're feeling—indeed, they probably don't even have the language to do so. Instead, you'll see other telltale signs on their sleep, behaviors, and emotions. Some children are especially sensitive to added stress and challenges in family and home life. Other children can naturally tolerate more stress. These are some of the classic stress indicators in children:

- **Stress can impact children's sleep.** It can make their sleep less restorative. They may have trouble falling asleep or staying asleep. They may struggle with nightmares and sometimes bed-wetting (although that is

172

sometimes unrelated to stress). They may also struggle with separating from you at nighttime.

- **Stress can impact how children eat.** Some children focus their control on how and what they're eating to manage the stress in their lives, which can be very dangerous if it leads to an eating disorder. Some children may overeat to self-soothe and comfort themselves. Some children may hide their eating habits.

- **Stress can impact learning, memory, and executive functioning.** When your child's brain is consumed with fending off stress, it has fewer resources to devote to the other important tasks they are trying to accomplish. This is especially true if your child experiences a significant trauma or is exposed to chronic toxic stress (i.e., abuse, neglect, or serious household dysfunction).

- **Stress can impact your child's immune system.** Serious stress problems that remain unaddressed suppress the immune system, putting your child at risk for developing serious health conditions, such as asthma, heart disease, stroke, an autoimmune disease, and cancer.

- **Stress can lead to increased physical aggression,** like hitting, kicking, throwing, and pushing.

- **Stress can lead to increased verbal aggression,** like yelling, screaming, teasing, and name-calling.

- **Stress can lead to increased defiance,** a refusal to follow directions, and talking back in a "disrespectful" tone.

- **Stress can lead to separation anxiety and even phobias.** My eldest experienced two hospitalizations, one in infancy and another as a toddler, and both hospitalizations required quite a bit of poking and prodding. When he was older, every single time we went to the doctor for an immunization, he experienced near-panic attacks. Once we came up with a plan to help him manage his anxiety better, he learned to tolerate the pain of the shots with more stress resilience.

- **Stress can lead to depressed moods**, irritability, quickness to anger, isolation, and unexplained tearfulness. In some cases, children make suicidal statements like "I wish I were dead." If your child says this, don't sweep it under the rug. It's a serious call for help, so please seek professional support.

- **Stress can lead to problems with peers**, like challenges with interactions, difficulty with conflict resolution, and controlling play behaviors.

These are all normal reactions to stress. Depression, anxiety, and irritability are coping mechanisms we use to adapt to the stress around us. And I want to be clear that these pages are not intended to be used as a tool to diagnose your child. Instead, I encourage you to recognize how stress may be impacting your child, adjust your response accordingly so you can help your child through it, and, if necessary, seek additional support from a licensed mental health provider who can support you with a more individualized approach as needed.

Additionally, you should never blame yourself for how your child reacts to whatever stressors that may be present in your family's life. Not only will the blame not serve you, but it's also misplaced shame and an opportunity for self-reflection, accountability, and personal growth. When you blame yourself, you keep the focus on you, rather than on your child. So, instead of blaming, take accountability for your actions. Say you're sorry when you mess up. Take the steps you need to repair and move forward with your kids. But be gentle with yourself in the process. Focus on how you're showing up now, rather than putting yourself down for not preventing the stressors in the first place.

Teach Your Child to S.T.O.P. Stress

When your child acts out, rather than immediately trying to stop the behavior (unless the child is hurting themselves or others), consider their behaviors in the context of any stressors they may be trying to process and make sense of.

It's important when we're processing the inevitable stressors of our lives that we approach it from a place of safety, protection, and nurturance. We want to acknowledge that it's happening, explain any steps we're taking to minimize stress, and help our children find other ways to tolerate and manage their own behavioral and emotional responses. The S.T.O.P. approach encourages children to pause and become better aware of their feelings while guiding them toward articulating what drives those feelings—and subsequent behaviors.

- "Slow your body down." Intentionally slowing down in a stressful moment helps give our body a chance to recover and connect on a deeper level.

- "Talk about what's bothering you." Children need to know that it's safe and acceptable to talk about vulnerable, hard subjects. Being open to having hard conversations deepens relationships on an emotional level.

- "Observe your feelings." You can't insulate your kids from stress or anxiety, but you can help them better manage stress by teaching them how to cope by identifying and naming what they are feeling.

- "Proceed with a new choice." Teaching children alternative ways to express themselves after confirming that you understand where they're coming from is an important way to correct challenging behaviors, without shaming or being critical or judgmental.

S.T.O.P. helps you address the impact of stress with your child, rather than rejecting their behavior outright. Involving your child in a discussion about a stressful situation needs to be done in a developmentally appropriate way, so please adjust any language I offer to suit your child. Here is how you might use S.T.O.P. after school when your child has some dysregulated behavior that confuses you.

- You could say, "I can tell something important is happening for you right now. Let's slow down together and talk about it. What's going on?"

- If your child shuts down, try offering a co-regulating activity like playing a board game and during play ask more specific questions: "What was it like at the lunch table today?" "What did you play at recess?" "Is there any bullying going on at your school?" The point is not to interrogate your child but to ask questions that can get them talking. Show them you are interested in what's going on, let them know that you are available to listen to them, help them when they're ready, and offer your support when they seem stressed or anxious.

- You may or may not get much out of your kid. Honestly, it is child dependent. You can offer your observations and invite them to self-reflect: "I've noticed that after school, you want to hit more, yell more, and blame others. That's why I wonder what your school day is like, so I can help you with this. What are you feeling inside?"

- Once you have a handle on what they're feeling, then you help them find new ways to express themselves: "It makes sense that you're feeling tired and afraid of getting in trouble. I remember that feeling at school, always feeling like I had to get it right all the time. That's exhausting. What are some safer ways you can express your tiredness and your fear of getting in trouble?"

S.T.O.P. is a practical strategy that allows you to be easier on your kids. It helps you build their stress resilience and teaches them to think consciously about their feelings and choices, connect their behavioral reactions to the stress they're facing, and find safety and trust in themselves and with you.

Being hard on your kid doesn't support their stress resilience, and it ultimately hurts your relationship. If you feel like you are being too hard on your kid, you probably are; if your kid says, "You don't understand!" you probably don't. It is hard to be a child. From an adult perspective, we feel like it's easy: they go to school; they play; they have someone to feed them, drive them, and do their laundry; and they don't have mortgages or the responsibilities of the family weighing on them. But if you have concerns about any issues, they probably pick up on it. It can be stressful for children to be told what to do all day. They don't often have a say in what happens and when. They are told what to do by parents, teachers, coaches, caregivers, extended family, neighbors—you name it. Is it any wonder that power struggles ensue?

Make an Empathy Book

The most effective tool I've found to help children cope with stress is an empathy book. These are homemade, short social stories that you create to help your child process the life events they're facing. Empathy books can be used to help children process the birth of a new sibling, the death of a parent, the transition to foster placements, their parents' divorce, or any tough, disconnected moment.

You can choose to make it ahead of time and then present it to your child, or you can make it with your child, depending on your child's emotional maturity and attention span. Play around with it and see what resonates more with them.

Empathy books are a collaborative tool that not only speaks to your child's lived experience but also helps to correct the faulty, incoherent narratives that children are prone to tell themselves, especially when they are stressed. Children aren't born as logical meaning-makers. They take bits and pieces of what they witness, weave them together from an immature perspective, and then tell a tale that isn't completely accurate.

We don't want our children perseverating on incomplete storylines that perpetuate their anxiety and distress. Instead, we want to create a beautiful emotional container. Using empathy books as a primary tool, we can help our children weave together a more complete storyline.

- Use stick figures. Don't go overboard with the illustrations (unless you really want to).
- Tell the story from your child's perspective.
- Have a clear beginning, middle, and end.

- Tell the story in the first or the third person, depending on your child's preference. Some kids don't like using "I"—it's too personal. Some children don't want it to feature a person: they can express themselves more freely through an animal figure.

- Keep the story concise and clear. You don't need to add every detail.

- Have the illustrations represent your child's real feelings and emotions.

- End the story with something hopeful and reparative.

Children don't require perfect, stress-free lives. They require a humble leader. Someone who isn't afraid to crack, but who also takes responsibility for the ways their breaking under pressure may sting others. My professional journey in guiding parents of anxious and stressed-out kids, plus my own personal recovery from anxiety and chronic stress, have taught me that managing the effects of everyday stress is a lifelong lesson for all of us. Your unique story will color in the lines, but the outline is all the same. We're all just out there, putting in our best effort, trying to survive the stress and trying to create as much joy, pleasure, and connection as we can.

As you feel more confident with how you manage your own stress, as well as the reactions you may have to your kid's inevitable feelings of anxiety and worry, you will be able to show up for your children in healed, whole, and new ways. You will correct whatever patterns of dismissing, rejecting, or ridiculing your child's stress that you may have faced growing up. You won't be able to eliminate stressors entirely, but you will be a guiding light for your child in terms of how to cope. Trust that you are the rock your child leans on for stability and strength in times of trials and tribulations. Eventually, they will internalize your steadfast demeanor as their own. When you falter and project more stress onto your child, be gentle on yourself. Repair, reconnect, and keep moving forward without being held back by the ball and chain of shame and self-loathing.

CHAPTER 8

• • • • • •

Ending Power Struggles

OR EIGHT-YEAR-OLD IRIS, EVERYTHING—AND I DO MEAN *everything*—was a battle. Her parents, completely distraught by the intensity of her strong will, found themselves in epic screaming matches almost daily. Basic requests like eating break-fast, getting dressed, completing homework, and preventing phys-ical aggression toward her three-year-old sister consumed a significant amount of their energy. A simple statement like "It's time for bed" would turn into a nightly brawl of chaos, tears, and frustration . . . for everyone. In our initial session, both parents broke down in tears: "Is it supposed to be this hard? How do we get her to stop and obey? We are sick of this!"

I certainly didn't blame them for feeling overwhelmed and ex-hausted. Their dynamic was not working. Parenting is *not* sup-posed to be this hard. When you get sucked into power struggles with your kids, everyone loses.

You are not alone if you're struggling with your child. It may be over bedtime, what to eat, morning routines, what clothes to wear (or not), getting out the door in a timely fashion, screen time; or with older kids, issues like friendships, homework, curfews, social media, or what sport, college, or career the child should pursue. Conflict with your kids is unavoidable.

The goal in ending power struggles isn't to prevent headbutting from happening altogether but to understand how (and why) they may trigger you and find artful, creative ways to help your child through the conflict. Approaching power struggles this way enhances collaboration among every member of your family, building a home environment where everyone's needs (and wants) are equally considered, even if we can't instantly honor them.

Know that this will take time. You're either going to spend time resisting your child, demanding your way, and feeling stifled by how much control you must maintain to trust your child, or you're going to put in the time cultivating a dynamic where mutual respect, mutual listening, and collaborative problem-solving are happening every day. It truly is your choice. Your kid is not baiting you. When kids resist their parents, it's usually because they have an unmet need. Parents typically stay committed to power struggles, because on a deeply unconscious level, they are enthralled by how powerful this dynamic makes them feel.

Redefining Respect

When a child submits to their parent's will, we call this respect. When a parent humiliates and shames a child to get them to do what they demand, we call this discipline that teaches respect. This is not respect. According to the *Oxford English Dictionary*, respect is a feeling of deep admiration for someone based on their abilities, qualities, or achievements. In the traditional parenting perspective, simply being a parent grants one respect, due to their position in the power hierarchy. They do not need to communicate in a respectful, compassionate way if their subject—oops, their child—isn't doing what they've asked. They will crush, criticize, and condemn their child's missteps and personal attempts for power . . . because that's how a good parent teaches their child to be respectful.

Exerting your power over your children is draining and costly. You won't get the respect previous generations believed they would get out of it. Instead, you'll get kids who feel resentful toward you and obligated to be around you, who don't necessarily enjoy spending time with you, and who feel guarded with you. When parents assert their authority in a dominating, overbearing way, children are less interested in working with them, because it's in our human nature to resist being controlled.

At our highest potential, humans are incredibly savvy, creative, and deeply collaborative. We have made achievements as a species because of our inherently cooperative nature. We've built lanes for travel on land and in the sky, discovered electricity, and built the internet to connect humans across the globe. We did all this by encouraging a collaborative attitude, honoring each participant's strengths, and bringing visions to life. This is the spirit that we can create in our homes to shift our family life from combat to collaboration. It's time to release your need for power and authority over your child's destiny. Stop telling yourself, *If I don't get a handle on this now, they're going to be doomed later.* Start telling yourself, *This is an area of growth for us. We both need more collaborative skills to improve this situation.*

Making changes in your family dynamic begins with you. We all exist as separate people who are part of different systems—family, community, school, work, government, religious, and social. As adults, we interact with those systems with an innate knowledge that we have the individual, personal freedom to do so—or to choose not to. It's not any different for our kids.

Children, like all human beings, are intrinsically sovereign beings. However, in the family system we often see kids as clay that we're responsible for molding, not free and autonomous beings. They're reflections of parenting achievements, so they better not make us feel like failures through their bad behavior or poor choices. We've deluded ourselves into believing that we have control over our children's outcome, causing us to double down in desperate need of the rule of law. And it is this delusion that keeps us trapped in the chaos of control.

You cannot shape your child into something they're not by demanding that they live their life to comply with your commands. This is the pathway toward future resentment, bitterness, and disconnection, which we're watching unfold as more and more adult children choose estrangement rather than staying in relationship with their dysfunctional, boundary-pushing family members. You can make a choice to connect rather than fight with your kids, and by making this investment, you can ensure long-term security in your relationship with your child.

The Origin of Power Struggles

Parents tend to operate in extremes. The helicopter parent hovers over their kid's every waking moment and doesn't let them make a move without parental involvement. They don't intend to be controlling. From their perspective, they are keeping their children safe and showing their kids that they love them by being extra attentive and engaged. Children, however, feel stifled by the parent's anxious need for control. We generally see more power struggles occur in parents who helicopter their kids.

The dominating parent aggressively challenges and commands their children to do as they say, not as they do, with the hope that this will raise sturdy kids who can pull themselves up by their bootstraps. In these homes, there is little room for error. Personal responsibility may be beaten into the children, demonstrating that you get what you want in life by overpowering those who are more vulnerable than you. There's a lack of investment in the security of the relationship with the child and a higher risk for long-term disconnection and tension.

The permissive parent, on the other hand, lets the children run the show, usually in fear of how the children might react to their boundaries, limits, or guidance. Many permissive parents will resist my guidance with, "My kid would never let me . . ." which signals the deep need for clearer guideposts in the family system. It's not about what your kid will or will not allow. Yes, they can have boundaries with you—something I believe in strongly. But it's also an important responsibility of childhood to learn how to cooperate and work with others. It's not about them not "letting you" do something, whether that's redirecting their behavior, validating their feelings, or anything else. It's about what skills you're willing to teach and what boundaries you're willing to hold. But, to keep the peace, permissive parents give their children too much control—too many choices, too much negotiation, and a lack of leadership and decision-making when it is necessary. While not necessarily controlling in an overt way, permissive parents often find themselves in the very power struggles that they desperately tried to avoid.

Sometimes, a parent's permissiveness is *so* hands-off that they become psychologically uninvolved, leaving the parenting up to the kids. This might sound like a kid's dream, but it's a nightmare. These children must fight for their parent's involvement. When the parent's disinterest becomes apparent, the child must work through complicated feelings like abandonment and rejection, both lonely psychological states for a child who relies on the safe, secure container of a mindful, attuned, responsive, and supportive adult.

Moving Through Power Struggles

Part of growing yourself as a parent is to unlearn the ingrained beliefs around your untouchable right to have power, control, and authority over your children. Instead, it's in your best interest to foster a mutually respectful dynamic that considers the thoughts, feelings, and needs of everyone in your family. When everyone in the system feels seen, heard, and understood, safety and security prevail, and that collaborative spirit can lead the way toward healthier, more fruitful interactions.

When your conditioning rears its ugly head, be kind and gentle with yourself. It's going to happen. That's part of the process. Your job is not to judge whatever need for control you have, but rather to have compassion for yourself and more awareness around what triggered it. You can accomplish this by using the M.O.V.E. Method. Remember those tools from Part One? We're going to come back to them here, just as you'll come back to them time and time again in your life.

Monitor Your Triggers

Observe Your Thoughts

Vary Your Perspective

Enact Change

Roger, Iris's father, initiated therapy so I could teach him how he could control her better. He physically overpowered her by yanking her around. He tried threatening and punishing her, and he even left her in her room for an hour during a meltdown, only to return to a completely destroyed room. The more he tried to control her, the more out of control she became.

First, Roger learned to **monitor** his triggers. Every time his daughter disobeyed him, he became enraged. He felt disrespected and couldn't understand why she didn't respect his authority. I asked him to sit with it. He practiced slowing down and really feeling the disrespect that shook him. He internally sensed it as a tightening in his throat and fists and a pit in his stomach. He felt trapped, so we talked to the trapped feeling. He grew up with an alcoholic father who used to fly off the handle in aggressive, drunken rages. He watched his mother get beaten as his father was deep in the throes of his addiction, expanding the shadow of a dark, wounded past that left Roger feeling unsafe, unprotected, and hypervigilant to any sign of threat. He feared the same dysfunctional environment was being created in his family, or worse, that he would become his father. While he wasn't an alcoholic, he felt the urge to use corporal punishment to gain control.

Second, Roger learned to **observe** his stressful thoughts. He tended to jump to conclusions with black-and-white thinking. *This is never going to stop! She is always going to be like this.* His inner child wanted to blame. *She's the reason why our family is such a mess.* Shame came pouring out in his "shoulds." *She should know better. It's not like we haven't had this discussion before!*

Third, Roger learned to **vary** his perspective. This conflict wasn't going to last forever (because nothing does), and it was his responsibility to make the changes that could help move things in a different direction with his daughter. Iris's behavior was challenging, and Roger's lack of effective collaborative problem-solving was contributing to the problem. He also needed more patience given that children require lots of repetition before they finally get what we're trying to teach them.

Finally, Roger learned to **enact** change. He had never tried asking Iris's opinion on bedtime, the morning routine, or her after-school commitments. He also wasn't very consistent in how he reacted to her. So, he committed to hearing her out, incorporating her ideas when it was reasonable, and maintaining a consistent stance that he would not escalate alongside her. He was intentional about grounding his body, pausing, and slowing down every time he saw her ramping up. He knew he had to be the change he wanted to see in her. This takes courage and heart.

In three days, Iris went from destroying her room in a nightly fit of rage to asking her father to read a book with her and falling asleep peacefully. They collaborated on a bedtime routine, which he wrote down and let her pick and choose the order. Instead of barking orders for her to follow, he simply sat on the bed and waited for her to complete her tasks, offering nothing but specific, positive feedback after she completed a step (like, "Great job getting pj's on!"). He maintained his composure and kept his inner child nurtured and safe, even when she became more disruptive on their first couple of nights trying the new routine. Iris felt her father's regulation, which enabled her to soothe her own nervous system and maintain their plan. Instead of him begging her to lay down so he could read her a book, she approached him when she was ready. He couldn't believe that only ten minutes had passed from the start of the routine to her being ready to settle!

Their family dynamic transformed from disempowered to empowered. Roger began treatment believing his daughter had a serious mental illness (she didn't), and he ended treatment four months later feeling much more confident in his ability to guide her and support her. He was tuned into his tendency to control her, and exercises like M.O.V.E. helped him transform his stuck energy into something more productive. Iris showed us her incredible collaborative skills throughout the entire therapy process and taught each of us never to underestimate a strong-willed child. They may have their own agenda, but that doesn't mean they aren't interested in, or capable of, expanding their skill set. Children need to know that you believe in them, have confidence in them, and that you're not going to squash them with your personal insecurities and unresolved wounds.

Changing the Power Struggle

Although many parents perceive control as a way of keeping the peace, over-controlling prevents children from learning how to cope with difficult emotions. You can't rescue your child from disappointment, frustration, anxiety, or sadness. An important part of life is learning how to be okay with not always getting what you want. That being said, we don't need to make that lesson more painful than it already is. Kids are organically open to learning. They don't fear their emotions; they want to *feel* them. It's our fear of emotions that influences their fear of their feelings. You are not doing anything wrong if your child feels all the feelings. You're also not doing anything wrong if you sometimes feel like a broken record. Let's be honest: parenting often feels like an endless loop of saying the same things over and over. You issue the same directions and the same corrections because that is how children learn . . . you keep putting in the effort until it finally sticks.

Imagine if your child's kindergarten teacher tried teaching the alphabet three times to your kids, then threw their hands up in exhaustion declaring that your kids simply aren't getting it, so what's the use in repeating themselves? Or what if they decided to ignore your child until they learned the alphabet? Worse, what if they decided your kid needed physical punishment, privileges taken away, and other consequences until they got it? Giving up, ignoring, and punishments are all illogical and ineffective when it comes to teaching children the skills they lack. I'd bet that you would never accept this kind of treatment when it comes to your child's academic success, and yet every day I see parents lament the incredible amount of teaching that is required for a child's social and emotional success. We're conditioned to resort to the less effective techniques because they feed the hierarchical delusion that the parent is above the child. It's not the kids who are keeping you stuck; it's your response to your kids that keeps you stuck in power struggles.

I Want the Squishy!

Silvia was often triggered by her toddler's demanding behaviors, and she needed more tools to get calm in her own body and help regulate with her daughter, Luna. I handed Silvia, who was rattled and anxious upon entering my office, some soothing magnetic putty to squeeze. Intrigued, Luna demanded, "I want the squishy!" Silvia calmly told her no several times, until she couldn't take the repeated begging. "Just stop! I said no!" she shouted. Every parent I know has experienced this type of interaction.

In these situations, it's more effective to acknowledge the child's desire, show that you hear their disappointment, and restate the boundary calmly, firmly, and lovingly. I call this holding the feelings and holding the line: "Yes, I hear that you want this. It's disappointing that it's not safe to have it. Still, it's not a toy for you." For young children, you can redirect them to something else: "You can squeeze this Play-Doh instead." For older children, you'll want to invite them to find ways to solve the problem at hand: "What's something else you can play with that's safe for you?"

Silvia tried this approach, along with redirecting Luna to kinetic sand, and while Luna got the message, she released her disappointment by stomping her feet, yelling, and bawling her eyes out.

This aggravated Silvia. She believed that Luna had a secret plan to manipulate her into eventually giving in to her demands. This is where parents get lost in the power struggle. They make grand assumptions about their child's motives and how a situation will resolve. They're quick to label their children, and thus limit their potential with projections of who they think they are.

There's a better approach that will leave you feeling good about these moments, rather than drained, annoyed, or totally exhausted. Next time, try staying in the present moment, validating your child's true emotions, and resisting the urge to fix, change, or control them. This is what Silvia did. She acknowledged once or twice, "I hear you. You really wish you could play with it." And within a minute, Luna wiped her tears and announced that she was ready to play with something else. She went from intensely protesting to accepting a redirection quickly and easily. What changed was how Silvia engaged with Luna.

I Want to Put on My Own Shoes!

Jani was a feisty two-and-a-half-year-old with a strong need for power and control. Her mom, Julie, easily became worked up when Jani made her demands. Jani was doing what she was developmentally designed to do—establishing her independence and personal control. As children reach the toddler years and beyond, they are driven to prove their competence—not just to you but to themselves. Doing so builds self-trust, enhances self-reliance, and increases self-esteem. Children need our support in their skill-building process to help them get there.

Every morning when Julie requested that Jani put on her shoes, it became a battle. Jani would scream, "I do! Not you! Go away!" Scrambling to get out the door on time for work, Julie found herself reacting in emotionally immature ways: "Fine! I'm never going to help you again!" After a few moments of self-reflection, she acknowledged that she was triggered and thus feeding the power struggle. Being triggered isn't the problem; it's what we do with the triggers that can be helpful or unconstructive. It's not the child's responsibility to never trigger us, but it's our responsibility to L.E.A.N. into the trigger and M.O.V.E. through it.

Julie's early childhood history revolved around her being the perfect daughter. She never made a fuss, stayed quiet and silent, and was always compliant. When her parents told her to put on her shoes, there wasn't room for defiance or error. She simply did what she was told, because she feared the verbal reprimands her older brother endured. In adulthood, she relied heavily on guidance from others and didn't believe her inner compass was worth listening to. She worried about making mistakes, failing, and getting punished quite a bit. This conditioning served her nicely for her corporate desk job, but it didn't serve her in motherhood.

Julie began to recognize that yelling at Jani to hurry up or forcefully putting on her shoes was sending the wrong message. Julie wanted Jani to build her competence in these important life skills, yet reacting in an overly restrictive way wasn't supporting their relationship (and was making their mornings more difficult). Julie's stress reflected her inner child wounds of doubt and insecurity, and she risked projecting those same wounds onto her daughter by means of her behavior, actions, and parenting choices.

Instead of complicating a very normal child-parent interaction, I encouraged Julie to set a clear boundary for Jani: "I see you are working on getting your shoes on so we can go. I'm going to finish a few things in the kitchen, and when I come back, if your shoes are not on, then I will help you finish so we can leave on time." By honoring Jani's developmental needs, Julie helped to heal her own inner child needs by becoming a supportive, attuned parent. Instead of receiving a message of incompetence, Jani felt encouraged by her mom's belief in her, as well as relief in knowing that if she needed help, Mom would be there for her, too. This is the power of using clear, loving, and consistent boundaries with your kids to deter power struggles from getting needlessly out of hand.

Clear, consistent boundaries build a cooperative and collaborative framework in your home. Boundaries help children feel safe. They give kids a fence (so to speak), and within the fence, they have the freedom to explore however they desire. In most families I work with, I see one of two boundary problems play out. Either the boundaries are far too restrictive and limit the child's freedom, or there simply aren't enough boundaries and the child is granted too much freedom. Both scenarios increase power struggles. Boundaries and setting limits in an age-appropriate way can help kids to learn to handle the freedom they crave, while also teaching them how to cope with what that freedom brings.

SIMPLE BOUNDARY FORMULA FOR KIDS

Keep it positive: "When/If [expected behavior], then [outcome]."

Example: "When you clean up your mess, then we can go to the park."

Example: "If you keep your hands to yourself, then we can continue playing."

Avoid the negative: "If you don't [expected behavior], then [punishment]."

Example: "If you don't clean up your mess, then we won't go to the park."

Example: "If you don't keep your hands to yourself, then I won't play with you."

This formula is especially useful for young children, although you can use it for children up to ten to twelve years of age. You will want to involve your tweens and adolescents in more discussions around the rationale for boundaries and assist them in building their skills in critical thinking, problem-solving, risk assessment, time management, and emotion-management.

Are Well-Behaved Kids Always Okay?

Traditional parenting approaches have declared that a compliant, obedient child is the A on your parenting report card. Parents who have kids who "don't listen" are apparently failing.

Building a cooperative, engaged relationship with your children is absolutely a long-term goal of the style of parenting I'm teaching throughout this book. However, excessive compliance and obedience—in other words, not asserting one's will—are not usually signs of a healthy child-parent dynamic. An exceptionally well-behaved child, while generally easy to manage, is likely an excellent mask wearer. I'm not talking about children who are generally well-behaved but push back at times, demand some autonomy, and take risks that they know may disappoint their parents. They are learning how and when to consult their parents' opinions while actively exercising the muscle of listening to their soul needs as well. There's a healthy amount of conflict, as well as active collaboration and resolution. These are healthy qualities in any relationship dynamic, and it's vital that these skills are exercised in the context of the child-parent relationship to prepare children for future relationships.

The children I'm speaking about are like ducks in a pond. On the surface, they appear to be floating easily, but beneath the surface, they are paddling hard to stay afloat. You may have been one of those kids. As children, they aren't usually identified as candidates for therapy and often end up in my office as adults. They cling so tightly to the label of being "good" out of fear of being "bad" and feel bulldozed by their children's emotions and behaviors. At the core of it all is that they never learned how to balance their own power needs themselves. Instead, they learned to give up their power in favor of the grown-ups' demands and desires. This is a cycle you can liberate your children from repeating.

Children wearing the mask of disproportionate compliance and obedience may be working very hard at keeping up appearances, not letting their feelings show, and doing whatever they can to keep the peace. It is very possible that you have a child who naturally has a laid-back, don't-rock-the-boat attitude, but the key thing is to be *curious* about their behavior (or, in this case, lack thereof). Have they always been like this? Are they like this only in certain situations? Are they afraid of disappointing you? Be conscientious about asking their opinions because these children often need permission to know that they can self-advocate, their needs aren't selfish, and grown-ups are tuned in to their inner world (not only enamored with how easygoing they appear).

I am not suggesting that we should push obedient children into distressing interactions with us to light a fire in them. That's not necessary. I am suggesting that there are some serious downsides to a child not learning how to manage their power needs effectively.

Some children decide they are done working so hard to keep it all together, and they rebel. My eight-year-old client, Chelsea, who was passed around in the foster system before finding her forever family, clung to the mask of perfection to keep her adopted parents' love. In her teenage years, she became overwhelmed after years of emotional repression and peacemaking and started rebelling through risky sexual behaviors and drinking.

Some children feel that pleasing others is the only way they can maintain closeness with them, putting them at risk for unhealthy relational dynamics where their kind and generous demeaner is taken advantage of. I've seen this in hundreds of women I've worked with who fear they cannot set boundaries around their partner's hurtful behavior out of fear that they will disrespect them. They would rather silently suffer through the pain of being repeatedly harmed in their intimate relationships than address the conflict out of fear that they will ultimately feel disempowered anyway.

Your compliant child needs just as much attention as your child who pushes your buttons, and you cannot overlook their lack of power struggles as something to be admired and not attended to. As parents, we're easily distracted by messy emotions and challenging behaviors . . . so much so that we miss the kids who feel there is no room for them to mess up. If you've dealt with people pleasing, perfectionism, peacemaking, emotional suppression, and/or silent resentment throughout your life, I bet you can feel this message in your soul. It's never a child's job to hold the family together. In fact, I'd argue that it's the child's job to rattle the cage of inherited wounds and lead us toward a more awakened and liberated path.

Pause, Connect, Collaborate

Power struggles with children are demanding and exhausting, often contributing to even more burnout in parents who are already feeling pretty crispy. The chaos of the power struggle makes you feel as if you're being pulled in two directions at once.

When your power-hungry child demands your attention or their way, you may not have the energy for it. When it comes to "solving" power struggles, you have a choice. You can choose to engage and go down that rabbit hole, knowing very well the conflict won't be very productive for either of you. Or, by using the Pause, Connect, Collaborate (PCC) approach, you can take charge and steer your proverbial ship away from the storm and into smoother waters.

Imagine that you tell your child to clean up and get ready for bed. They quickly snap, "No, I'm not going to clean up, and you can't make me!" They run away, laughing like some evil genius, and you're fed up because it's been a stressful day and you are done repeating yourself. You're gently parenting, but these kids aren't gently childing. You begin to feel frustration rise within you as you think the thought that crosses practically every parent's mind a minimum of once per day: *Why won't these kids just listen?!?!*

Pause

First, pause. Take a deep breath. Notice what's happening inside your body. Do a full scan from head to toe, making note of areas of tension, disconnect, heat, and imbalance. Use any of the tools you learned in Part One that help you assess your internal state. If you or your children are not in danger, you can pause, center yourself, and get grounded. Ask yourself:

- Am I triggered? Annoyed? Pressed for time? What am I feeling emotionally?

- Is my inner drill sergeant taking over? Am I checking out and giving up?

- Can I see my child as a separate human being worthy of connection and respect, even if they seemingly "defy" me?

- Can I release my need to feel respected and embrace the truth that my children don't owe me anything? That I'm responsible for them, and not the other way around?

- Am I open to my role as teacher and guide, someone entrusted to nurture and support my child along their unique soul journey?

The more comfortable you become with self-reflection, the quicker this scan will be for you. In the beginning, it may feel challenging to allow yourself to pause and do this inner work prior to responding to your children. That's okay. Most of us are quick to react to our children. The Pause teaches you to slow down, attune, and respond more intentionally. Try to resist the urge to rush this process. Wait until you feel more grounded, regulated, and collected on the inside. You can still feel frustrated but together (rather than explosive). You can still feel annoyed but regulated (rather than critical). Giving yourself a chance to pause teaches your body to take charge of your own emotions. It helps you to be aware of what's coming up for you personally, allowing you to respond to the moment instead of acting out your inner child wounds.

Connect

Second, connect. We are often quick to correct the behavior, thus missing a vital opportunity to connect to the meaning behind the behavior. Connecting with a child in a discipline-related moment is usually the hardest step for most parents. Many parents tell me, "I can't notice their feelings, because I'm too focused on them not listening to me!" Take a breath and take a knee. Get down to your child's eye level. Doing so will tell both of your brains that this situation is not a threat, and you are capable of working this out together. Allow your facial expressions and your body language to mirror your child's. For example, if your kid is screaming and they're angry, your face and body can reflect some of that anger and frustration they're feeling. You don't want to become too dramatic here, so the rule of thumb is to mirror back at about half the intensity you see in your child. If your kid is crying, don't cry with them; simply put your hand on your heart and nod along, allowing your face to capture your genuine concern and care. Your goal in connection is to watch, listen, and understand what's happening on the inside for your child.

If you have asked your child to clean up and they dart away from you, it's perfectly appropriate to limit their problematic running by saying firmly and lovingly, "Stop your body, please." Walk slowly and deliberately toward your child. If they're young and they think this is a game, they will eventually find themselves in a corner. Once you're face-to-face with your child, get down on one knee, hold their hand, and validate where they are emotionally: "You really wish it wasn't clean-up time. I understand." Let your face communicate that you get that they wish they could keep playing. If it sounds simple, it's because it is. We don't need to over-complicate connecting. Here are four easy connection starters to use with your children in a challenging moment:

- "I hear you."

- "I'm with you."

- "Yes, this is hard."

- "You really wish . . . I understand."

As mentioned earlier, part of connecting with children is also providing guidance for behaviors that are unproductive and do not serve them well. Clear, consistent boundaries help your child understand exactly what you expect, and they build the threshold for more interpersonal success. We want our children to feel in control of their bodies and confident in their relationships. This means that they need loving, firm, and clear guidance for their behavior. Try not to overcomplicate this by focusing on "doing it right." Instead, practice telling your child clearly exactly what is okay and what is not okay.

You might say, "Running away when I make a request is not okay with me." The boundary is the line in the sand. Children aren't fragile, and they can certainly tolerate knowing when they've crossed the line. We can communicate that without shaming, ridiculing, humiliating, or harming them. You're forming a partnership with your children when you approach power struggles this way. Here are four simple boundary starters that you can adapt to encourage more accountability in your child:

- "I'm not okay with . . ."

- "That's not a safe way to express ourselves."

- "I can't let you . . ."

- "This isn't working."

Collaborate

The last step is to collaborate. Starting at an early age, begin asking your children, "How can we find a way to work together?" Children as young as three will be eager to provide their perspective. Sometimes you'll follow your child's lead, and other times you will be the one who makes the final decision. By trying to strike a balance between the two, you help your child learn the art of negotiation, while also helping them feel like a valued member of the family (which they most certainly are).

Collaboration is an active problem-solving skill that involves contributing ideas and coming up with a joint solution. Remember that children need to learn how to think about problems. Rather than seeing you or the relationship as the problem, they need to see the problem as the problem, so they can find a way through it. Children need support with learning the strategy behind solving problems if we want them to have fewer power struggles.

Power struggles are ineffective conflict-resolution skills. Good problem-solving skills involve anticipating that a problem may occur, identifying what the problem is, listing pros and cons, deciding on a solution, and then evaluating the outcome. A fun way to teach this skill is through strategy games like checkers. Resist the urge to tell them where to move because that would be doing the strategy for them. Instead, tell them the problem: "Your red piece needs to move into my home, but my black piece could jump you." See if (and how) they experiment with different solutions to the problem.

Children have different problem-solving skills depending on their developmental stage. Based on my work with children, I've devised some general guidelines for helping them collaboratively solve problems:

Toddlers: When given two choices, they will most likely choose one. Sometimes you will need to choose for them. Stick to two choices, because adding more is often overwhelming for our littlest ones.

Children three to five years old: They may be able to come up with an idea or two to solve a problem, but they will probably rely on some choices provided by you. As they reach kindergarten, the desire to critically think about problems and find solutions becomes more focal. Your job is to present them with the opportunity to think through their problems: *How should we solve this problem?* And then nurture their process by helping them come up with ideas.

Children six to ten years old: They can actively problem-solve by clearly defining the problem, imagining two to three solutions, identifying the pros and cons of each potential idea, then following through on implementing a plan. Children this age may require adults to oversee the implementation process, need parental ideas to get the ball rolling, and can benefit from adults helping them evaluate the effectiveness of the plan they collaborated on.

Tweens and teens: Parents need to step back and let their adolescents take the lead on examining the problems they face and coming up with an appropriate solution. Your big kids will appreciate knowing that you are available to support if requested, but this age group is actively working on taking risks, exploring, and learning about mistakes and repair on a whole new level. This does not mean that parents disengage and give up. This means that if their room is a mess, you don't harp and lecture on how dirty they are. Instead, follow this process:

- Help them identify the problem: They're struggling with organization and tidiness.

- Have them name three possible solutions to the problem: They may need clearly marked drawers or bins, visual reminders, or a clear limit to motivate them, such as "When your room is picked up, then you can head out to your friend's house."

- Have them name the pros and cons for each potential solution: The bins will help them stay organized, but they will cost some money to purchase. The visual reminders will jog their memory, but they don't necessarily make organizing any easier. The clear limit will hold them accountable for their choices, but they may feel frustrated when the boundary is held.

- Encourage them to pick a solution and try it out: Your child may choose to have the bins. Encourage them to create a system and offer support if needed. Do not stand at the door and dictate your tween/teen's every move. Let them figure it out as independently as possible.

- Teach them to assess how they feel the plan is going: If tweaks are necessary, help them make those tweaks. If it's going smoothly, celebrate their accomplishment and express your gratitude for their openness to learning new things. If your tween/teen struggles with this process, it's not because they're lazy or because they don't care about your house rules. It's probably related to an executive functioning issue, and the messy room is a sign that they need more support with organization, structure, and planning.

WHERE COLLABORATION IS HELPFUL IN REDUCING POWER STRUGGLES

- Screen time boundaries for school-aged kids and adolescents
- Family responsibilities of housework (dusting, vacuuming), cleaning up (toys, kitchen, rooms, shared living spaces), laundry, groceries, mowing, and gardening
- Kid responsibilities of homework, academics, friendships, extracurriculars, and sibling relationships
- Personal needs like hygiene, nutrition, mental health, and physical health
- Committing to respectful, loving, and mindful communication as a family

As your child's guide, you're tasked with helping them learn how to create collaborative solutions for whatever challenges they may face. Sometimes this process plays out smoothly, and other times you'll notice that your child may still struggle to cooperate. That's okay. Learning how to work together is a skill that takes time to embody. When this happens, trade in your Collaborator hat for your Director hat, and be intentional about communicating your warmth, compassion, and firmness. Here are four sample statements you can say to your child to signal that you'll be taking the lead on the problem-solving front:

- "I'll give you a minute to choose, and then I'll choose for you."
- "It looks like you need some help. Here's the plan."
- "I want to hear your ideas, but you must share them. Otherwise, we'll go with my plan on this one."
- "Thank you for sharing your opinions. We're going to go in a different direction. While I know that might be disappointing, I feel this is best for everyone."

On those days when you don't feel warm and fuzzy, take a deep breath, give yourself some grace and kindness, and remember that you don't need to get it right all the time. It's about getting it right some of the time and repairing the rest of the times you got it "wrong."

The Do-Over

When you find yourself acting out and wishing you hadn't, I encourage you to be humble enough to apologize, make amends, and keep trying. Guilt and shame for every mistake will eat away at your soul. One of my favorite ways to apologize and make amends is to model a do-over for your children. Any time you catch yourself behaving in ways you know you'll regret, pause. Say out loud in front of them: "Whoa, I don't like what I'm doing. Let me try it again." Take a nice deep breath and rephrase whatever you meant to say. Your children will see you actively correcting your own behavior in the moment, which will encourage them not to fear making mistakes themselves. You are giving them the gift of owning their humanity, rather than fearing it.

I noticed a pattern that every time we got into the car to drive to school, both of my boys would argue about whose turn it was to choose a song. It was an aggravating way to get the workday started. I would often feed the power struggle by saying something like, "You kids can never agree, so it's no music, then!" This response was about my need for power and control and didn't actively teach my children anything about navigating their needs for power, control, and cooperation with each other. I decided to make a different choice.

I chose to pause. On the days I had the energy, I led with connection: "Boys, you're both frustrated, because you both want to be first." Naturally, they logged their individual complaints: "He got to choose first yesterday!" "Well, he got to choose the first book last night!" After they got their hurt feelings off their chests, I put on my Collaborator hat: "So, how should we solve this problem?" This was too broad of a concept for my youngest, who at the time was less than three years old. But my eldest (at five years) was ready to engage: "We can go back and forth. I get to choose the first song and the first book on Tuesdays and Thursdays, and he gets to choose them on Wednesdays and Fridays." The little one agreed to the plan, and so now it was time for the do-over. I said, "Let's try it again. Instead of starting our drive to school with all this screaming, ask me what day it is, so we can figure out whose turn it is to choose the first song." They delightfully followed through and were both on board with the plan.

After all this collaboration and role-playing, your children will still need reminders and encouragement. Please don't take this to mean that your approach is ineffective or "isn't working"; rather, it is because these concepts require a high degree of psychological development to integrate seamlessly into your child's day-to-day routine.

If you're easily discouraged, I want you to know something: when you're learning to embody this work consistently, it truly is a split second before rage, frustration, anxiety, or fear attempt to sink the ship. You are not on the *Titanic*. There are more than enough lifeboats, and your ship is not going down. If you engage in the power struggle by bickering, demanding compliance, or threatening with punishments and consequences (. . . we all do it!), you have the power to turn the ship around at any moment.

CHAPTER 9

Mastering Discipline

KIDS MAKE MISTAKES—LIKE EVERY HUMAN ON THE PLANET— and it's the parents' job to help them learn from those mistakes. In the same way that doctors take an oath to do no harm, I invite you to adhere to this same policy with your children. As an adult, you are ostensibly in a position of authority, but that doesn't mean you can freely crack the whip or that you're not accountable for your impact. How you support your kids through developmental challenges sets the stage for how they navigate life's difficulties in the future. What you say and do matters. And if I've learned anything from my child clients, they're not looking for a lecture, blame, or punishment. They're looking for your guidance and need your sage wisdom about how our world functions. They're looking for your support and understanding when they fail, so they can feel inspired to get up and keep going. Most important, they are looking to work *with* you.

Discipline Means to Teach

The original definition of "discipline" did not mean to punish, despite the modern colloquial use of this word, which has its roots in the Old French translation. The word "discipline" comes from the Latin word *disciplina*, which means "instruction and training." It is derived from the root word *discere*, meaning "to learn." Therefore, to discipline means to instruct and to teach, and to be disciplined means to learn. Nowhere in this definition does it require someone to be punished to learn, yet this is the message parents have received for generations.

As a parent, you are being called into a teacher role. Consider yourself a coach. A guide. A shaman. Whatever the archetype you envision yourself to be, see yourself as a leader who observes and supports from the sidelines as the learner (your child) embarks upon their journey. You are there to offer moments to reflect on past or future steps and offer course correction as needed, but allow your child to play on without undue interference.

We all learn through doing and repetition. You don't shoot one three-pointer and call yourself Kobe Bryant. Parents tend to respect the process of learning when it comes to reading, writing, math, riding a bike, and so on. But when it comes to social and emotional learning, parents have historically had a misguided understanding of a child's innate capabilities. In fact, in a Zero to Three national survey conducted in 2016, about 50 percent of parents reported that their children were capable of self-control and other developmental achievements much earlier than they are. It is this "expectation gap" that can be incredibly frustrating for parents . . . probably more frustrating than the difficult developmental behaviors themselves.

When you level your expectations for your child's social and emotional functioning the way you do with your child's achievements in other developmental milestones, you won't find discipline as daunting. Exhausting, yes. But blame your exhaustion on the job. Being an *effective* teacher is a challenging endeavor. Disciplining through teaching is especially exhausting when you have a reservoir of untapped and underacknowledged wounds. Parents who prioritize parenting themselves first find that they can roll with the punches of discipline more easily after they embody the skills learned in Part One.

Perhaps punishment became the mainstream form of discipline because it's less challenging in the moment to yell at, humiliate, swat, or spank a child, and it produces immediate results. In general, children will instantly comply with your commands when fear-inducing tactics are used, but not necessarily out of respect for your rules or your authority. They comply out of fear of feeling harmed by you, rather than learning how to work with someone. Under these conditions, the child-parent dynamic is focused on who has all the power and the control . . . and who is oppressed by it. In a functional dynamic, power and control are a shared responsibility between the child and the parent. The child must learn how to assert their power without hurting or harming others . . . and the parent must do the same.

It is "easier" to use harsh discipline strategies that require zero self-control on your part. It is "easier" to react in an emotionally immature way than it is to be mindful of yourself and choose a more collected way to guide a child. Yet even the parents surveyed who physically punished their children reported that spanking and yelling were not the most effective ways to teach their children—30 percent said, "I spank even though I don't feel okay about it." And 69 percent of parents recognized that "verbally putting down a child or calling them names can be as harmful as physical abuse." Of the parents who spanked their kids, 77 percent "do not count it as one of the most effective methods of discipline."

Despite their (at times) unruly protests, children long to receive your guidance, but they will always resist your control. Punishments, threats, emotional manipulations, coercion, or other control-oriented strategies intend to "teach" by inflicting pain and thus eliminating the behavior. You're conditioned to believe that a little bit of suffering (or, in some cases . . . a lotta bit) "teaches" a child not to repeat the "bad behavior." However, the exact opposite is true when you consider this through a child development lens. If a child does not have the skill to do something, they won't do it. If a child hasn't learned how to control their body when they're angry, hitting them when they hit will do nothing toward teaching them not to hit. When it comes to a child's behavior, it's not about *will*; it's about *skill*. When we punish, we teach our children to fear us. When we isolate a child, we teach them that loneliness is the result of not pleasing others. When we control our children, we teach them to resist our grip and push harder against us.

What Is Effective Discipline?

There are two discipline extremes. The Drill Sergeant Parent is usually overly strict and stern, ruling with an iron fist. Their motivation is, *I won't raise an entitled brat*. The Permissive Parent is highly nurturing and supportive of the child's emotions, but usually lacks consistency, reliability, and predictability when it comes to healthy boundaries and limits. Their motivation is, *I need my kid to like me*.

But effective discipline (what you're aiming for) takes a different approach. An effective disciplinarian looks more like Mary

Poppins—she serves up the bitter medicine, yes, but she sweetens the deal with some sugar. Mary Poppins holds the line and the feelings . . . at the same time. The Drill Sergeant is great at holding the line but misses the mark with the feelings. And the Permissive Parent is phenomenal with the feelings but struggles with the line. To find the sweet spot between the two, you'll want to embody these qualities observed by researchers of authoritative parenting (first researched by clinical and developmental psychologist Diana Baumrind in the 1960s):

- Warm with high standards
- Affirming with clear limits
- Collaborative and consistent

Baumrind's research found that children raised with these qualities had a lively and happy disposition, believed in their ability to master tasks, were resilient in the face of challenges, and displayed well-developed emotional regulation and social skills. Additionally, further research supports that these children often go on to be independent, self-reliant, socially connected, academically successful, confident, caring, and high-achieving people. This style of parenting can reduce the risk of your children developing depression and anxiety, as well as the likelihood of engaging in school delinquency and drug use.

Becoming an effective disciplinarian won't happen overnight. It takes repetition and patience. It also takes a great deal of self-control, which might be the hardest part of mastering this skill. You do not need to be a master to get started; you just need to take the first step. Believe that your child is capable and that they want to listen to and learn from you. Know in your heart that your child is wired for empathy and is poised for immense physical, psychological, and spiritual growth while under your care. Keep in mind that your child longs to feel like an important—and valued—part of your family. Never forget that in the hard, stressful moments, you and your child are on the same team.

The more you embody these truths, the more you will intrinsically realize how ineffective traditional discipline strategies such as rewards and punishments are. You'll recognize that the underlying current of these tactics is to shape and mold the child, rather than encourage the child to discover exactly who their soul is destined to be in this lifetime. You'll no longer view misbehavior as disrespect. Instead, you'll see it as a sign that your child is working on a developmental skill, and you'll feel more equipped to guide and support them along the way. Collaboration will begin to feel intuitive, logical, and achievable.

The traditional endgame for discipline is to get a child to behave according to the rules and regulations set forth by the parent, to be more compliant, follow orders immediately, not push back, and respect authority. However, the true goal of discipline is getting a child to work with others cooperatively and collaboratively. Many parents operate with the conception that if you give a child an inch, they will take a mile.

The truth is that when children *know* better, they *do* better. And to help them do better, your discipline approach should aim to help them learn physical control, emotional awareness, and self-motivation.

- When your child is out of control, you teach them exactly what they can do to get back into physical control.
- When they're acting out their emotions, you help them identify their feelings and how they're impacting their choices.

- When your child is struggling with something novel or difficult, you tell them that they can give up on a good day, when it comes easily and they're enjoying it. But not to give up on the hard days, and instead be curious about new ways to face the problem.

Effective discipline does not produce a "perfect" human or ensure that your children live up to the socially sanctioned ideas of "success." Rather, effective discipline raises humans who express themselves authentically and in a functional manner, don't intentionally cause harm to others, take accountability for their impact when harm is caused, and are internally driven to express their highest potential through compassion, empathy, curiosity, kindness, and grit. You can help your children achieve this by holding them accountable without shame.

Accountability Without Shame

My son learned from his fellow kindergarteners how to throw an insult, and one morning, he decided to try it out. Seemingly out of nowhere, he announced, "I would prefer it if Mommy were dead." Immediately, he busted up laughing, believing he had cracked a funny joke. How do we respond in moments like this, when we know the child doesn't really "know better" (i.e., lacks social skills and a nuanced understanding of what they're saying), but we also don't want them going around saying these things, as they could offend or hurt others?

Had I said something like that growing up, I imagine my mother would have reacted disproportionately with fury. No doubt she would have shamed me with something like, "Fine, consider me dead and do everything for yourself now!" followed by her slamming her door, locking herself in her room, and smoking a Virginia Slim.

Shame and disconnection are common ways we attempt to teach children about the mark they're leaving on the world, but it doesn't stop or prevent misbehavior. We act out our hurts, pain, and wounds, sometimes in an overly dramatized fashion, just to prove a point. Children need to witness our emotional maturity while being held accountable in an appropriate way. They need us to teach them about what's happening internally for them, how to read what's happening internally for others, and how to course-correct when their impact and intentions are misaligned.

My son intended to make me laugh and was completely un-aware of the fact that I am especially sensitive to comments about dead moms, because I'm a motherless mother and often long to hear my mom's voice again (even if she was a complicated source of comfort and pain for me). It's not his job to be sensitive to my childhood wounds, but it is his job to become more mindful about how his choices may impact others. By not overreacting to his be-havior, I gave him the grace and compassion he needed so that he could take accountability. I simply said, "Son, have a seat and please think about the words you just said. Then, we will discuss what you learned."

Because we have a relationship that is rooted in the Six Seeds of Connection (attunement, curiosity, co-regulation, playfulness, reflection, and repair), he was cooperative and agreed to work with me. After a few minutes, he stood up and said, "That was a mean thing to say. I'm sorry. I didn't mean it." I gave him a hug, accepted his apology, and affirmed his intentions: "I know, bud, you just wanted to make me laugh. Our words are very powerful. We never know how others may hear what we have to say, and I'm grate-ful you took the time to think about it and correct it." That was it. He was held accountable for his choices without making it about my unmet needs or inner child wounds, and we reinforced that disappointing, difficult, or uncomfortable moments are redeemable.

As with most things parenting related, it is important to factor in your child's age and development when holding your child accountable without shame. In the first five years, children are known to be egocentric—this means that your child isn't mature enough to understand other people's perspectives and believes that everyone thinks, feels, and sees things the way they do. If your young child hits you and you say, "Stop it! You are hurting me!," you are expecting them to see the situation from your perspective, which they are not yet ready to do. Perspective taking is a developmental skill that takes many years for your child to attain, which is why it is so valuable for us to remain focused on expanding their skill set rather than punishing them for milestones they haven't yet achieved.

Very simply put, your child's *developmental* age is how old they feel with respect to their unique path of social and emotional development, and their *chronological* age is their actual birth age. For example, a young child of four may have the language skills and the height of a six-year-old but the emotional regulation skills of a two-year-old. When looking at and interacting with this child, your mind may make you believe you're interacting with someone older; and then, when they have a temper tantrum because you said no, you may unconsciously expect them to behave according to their chronological age (four years) and the age they physically appear to be (six years). This will get you into some hot water, and you'll both be left feeling dissatisfied.

I invite you to ask yourself, *How old does my child feel right now?* If your child feels younger to you, then your goal is to intervene according to their developmental age in the moment. Doing so will allow your child to feel seen, heard, understood, and safe with you, and it will allow you to expand their developmental capabilities by "nurturing them up."

How to Teach Accountability Without Shame

- **From birth onward:** Describe your child's emotions as you see them: "You're sad, I'll hold you." Narrate your child's behaviors without judgment, and set simple boundaries: "You're biting. Let's take a break and try again later." These two foundational approaches will evolve as your children age. For children to internalize self-accountability, they must have a firm grasp on their emotions, impulses, and needs.

- **Twelve months and up:** Teach your children how the actions of *others* impact *them*: "Mommy said no, and you did not like that." "They took your toy, and you weren't ready to share." At this age, young children still don't have great self-awareness but can begin to understand emotions and actions based on how others affect them.

- **Eighteen months and up:** Teach your children how *their* actions impact *same-aged peers* and help them follow through with a resolution: "You threw his ball over the wall. Now he's crying. He's sad, and he wants his ball back. Let's go help him find it." This teaches children that mistakes aren't fatal and most problems can be solved collaboratively. If your child runs away and doesn't participate in the follow-through, hold their hand and guide them along. Remember, you're aiming for warmth with high standards, affirming with clear limits, and being collaborative and consistent.

- **Four to six years and beyond (depending on their emotional maturity):** Teach your child how *their* actions impact *adults* using non-shaming language. Validate their perspective, concisely explain the problem, and clearly define your boundary and/or expectation.

    - *Young kid:* "I'm not okay with you hitting me in the face. I know you're upset, so please find another way to express your anger."

    - *Older kid:* "I know you've been having a hard time at school, but it's not okay for you to curse me out, even if you're struggling. I will always be here to help you, love you, and support you. And I need you to find another way to let me know if you need some space."

Unless your child developmentally feels like a very young toddler, try to resist the urge to direct your child too much in these types of situations (e.g., "Take a deep breath."). While I encourage you to actively model more constructive ways to deal with emotions, we ultimately want our children to be the ones who do the heavy lifting. If you're consistently handing them the tools, and essentially "doing it for them," they won't learn how to hone their own tool kit.

Guilt for misbehavior is appropriate. Remorse helps build character and guides morality. Shame for misbehavior teaches your child that they are bad. Believing that one is bad becomes a self-fulfilling prophecy. Children start to feel a little guilt as young as three years old. You don't need to force it. Let life be your child's best teacher, and focus on teaching and guiding your children with love, compassion, and kindness.

Teaching children personal accountability without shame is a process, so be in it for the long haul. It's okay if you encounter resistance even when you're keeping shame out of the equation. Resistance doesn't mean this approach isn't effective. It simply means that change is tough, most people don't enjoy being called out, it feels vulnerable to acknowledge that you've unintentionally caused harm, and it takes a ton of courage to make things right with others. With this developmental framework, you're guiding your children to make more conscious and intentional choices, enabling them to better understand the complexities of human relational dynamics as well as exactly what they can do to repair a situation and move forward.

Be Clear, Consistent, and Connected

If you feel your children are out of control and they "never listen," it's possible your dynamic is missing one or more of the three Cs of discipline: clear, consistent, and connected. All three must be present and balanced for parents to feel effective in their discipline approach.

Be Clear

Boundaries and directives must be stated clearly and in a developmentally appropriate way. Your commitment to clear communication takes the guesswork out of the equation for your child, enabling them to trust your guidance.

During lunch, Marcus asks his dad for candy, and Dad replies, "Later." Shortly after finishing his lunch, Marcus asks for candy again, and Dad says, "You can have some later, but not right now." Marcus then throws his fork in protest, and Dad wonders why his kid isn't listening to him. Being incredibly clear can not only turn this problem around in the moment, but it can prevent it from happening in the first place. Dad can say, "Candy is on the menu for dinnertime. Right now, you have mac and cheese with peas to eat." If Marcus protests, all Dad needs to do is repeat the boundary clearly until Marcus respects the limit. If he refuses to eat because only candy will do, Dad's job is to stay committed to clear communication.

Be Consistent

Boundaries and directives must be repetitive, reliable, and predictable for children to internalize them. Consistency gives your child a firm structure they can depend on.

Raj refuses to pick up his toys, making it a regular everyday battle. His parents either scornfully scold him or do all the cleaning themselves after he goes to bed. Due to their lack of consistency, structure, and follow-through, they all miss an important learning opportunity. This problem can be fixed by creating consistent and reliable routines, and perhaps using visual reminders like checklists to support Raj. His parents cannot rely on him to implement the necessary structure and follow-through—the oversight of any task completion is on the parents until children are mature enough to do it independently. So, if you are like Raj's parents and you struggle with this, you'll need to put some systems in place to support your own organization and follow-through. It takes about ten weeks for a new habit to be formed, but it could take anywhere from eighteen to 254 days to break a habit. This means that it's relatively easy to learn something new, but old habits die hard. You will have to be mindful of the patterns that prevent you from being consistent in the first place. Children are not robots who will instantly comply with what we ask (no matter how much we want them to). They need us to consistently follow through on the standards we've set for them to achieve what is being asked of them.

Be Connected

Boundaries and directives must lead with the energies of compassion, empathy, love, and grace. Connection softens your child's heart to whatever correction you may be required to give to support their social, emotional, and relational well-being.

Six-year-old Leo constantly pushes back on his mom's requests. He rarely seems interested in working with her. She believes he is trying to manipulate or trick her into getting his way. The brain structure in children seven years old and younger is not mature enough for such advanced cognitive tasks, despite how much it may feel like they have something up their sleeves. Mom is quick to judge and criticize his mistakes and labels him as bad when he messes up, contributing to this ongoing rift in their relationship. This can easily be shifted the moment Mom chooses to lead with understanding to get his buy-in: "You don't like that I asked you to please stop playing and get ready for bed, is that right?" She can then offer a clear and consistent correction: "Still, slamming doors is not an acceptable way to say we're angry. What do your angry hands wish they could say right now?"

But Effective Discipline Isn't "Working"

When this style of discipline feels like it's "not working," ask yourself if you're experiencing a lack of clarity, consistency, or connection in discipline moments. Perhaps you're great at maintaining the connection, but you're not consistent or clear in your directives.

Or you're extremely clear, but you lack the necessary warmth and dependability. Too much or too little of any of these essential ingredients is often what leaves parents feeling defeated and run-down.

Instead of assuming the discipline isn't working because there's something off with your child, start by conducting an honest self-assessment. When you set a boundary, offer a correction, or give your child a command, how clear are you in terms of what you say and your expectations? How structured and consistent are you with your rules? Do you let some moments slide? Do you sometimes flip out but are patient at other times? Do you lead with connection or critique? You can always use Part One's exercises to explore the why behind any of your actions, especially if it's not in alignment with how you desire to be as a parent. Otherwise, give yourself the grace needed to internalize these teachings by trial and error. Just as experience is your child's best teacher, life is the greatest teacher for all of us.

1:10 Ratio for Debits to Deposits

Every directive you give to your child is like a debit of their emotional and physical reserves. Stopping them in their tracks, redirecting them to something else, correcting their acting-out behavior, or calling them out for something inappropriate and teaching them something more acceptable "costs" your children something internally. They must stop their interests to follow whatever lead you're giving them. Debits are an inevitable part of being in a human relationship, so I don't want you to fear having debits with your kids. But you can counter the effects of debiting by having more deposits than debits by playing with your child, telling them you love them, showing interest in their activities or hobbies, and telling them that you see how hard they're working.

To maintain a balance in your child's emotional reserves, keep the debit-to-deposit ratio at or around 1:10. For every one debit, aim to have about ten deposits. This way, your children will not burn out on your requests, and your relationship will feel warm, collaborative, and genuinely connected.

Think of the last time you ate at a restaurant. You're sitting in the booth watching your children behave as if they have never been in an establishment where social rules are expected to be followed. You hear yourself correcting them for many (legitimate!) issues: bouncing in the booths, talking loudly, or having a wrestling match under the table. You're not unreasonable to want to eat a meal without accidentally kicking a kid under the table! But remember that every ask you make of them is debiting their emotional reserves. Those reserves are probably already a little low, because you're inviting them to do something that is socially challenging. Keep these stressors in mind as you navigate these everyday moments.

Instead, find the delicate balance. If you're criticizing their every move, eventually they may dread going out to eat with you. If you're passive and let them do whatever they please, you may dread going out to eat with them. Prepare before you go and bring card games, activity books, small puzzles, or something accessible for everyone to enjoy. (Try to avoid the screens, if you can—that's not teaching kids the kind of attention and resilience you're seeking to instill.) Be mindful to balance correcting their behavior with enjoying them as people. You can tell your children to sit on their bottoms in their chairs and then offer them a high five with a big smile once they follow through. That type of interaction is a net positive: the positive acknowledgment of their efforts cancels out the debit.

The Dos and Don'ts of Effective Discipline

1. DO start by giving one direction at a time. This will give your child the opportunity to feel successful in listening and following directions. The more success they feel, the more they'll feel motivated to keep trying. Rather than saying, "Clean up your plate and put away your toys, then hurry back for your bath because we're running late for bed," consider saying, "Please bring your plate to the kitchen sink." Once your child can do this easily and automatically, increase the number of directions.

2. DO state your boundary clearly. Tell your child what you want them to do, rather than what not to do. "Walking feet, please," rather than, "No running." If your child doesn't understand your boundary, they will be more likely to violate it.

3. DON'T give a directive and then walk away without overseeing your child's success. They will not take you seriously. Furthermore, if your child has any issues with organization (or if they are younger and their organization skills aren't fully developed yet), walking away without seeing the directive through will usually lead to failure on the child's part. You'll get frustrated because it will seem like your child isn't listening to you. You can avoid this by waiting for your child to complete whatever task you asked them to do before you rush off to something else. I respect that you may be running a tight ship (as I am), but you've got tiny passengers on board who don't have the years of practical experience that you do with planning, organizing, and executing. They need lots of repetition before something as mundane as the morning routine, the after-school routine, and so on feels like second nature.

4. DO give assistance when needed. A child *will* do when they *can* do. This means that if they aren't following your requests, you may need to support them to complete the task at hand. Rather than saying, "Fine then, I'm going to throw away all your toys, because you refuse to keep them tidy," consider saying, "I see it's a challenge for you to keep your toys organized. Let's work on this together. Make a pile of all your make-believe toys. I'll create a separate pile of all your building toys. When we're done with the piles, we can figure out where things should go, and we'll label everything with pictures, so you don't forget in the future." The child's perspective is validated, the problem is defined, and the solution is discussed collaboratively.

5. DO have a plan in place for new or difficult situations. Novel situations like the first day at a new school, a new babysitter, or trying a new class can bring unexpected challenges. If an experience is new to your child, you want to help them understand the expectations clearly and try to anticipate any boundaries you may need to uphold. If your child is starting a new soccer club, let them know the plan: "It's indoors, it may be loud, and there will probably be several classes playing at once." Be clear about your boundaries: "You can go out there and play when you're ready. I'll be sitting in the bleachers during your class. If you choose not to play, you can wait with me on the sidelines until you're ready."

Common difficult situations parents repeatedly run into are issues like the morning routine, evening routine, sibling fights, the candy/toy aisle, and screen time. Planning behavioral expectations and boundaries with them helps to move them along and are helpful for bringing more peace and joy into your home. If you know your child has a hard time leaving the store without throwing a fit over the candy aisle, then prior to going to the store, let your child know the plan: "We're going to the store to get XYZ. You can choose one item." Be specific about what their options are and be crystal clear about your boundary: "Even if your body gets angry and you scream and cry, we will not get more than that one item." The plan is exactly what you fall back on when you're holding the feelings and holding the line.

Have your child confirm their understanding by repeating the plan. Then, go back to depositing something positive: "High five for working together! I love our teamwork!"

Once your child honors the boundary, follow through with more positive feedback: "Thank you for working together with me. I said you could choose just one item. And you chose it, all while keeping your body cool as a cucumber in the process. Way to go! How did you do that?!"

6. DON'T say, "Why would you do that?" Not only is the response likely to be "I don't know," saying this triggers shame within your children. It makes them feel doubted and questioned by you, giving way to feeling insecure and a lack of self-trust.

Consider saying, "What was happening inside of you when you made that choice?" If your child requires more specifics to answer you, ask, "What thoughts were you thinking? What emotions were you feeling?" And then connect the dots between when they were thinking and feeling to what they were doing.

For example, "What was happening inside when you chose to lie about how many pieces of candy you had?" Your child may reply with something like, "I was afraid I was going to be in trouble. I didn't want you to get mad at me." Then, you get to connect the dots: "I see. You were afraid of getting in trouble, and so you chose to lie to avoid a punishment." You can then empathize and offer a correction: "My love, this is a punishment-free home, and you'll never get in trouble for telling the truth. So thank you for telling me. Everyone makes mistakes, and you ate more candy than was available for you, making it so that your sibling couldn't get any. Please decide with your sibling about how you will make good on the candy you took from them." (Bonus points if you're able to see that this scenario is an impulse-control-related issue, and you create more structure in your child's daily routine to support them developing better self-control.)

7. **DO focus on the rule rather than the exception.** If you occasionally overreact and you follow up with an apology and an intentional repair, that's not the same as consistently using punitive discipline to get your kid to comply with you. If your inner critic likes to point out your every misstep, keep a log of all your wins and setbacks over a week's time to gain clarity around what's really happening in your home. Nearly all my clients who I've asked to do this return to their following session with a sense of relief because they realize they aren't messing up as much as it feels like they are in their heads. And I bet it's similar for you, too.

Consequences Should Be Natural, Not Imposed

I often hear, "If I don't give my child a consequence, how will they learn not to do this anymore?" or "My kid is acting out and needs a consequence. I don't want them to grow up spoiled or entitled. I'm the parent. What I say goes."

These common fears are upheld by a social system that routinely mischaracterizes the motivations and intentions of children. We forget that children are getting their first experiences under our care. They don't know what acceptable or unacceptable behaviors are, so it's our job to teach them gently and respectfully without being "too soft" or "too permissive."

I am not anti-consequence. "Consequence" is a neutral term that means a reaction to some action. We are constantly making choices every day, and our different choices bear consequences. If I stay up all night, I will bear the consequence of feeling exhausted and foggy the next day. However, when it comes to kids and consequences, we typically use it to mean that a parent needs to "give" a consequence to a child to get them to "learn" not to do something we want them to stop. I don't support parent-imposed consequences in most circumstances, because they function more like punishments while emphasizing the parent as the child's motivator for good behavior, rather than the child finding it within themselves to behave in appropriate, adaptive ways.

Natural consequences, on the other hand, invite children to experience cause and effect. Allowing children to experience the natural consequences of their decisions teaches kids to analyze their choices and look inward for how to move forward. An example of an imposed consequence is "Because you didn't get in the car when I said so, we are not getting ice cream later." Sure, your child may "learn" to rush to the car as soon as you tell them in the future, but the more you rely on this, the more their brain becomes wired to need an external motivator—you and the threat of losing ice cream—to get them to follow directions.

Over time, parents become exhausted by having to impose consequences because they need to keep doling them out to keep the child in line. Policing someone's every action to ensure that they are "good" doesn't feel good for anybody.

You can set your kids up for success by giving a clear, consistent, and connected directive: "We need to get to the car quickly so we can have time for ice cream later." If the children dawdle, the natural consequence might be "Kids, I'm sorry, but we won't have time for ice cream. I needed you to move quickly when I asked. Next time, we'll try again!" The consequence should naturally occur and be appropriate for the problem itself. If you need to think of a consequence to give your child "a lesson," it's not naturally occurring.

EXAMPLES OF NATURAL CONSEQUENCES

Your child refuses to keep their room neat.

Imposed consequence: You ground your child until they can keep a clean room.

Natural consequence: You and your child go through their things and donate the excess.

Your child refuses to do their homework.

Imposed consequence: You give them extra chores so they can "learn their lesson."

Natural consequence: They get a 0 for their homework that day.

Your child hits a friend.

Imposed consequence: You send them to bed without supper.

Natural consequence: They may lose that friendship, the playdate ends, or they must find a way to make amends to preserve the friendship.

Your kid draws on the walls with crayons.

Imposed consequence: You destroy something of theirs so they "know how it feels."

Natural consequence: They need to clean it up, and that may cut into the time they could have spent doing something else.

If your child is repeatedly getting the same natural consequence, they might not have the skill set (yet) to be successful in the task you're asking them to perform. When you notice this happening, simplify the task to make it more easily achievable. If they are routinely getting one fewer book per night because their dawdling eats up the time you've allotted for the bedtime routine, simplify how many transitions and directives you give for bedtime. Give your child a visual chart so they can easily see what you're expecting and teach them to look at their chart anytime they go "off task."

Unless a situation is highly dangerous, it's helpful to stay out of the way and let your child learn through natural consequences. Let your child make their own mistakes and help them process how their decision-making led to what happened. Additionally, you can encourage them to think of alternative choices they could have made as well as what potential outcomes could have happened as a result. By processing their mistakes in this way, you lay a foundation for seeing missteps and mistakes as a normal and important part of life, rather than something to fear and avoid at all costs.

A Word About Scripts

Social media influencer culture—especially in the parenting space—has undermined parents by convincing them that there are perfect words to say to their children to "get this right." While I offer language suggestions, I'm not giving you a script that you can parrot back to your child that will magically transform all your daily interactions with them. How you communicate in difficult moments matters. How you read the subtext behind your child's behaviors and your body language, as well as your choice of words and actions, will ultimately influence how your children feel about themselves, their relationships, and the world around them.

You are not an actor in a play, but a parent in a relationship with your child who is trying to do better. I applaud you for that. I don't want you trapped inside your own head, doubting if you're saying the right things or wishing someone could rescue you from a stressful interaction with a perfect response. Effective discipline requires getting out of your head and into your body, being in the present moment, and pausing and really listening to yourself and your child. It is measured not by a perfectly behaved child, but by our willingness to fail, dialogue about our missteps, find love in the process, and move forward. It's okay if you stumble over your words or feel awkward when speaking with your children about a discipline issue. Kids will appreciate authenticity—they have very highly developed BS detectors, and if they feel like they are being talked down to, they will tune you out.

This Is Worth Your Time

Many parents have said to me, "This approach takes too much of my time and energy. I don't have all this time to give." Realistically, you're going to put in the time no matter what. You're going to put time into battling your kid, screaming at them, telling them to go to time-out, and constantly policing their behaviors into adolescence until they rebel, or you're going to put in the time now to help them understand their behaviors, learn about boundaries, take accountability, and discover new constructive ways they can choose to express themselves. The research is too evident to ignore the reality that putting in the time when their brain is still developing and they're still wanting to learn from us is well worth your investment.

The child-parent relationship is special because the way we choose to be in relationship with our children sets the stage for how they will instinctually be in relationship with others for the rest of their lives. They learn whether they can mess up and disappoint someone based on how we respond to them. They learn to excessively please at their own expense the more transactional we are with our time, presence, and affection. They learn how to set and hold their own boundaries depending on what we model and what we allow within our relationship with them.

When you treat them in the respectful, compassionate, and consistent way I've laid out for you throughout this book, you're teaching them how they deserve to be treated in the world and how to treat others that they meet in the world. Without sounding melodramatic, you are quite literally changing the world by how you're choosing to support your child throughout childhood.

Your clear, consistent, and connected boundaries create a safe container within which your children can freely explore the world. As they start to push back on your boundaries, you can begin inviting their options and ideas on how to solve whatever problem you're facing, effectively giving your child more responsibility (and thus more opportunity to "fail" and learn from their mistakes).

This is not to say that your child will always have the final word. Many parents fear that collaboration with a child results in their taking over and ruling the roost. If you're tiptoeing around their feelings because you're afraid of your child's emotional reactivity, then yes, it's highly likely that they will take charge (but only because you've let them). If you're embodying the teachings of this book, it's unlikely that this will be your outcome. Try to remember that sometimes you'll make a final decision because it's reasonable and it suits the needs of everyone in the family as fairly and diplomatically as possible. At others, your children's request will be reasonable, and you will accommodate them. There isn't a strict set of rules for you to follow in any given circumstance. You've got to commit to being in the moment, being mindful of your own triggers and unconscious projections, and tuning in to your child's inner thoughts, feelings, and needs. This is the mindset that leads you to becoming a master decoder, and an effective interventionist, whenever you are needed by your child.

I want to acknowledge that there are plenty of parents who are burning the candle at both ends to make ends meet and provide for their children. If this is you, please know that by making a habit of connecting with your children in challenging moments, even if you have limited time because you're endlessly working, you are teaching your children how to transform a conflict into dialogue . . . and ultimately into a connection.

PART THREE

· · · · · ·

Caring for the Whole Family

. . . . . .

CHAPTER 10

Navigating Sibling Dynamics

RAISING MORE THAN ONE CHILD IS DEMANDING. NOT ONLY ARE you navigating the differences in personalities, you are also constantly having to find creative ways to maintain harmony in family dynamics. Rarely, if ever, do you parent two children the same, because each child elicits something completely different from you. And you are a different version of *yourself* with each of them.

My client Katie was a single mom who was fiercely loyal to her two daughters, Claire and Vera, who were polar opposites. Claire was outspoken, demanding, and rebellious; Vera was anxious, eager to please, and clingy. As was common with siblings, they often competed to see who the favorite was. "Why do you always let Vera do things that you don't let me do?" Claire cried. Vera felt like she never got the attention that Claire did, a sentiment that had some truth given that Claire struggled with emotional and behavioral regulation issues because of her ADHD.

Katie anxiously hovered over Claire to correct her missteps and walked around in fear, hoping that by doing so, one of Claire's epic (and usually violent) meltdowns wouldn't happen. For years, Vera watched this pattern and eventually began to mirror Katie's anxiety. She, too, would minimize her needs and acquiesce to Claire's demands, which created a storm of discontent and resentment in the home. Katie saw a lot of herself in Vera and found herself wanting to "protect" Vera from Claire. Unconsciously, Katie had interfered in their relationship right from the very beginning.

The Sibling Relationship

Navigating the sibling relationship is challenging. Parents often unconsciously align with the child who complements their own inner needs—for example, your easygoing nature may conflict with your child's rigid temperament, yet you may feel more easily connected to your laid-back, go-with-the-flow child. And no matter what we think, the other children *will* notice any hint of preferential treatment for one sibling and chalk it up to favoritism. Then, when they call us out on it, rather than taking time to reflect on the accusation, we often respond defensively and blame the child for not living up to our expectations: "Well, your brother doesn't stir up as much trouble as you do, so he's easier to deal with. But I love you both the same."

Many parents have more children with the expectation that they're giving the other child a "best friend" for life, without understanding that this is a lot of pressure. It's helpful to focus less on "I gave you a sibling, so you'll always have a best friend" and more on "Having a sibling is a special bond, and I'm going to help you all learn how to do life together." Sibling relationships are usually the longest relationships we maintain throughout life, but they are not automatically harmonious and mutually enjoyable. Personalities may clash, and interests may differ. It requires intentional effort to help children respect these innate differences, discover commonalities, and celebrate individuality in the family.

Multiple children complicate the family dynamics. With more mouths to feed and bums to wipe comes more chaos and pressure but also more laughter and play. Siblings receive the benefit of routinely practicing social skills with each other. At the same time, you may feel less regulated to model and teach the skills you're wanting to impart upon the kids solely because you're stretched thin with caring for them. Two kids are not simply double the work, as any parent of siblings can tell you. It's more like triple or quadruple the effort!

Many parents are conflict-averse, underscored by an almost involuntary reaction to pick a side when faced with a sibling conflict. Rather than being the mediator who hears both sides and tries to find a mutual resolution, we instinctually want to assign blame. Instead of guiding our children's problem-solving skills, we behave more like children ourselves by pointing the finger, which interferes with the sibling relationship, making their conflicts centered on who will gain our approval and who will be proven wrong.

When Claire was angry about Vera repeatedly snatching her toys, Katie would side with Vera by justifying her actions: "Vera is younger than you. Plus, you've taken her toys, and she didn't complain about it. She doesn't know better. Let her play and go find something else to do." Claire received the unspoken message that no matter how unfair Vera's behaviors felt, Mom would choose Vera's side. When children pick up on these perceived injustices, it often increases negative behavior and sibling tension as they repeatedly test their parents' loyalties.

To be more effective in nurturing a collaborative relationship among your children, you must first determine if you're acting out old wounds from your own sibling dynamics. Katie was herself the youngest of five kids, and as a result she often felt overlooked. Her parents poured a lot of thoughtful energy into her older siblings, but by the time they got to her, they were too tired to support her in the ways she needed. She was often teased, humiliated, and ridiculed by her older siblings, which is a pattern often found in dysfunctional families. When she asked her parents for help, they told her, "Just don't play with them," which gave Katie little guidance on how to advocate for her needs, stand up to mistreatment, and resolve conflicts without avoidance.

Sibling abuse is an overlooked and underreported form of bullying, and it's different from sibling rivalry. Sibling rivalry, common in many families, includes bickering, jealousy, and competitive behaviors, often to gain the attention of the parent. Sibling abuse, however, includes repeated unwanted acts that aim to harm, manipulate, or coerce a sibling, such as ordering a sibling around, poking fun at them, intimidating them with threats, shaming them, persistent name-calling, hitting, tickling, pinning them down, hair pulling, sexual abuse, and more. In environments where effective discipline is lacking, older children may feel compelled to release their rage onto younger siblings, who often wish to please their older siblings, thus perpetuating the abuse of power and chronic victimization.

It is believed that up to 80 percent of children experience mistreatment from their siblings, yet rarely is it addressed appropriately. This is learned behavior that is modeled by parents in both overt and covert ways. Many parents believe that fighting in such damaging ways is normal sibling rivalry, and they don't recognize that these kinds of interactions carry the risk of long-term trauma.

Katie had to acknowledge that her repressed anger over not feeling protected against the verbal harm from her older siblings was what compelled her to consistently "side" with Vera and thus project her childhood need for power onto Claire, making it Claire's burden to carry for her.

Katie's commitment to self-reflection allowed her to consciously choose a new style of interaction when her girls had a conflict. Instead of reacting, she learned to hold space for that wounded part of herself and at the same time hold space for both of her girls' wounds in the moment. Now, when Claire complains that Vera stole her toy, Katie replies, "I see two sisters having a problem. Let's try to figure this out together."

SOURCES OF SIBLING RIVALRY

The following are common issues that appear to fuel competition issues, jealousy issues, and a general sense of disconnection between siblings (as seen in my practice).

- The older child feels replaced by the cute, younger child.

- One child gets more attention than the other, for whatever reason . . . even if it's due to negative behavior.

- One child feels moody and takes it out on the other child.

- One child retaliates for something that happened earlier.

- The older child is put in charge of caring for the younger child, which often leads to resentment. For example, a twelve- or thirteen-year-old sibling being expected to babysit younger siblings or high schoolers being expected to carpool younger siblings. I'm not suggesting that it's a bad idea to ask older children to be involved; however, be mindful if you start to see more rivalry or competition among the children. Reduce the demands on the oldest and see if doing so supports the relationship.

- The younger child is let off the hook for being younger.

- The older child is blamed because they're older and should "know better."

- Asking one child why they can't be more like another child.

- Overpraising and clearly favoring one child while criticizing and/or humiliating the other.

- Significant differences in abilities: For example, when one child is disabled or is neurodivergent while the other siblings are able-bodied or neurotypical, there can sometimes be hidden (or obvious) expectations that the able-bodied and/or neurotypical child operate more independently so that the parents can better support the child with special needs. This can sometimes be a complicated dynamic, and so I usually suggest family therapy to work out whatever is at play here.

No Comparison, No Competition

Growing up, my younger sister, LaDare, was often compared to me by our parents and teachers. We are thirteen months apart, and our personalities couldn't be more different, but she felt like she lived in my shadow. I was annoyed by how much she was expected to emulate me. Teachers taunted her with questions like "Why can't you be more like Bryana?" Rather than being seen as her own person, with unique talents for caregiving and joke telling, others expected her to be like me, which had a crushing effect on our relationship.

When we were little, she complained that I was too loud and too embarrassing to be around, a sentiment that my mom agreed with, fueling a competition between our fundamentally different ways of self-expression. My mom insisted that I stay away when her friends came over, feeding the competitive vibes and further splitting us apart. LaDare, naturally funny and great at conversation, was always much better at making friends than me, something I envied rather than admired. I was emotionally quite sensitive, so when LaDare began to throw shade like a true queen, she was celebrated for her wit and I was ridiculed for being easily hurt. This became another wedge between us.

The years of chronic comparison and a competitive environment sucked the soul right out of our sisterhood. The only thing that was keeping us together was the fact that we shared a bloodline, which was a miserable feeling. I decided that I wanted to improve things with her, to really know her and for her to know me. So I became clearer with my boundaries around any of her behaviors that provoked shame in me, and we've since repaired what couldn't be addressed in childhood.

So much heartache and resentment among siblings could be avoided if parents learned to foster a healthy, collaborative relationship right from the start. Comparison (particularly done by adults) does not belong in the sibling dynamic. Children, by nature, will compare themselves to one another. In fact, we all compare ourselves to peers to measure our success or competence. Your kids are already noticing the differences they have with their siblings. One child may see that the other child is academically inclined and may fear they're falling short because school doesn't come as easily to them. When adults add to the comparing by saying, "You need to get your grades up like your sibling," they unintentionally give credence to the child's self-assessments. They come to believe, *I am falling short. There's nothing that will help me measure up. I'm hopeless.*

When children are compared with one another—especially using labels—it often backfires. When your child hears you say, "He is my smart one," your other child hears, "No one else can be smart." When your child hears you say, "She is my athletic one," your other child hears, "No one else can be athletic." Labeling and comparing children only pits them against one another, forcing them to compete to keep their "title." Enzo might assume, "If Gianna starts doing well in sports, then it means I'm doing bad! If I'm not good at sports anymore, then my parents won't love me or want me." Enzo would be more likely to draw this conclusion if being identified as the "athletic one" has earned him the most favor and love from his parents. It may not be rational, but it is how the mind of the child works.

Although comparison seems to be part of human nature, we want to avoid fueling that fire because comparison drives competition. For example, after hearing what a great baseball player his sister is, Enzo may start to tease Gianna—maybe he'll tell her that she looks stupid in her cleats and she should stick to dancing, because girls aren't good at baseball anyway. Suddenly, the seeds of rivalry are sown and sprout, and the children must unconsciously compete for their title . . . and your attention.

When you take the comparison and competition out of the equation, you create more room for collaboration.

- Resist the urge to label your kids (e.g., "my social butterfly."). Kids can have different interests. They can have the same interests. It doesn't matter. Focus on what makes each child unique and encourage them to encourage each other's interests and hobbies.

- Try not to make an example out of one child for the other children to learn the lesson.

- Don't set up the kids for competition, but ask them to work together. Rather than "First one to the car gets a prize!," try "We have five minutes before we need to be in the car. Kids, see how fast you can work together to get ready and meet me there!"

- For kids eight years old and up, consider team-oriented responsibilities instead of individual responsibilities. Instead of "Whoever cleans the most will get a bonus in their allowance this week," say, "I need you all to work together to get the bathroom and the kitchen clean, please!"

- Have "community" items that your children learn to share and personal items that they're responsible for. Help your children learn how to set boundaries around their personal things, as well as how to take turns with things available to everyone.

- Feed the hungriest first. You won't be able to meet everyone's needs at the same time. Sometimes one child will demand more attention before you can get to the other. Learning how to wait is an important part of having siblings. If it's happening consistently that one child is often the "hungriest," be sure to explore any environmental stressors or underlying needs that may be unmet for that child and make it a point to show up for the other children in a more intentional way.

- Always focus on the exact problem in the moment. Resist the urge to bring in history. Rather than "You're always interrupting his piano practice!," try speaking to the child's needs and stating the problem: "It's hard for you to wait for him to be done. He needs you to practice respecting his boundary, please. He wants to focus."

- Don't take the bait when they say, "That's not fair!" Instead of "I took your side last time, so you should be grateful," focus on the underlying need: "Tell me more about what's happening inside you. I want to understand."

Fostering the Collaborative Spirit

Conflict is an inevitable part of life, but rather than fanning its flames, we can help our children learn how to navigate it by fostering a spirit of collaboration. Embodying a collaborative spirit aligns you and your family against a problem, teaching your children to view the problem as the issue, rather than one another as the problem. In the traditional "who's to blame" style of raising siblings, the kids don't learn to tackle problems together. They learn to tackle one another (figuratively . . . and sometimes literally) to avoid punishment, judgment, or shame.

The collaborative spirit doesn't always come naturally. Navigating the needs of more than one person, trying to be fair, and having your own internal reactions can cloud your judgment and make it harder to be in the present moment with your children. Invalidating, dismissing, denying, or rejecting children often leads to more sibling problems and less conflict resolution.

Blaming Leads to Shaming

Sister: "Johnny took my toy, and he won't give it back! I hate him!"

You: "Well, that's not a very nice thing to say. Were you even playing with it?"

Sister: *She doesn't get me. She thinks I'm a bad kid.*

Brother: *I knew I could count on Mom to stand up for me against my monster sister!*

Accusations Lead to Revenge-Seeking

Sister: "Johnny took my toy, and he won't give it back! I hate him!"

You: "Johnny, you know that's her favorite toy. Give it back now!"

Sister: *See, I was right! He was wrong.*

Brother: *I can't wait to get back at her for this.*

Lack of Direction Leads Nowhere

Sister: "Johnny took my toy, and he won't give it back! I hate him!"

You: "You two kids are helpless. When will you learn to be friends?"

Sister: "Give it back!"

Brother: "*No!* I was playing with it."

More chaos erupts.

Punishing Leads to Disconnection

Sister: "Johnny took my toy, and he won't give it back! I hate him!"

You: "You know what, since you both obviously can't play nice, I'm taking the toy away!"

Sister: *He ruins everything!*

Brother: *She ruins everything!*

In each of these scenarios, notice how the parent's intervention did not support a collaborative spirit between the children, as well as how children may internalize our attempts to end their conflicts. Helping the kids learn to get along is one of the trickiest issues to navigate as a parent, but not every moment requires your intervention. If it's a little quibble, give them some space to figure it out independently. Bickering is normal for kids, even if it's annoying. Try your best to ignore it, but if things are heating up (or you sense they could use some support), intervene with the intention to help your kids build some perspective so they can creatively solve the problem together. Perspective taking teaches them to empathize with others, compromise when needed, and take accountability for their missteps.

When you consistently nurture the collaborative spirit, you will see notable changes in your children's bickering, squabbles, and battles. By implementing this four-step framework into your daily lives, you can expect that your children

- Will learn to slow down, rather than ramp up, when they're facing a problem.
- Will listen to you and one another better.

- Will communicate with more emotional intelligence and awareness.
- Will feel more equipped to take missteps in stride.
- Will generalize these skills with peers over time.

Step One: Separate

Separation is reserved for physical altercations or when the yelling is getting so intense that everyone needs a moment to cool down. Say, "WHOA! This isn't safe. I need you to separate now." "Kid A: go over there." "Kid B: go over there." "When we're feeling calm in our bodies, we'll discuss this."

Screaming, "What's going on here?!," "Who started it?!," or "What are you thinking?!" projects shame and doesn't get the children to safety quickly, which is the top priority in such circumstances. Do not allow your children to physically beat up one another. We should also be careful not to normalize the gender stereotype that brothers physically fight because "they're boys." All children need to learn how to internalize emotional regulation and impulse control.

Create some physical distance between the children. In more intense scenarios, you may have to physically remove one of your children from the other. If physical altercations of this nature are the rule rather than the exception in your home and your children are seven years old and up, it might be helpful to work with a family therapist. There may be some underlying factors, like neurodivergence, that need to be addressed to resolve this problem.

From the moment you intervene, your tone of voice is important. If you're hesitant or anxious to get them to stop, your kids will sense your insecurity. If you're overbearing, angry, or overreactive, your kids will react to your stress. If your tone communicates fear or fury, your children may not take you seriously and may continue escalating. Your mission is to contain the chaos by separating them and immediately lay the groundwork for connection by keeping your tone clear, neutral, and firm. Remember: you can be stern and respectful at the same time. It's appropriate for your children to hear a serious, no-nonsense tone from you when their behavior is physically getting out of hand . . . even if they don't "like" it. This will not damage them, and besides, it's not your job to make them "enjoy" being corrected.

When you first start this practice, your kids might immediately complain. "He started it!" "She said my painting was ugly!" "No fair, I didn't do anything wrong, it was all their fault!" They may continue to emote passionately from their respective spaces. That's okay. Pause, breathe, and remember that this will pass.

If your children refuse to separate when you say so, you may need to use a more serious and firm tone. Be careful to avoid becoming threatening: "Separate now, or you're both going to miss baseball practice." When you react like this, you're opening the door for a power struggle. You're making it about your need for control rather than their need to cooperate with you and collaborate with one another. Additionally, this type of reaction will only activate them further and decrease their willingness to work with you.

Being firm and serious could sound like, "Kids, you can separate on your own, or I can help you." Count to three, then follow through. Be careful, because you are much stronger than your children. Your consistency and predictability holding this boundary will help your children come to respect the limits you're providing. If the conflict is between a bigger child and a smaller child (for example, a sturdy toddler and an infant), you will need to act quickly: "Toddler, stop your body." Then quickly remove your infant and explain: "Our bodies aren't being safe. We need to separate for a moment." Your toddler may be upset, but that's okay. Physical safety for all children is the priority.

In my practice, I've observed that many parents hop in and separate too early, sending the message that the kids can't resolve things on their own. Of course, the parents' intentions are to help end the conflict. But if children learn they need their parents to stop them and direct them in times of conflict and distress, it undermines the children's developmental process and manufactures overdependence. Instead, reserve the Separate step for when your kids are getting hands-on and physical safety is at risk. Or when they're screaming so intensely that it will likely escalate to something potentially risky or dangerous if you don't intervene. Wait for your children to be more regulated before you move onto step two.

Step Two: Validate

When things have heated up and your kids need your support, validate each child's perspective without taking sides: "Kid A, what's your side?" "Kid B, what's your side?" Then, reflect back the problem as you heard it: "Here's what I'm hearing."

You're helping your children learn to listen to multiple perspectives. You are not telling one child they were right or assuming that any child is to blame or at fault. Instead, you're focusing on creating a space where all sides can be heard and understood.

You: "Hey, kiddos, let's take a pause and figure this out. Wren, what's your side?"

Wren: "This is my car, and I was playing with it, and he keeps trying to take it from me."

You: "Okay, and, Theo, what's your side?"

Theo: "I told her she could borrow it, but it's really my car, and I want it back."

You: "Here's what I'm hearing: You both want to play with this car and disagree about who it belongs to."

You may need to express a limit around unacceptable behaviors, especially physical aggression of any kind. When necessary, state the limit simply and immediately get curious about your child's perspective. If Wren had shoved Theo, you might say, "Wren, you cannot get hands-on, even if you're upset. What's your side?"

Step Three: Collaborate

Once you validate their respective sides and reflect how you understand the problem, your next step is to help them move into collaboration mode. Remember, it's not about will, it's about skill. When children fight with one another, it's because they haven't yet fully grasped how to compromise, cooperate, or find creative solutions to whatever problems they're facing. Each new tiff (even if it's a recurring one) is an opportunity for them to practice finding new ways to work together.

Your child may sometimes divert all the blame away from themself and onto someone else. "It wasn't me who did it, it was brother!" or "You're the worst parent ever!" In situations like this, stay focused on teaching your children how to solve the problem they're immediately facing. Here's how you can navigate collaboration between siblings in a developmentally friendly way:

- **Birth to two years:** Narrate and solve the problem. Your newly turned two-year-old drops a toy close to your small infant's head and startles her. Because the infant wasn't harmed, first validate: "Toddler, what's your side?" If they aren't verbally communicative, simply narrate what you saw: "Your sister felt scared when you dropped that toy close to her head." Then, collaborate: "Here's another way you can show sister your toys." Model what you want to see. Offer positive feedback when they mimic the appropriate way to interact: "That's a safe way to play."

- **Two to three years:** Offer two choices, both of which you approve. Your three-year-old twins get in a fight over a beloved stuffed bear and tear the bear. First, validate: "Jaxon, what's your side?" He tearfully mumbles that he wanted to snuggle Beary. "Mason, what's your side?" Angry, he accuses his brother of ripping his bear. "Here's what I'm hearing: You both wanted to play with Beary, and you're both sad and upset that he ripped in half. You didn't expect that to happen." Then, collaborate: "Here are our options: we can try to sew Beary back up, or we can say goodbye to him and look through all our favorite pictures with him. Work together to decide which option you want." If your kids don't agree with your ideas and/or each other, remind them to find a way to work together. Convey your trust that they are competent enough to come up with an agreeable solution. Try not to rush their process. If you must step away and give them some time to work on it together, that's okay. You don't have to hover over them.

- **Three to five years:** Encourage them to come up with a solution and support their follow-through when necessary. Four-year-old Meg pulls six-year-old Brody's hair, and he gets angry and screams, "You're so annoying! I hate you!" First, set a clear limit, then validate: "Meg, you may not pull your brother's hair, even when you're frustrated. Use your words and say what the problem is, please." With her arms crossed and her brows furrowed, she claims Brody said her LEGO tower was boring and he could build a better one. "Brody, what's your side?" He says that she's always in his way and doesn't give him any space to play on his own. "Here's what I'm hearing: Meg, you worked hard on your tower and felt hurt that Brody didn't like it. Brody, you don't like that Meg keeps getting into your bubble space. And it wasn't okay that she pulled your hair. This is a tough one." Then, collaborate: "How should we solve this problem?" Encourage the children to come up with a few ideas. If they need help, you can facilitate the process: "Meg, what's one idea you have to resolve this?" She suggests that both her and Brody build, but instead of building the best LEGO tower, maybe they can build the silliest one. "Brody, what's your idea?" Brody thinks they should have ten minutes of alone playtime and then do the silliest LEGO tower contest. "So, kids, what's your plan?" They decide that Brody's idea gives them both what they want. Kids this age often need help with the execution, so you can offer your support: "I'm available to help if you need me. I'll be right over there." The key is to find a balance in over- or underestimating their confidence, while also finding the right amount of help you can offer.

- **Six to twelve years:** Encourage them to resolve the conflict independently and support their follow-through if necessary. Ten-year-old Nessa is tired of her sister always copying her. Fifi, six years old, looks up to Nessa and feels hurt when she is told to go away. First, validate: "I see you two having a problem. Nessa, what's the issue?" She says that Fifi has been stealing her eye shadow. "Fifi, what's your side?" Fifi says she took it because when she asked nicely to use it, Nessa wouldn't let her. "Here's what I'm hearing: Nessa, you don't want to share your eye shadow. I know you worked hard to afford that on your own. And, Fifi, you felt that by asking nicely, Nessa should have let you borrow her makeup. Thank you for being honest about taking it. I know you know that wasn't okay. I can see why this feels frustrating for both of you." Try not to engage in a he said/she said argument if children accuse each other. However, if one child admits wrongdoing, thank them for their accountability and reiterate the limit. Then, collaborate: "I look forward to seeing how you find a way to solve this problem. Let me know if you'd like my input." Kids this age will sometimes need support with following through, in which case, help each of them come up with a solution until they find something they can both agree on.

- **Teens and young adults:** Witness their conflict and express confidence in their skills. Your teenage kids get into a fight over who gets to be friends with Rebecca. First, validate: "Morgan, what's your side?" She says Rebecca was her friend first, and since Jordan is so popular, Rebecca won't want to hang out with her anymore if she joins his friend group. "Jordan, what's your side?" He shares that he's known Rebecca his whole life, and he doesn't understand why they can't all just be friends. Then, collaborate: "I trust that you two will be able to figure out a mutually agreeable solution. I am here to be a sounding board. If you want my specific advice, I'm happy to offer it with no expectations that you take it." It's important that teens are given the opportunity to independently solve problems without always having your input. Leaving it up to Morgan and Jordan to navigate this together may give Jordan more empathy for Morgan's fear of losing an important relationship. It may also give Morgan more compassion for Jordan's perspective because he also considers Rebecca a good friend. It could help them learn to have each other's backs and be supportive of each other with a mindset of abundance rather than competition.

Step Four: Try Again

The last step in fostering the collaborative spirit is to try again. This is when you encourage your children to find fruitful ways forward with each other, make amends, and fully resolve fights amicably and respectfully. It's their chance to rehearse the new skills they've built together. I learned from my theater training that you've got to get the lines and the stage directions out of your head and into your body, and you can't do this without adequate rehearsal. When it's practical and your children are willing, encourage them to try the entire interaction again, but this time incorporating the solutions they've agreed to.

Scenario: "He took my toy and won't give it back! I hate him!"

When you hear the kids arguing over a toy, you first listen for a few moments to see if your intervention is needed. Things start to heat up when you find them tugging at a toy. As soon as Sharri (six years old) sees you, Johnny (five years old) takes advantage of her distraction, snatches the toy, and hides in the corner. She wails and clings to you.

Validate: "Let's take a pause and figure this out. Sharri, what's your side?" She says that he took her toy and won't give it back. "I hate him!" You nod empathetically and resist the urge to correct right away, even though you know "hate" is a strong word. "Johnny, what's your side?" He claims that he was playing with it first and she took it without asking when he went to the restroom, even though he asked her not to touch it. "Here's what I'm hearing: You both want to play with this toy, and you cannot agree on how to share it. This is a tough one."

Collaborate: "How should we solve this problem?" Prompting them to see sharing rather than each other as the problem will help them move through this common quarrel. Sharri suggests they set a timer to play with it. Johnny asks if he can have it for the first round since he's already been waiting. They both agree to this plan. Then you chime in: "And I'd like to add: it's important that we're careful with what we say, even when we're angry. Saying we hate someone can be hurtful. But saying you feel angry doesn't hurt others." Sharri turns to Johnny and apologizes unprompted, to which he says, "That's okay."

Try Again: "So let's try it again and practice what we're learning. Johnny, pretend that you're coming back from the bathroom and, Sharri, play with his toy. Let's use our words and focus on solving the problem." Johnny enters and says, "Hey, that's mine!" Sharri rebuts, "But you weren't playing with it." When kids are a little young, they may need some prompting to keep going with the role-play. So, you coach Sharri to suggest a way to solve it, and she says, "I have an idea. Why don't we set a timer so we can both get a turn with it?" You give Johnny a nudge to assert himself, and he says, "Sure, that works, but I want it first since I just got it out and wasn't using it very long." Sharri sets the sand timer, and they both carry on with ease.

If your child refuses to participate in the role-play, there is no need to push it. You can also play the role of the child, and they can coach you. Kids often love doing this, because it's silly and they get to show you what they really know. You can also choose to role-play with their figurines or other toys; stuffed animals, Barbies, dinosaurs, superheroes, or cars can be "humanized." But if they're not into it, that's okay. Trust that this situation will present itself again, giving them a fresh opportunity to keep growing.

Jealousy

Jealousy is a perfectly normal emotion, and siblings get extra practice with it. Excessive doting over one child, clear patterns of favoritism, comparison, constant competition, and the birth of a new sibling can all trigger feelings of jealousy inside your children given that they threaten your child's sense of relational security.

Rather than talking it out, children are prone to acting it out. For example, when they feel jealous because you're giving another child a compliment, they may demand your attention. Or they may start doing what the other child is doing, but in a more dramatic way. They may pout, "You didn't tell me I did a good job. You like them better than me." They may try to take something away from the other child to gain some power over how powerless jealousy can sometimes feel. Possessiveness is a common sign of jealousy among children. They may doubt their skills if they perceive someone else is better than them.

Regardless of how your children express their jealousy, they need your support with helping them make sense of this emotion and what it's driving them to do. They don't need you to minimize or erase the feeling, nor do they need you to judge it. This is an opportunity to help your child feel seen, heard, understood, and safe with you. Use the PCC to work through jealous moments effectively:

- Pause: Be honest with yourself about what your child's jealousy is triggering within you. If you have an inner child wound, remember that's yours to tend to. Resist the urge to make your history with jealousy your child's burden to carry.

- Connect: Validate their perspective: "I hear you saying that when I notice your sibling's accomplishments, it makes you feel like no one likes you or cares about your hard work. That makes sense."

- Collaborate: Try to support your child by expanding their perspective: "Is there another way you can see this situation?"

When Jealousy Turns Competitive

Sometimes, children intentionally provoke one another to get a reaction. Often, issues like a lack of confidence and impulse control operate behind the scenes of jealous, competitive siblings. They want to work together, but they're stuck in a rut of inadequacy and insecurity and thus cannot access collaboration the way they need to, so they taunt one another: "Ha-ha, I'm smarter than you!" "Your friends are boring. Mine are much cooler." "Look at this sick new rock I found. Yours is nothing special." "Mom said I'm her favorite. That's why she gave me more ice cream than you." This was the case with Asher (nine years old) and Andy (six).

Justifiably exhausted, Asher and Andy's parents grew tired of trying to stop the boys from constantly being at each other's throats. Eventually, they gave up, and things quickly got out of hand. The boys needed the three Cs of discipline: clear, consistent, and connected. When they first came for treatment, if Mom or Dad gave any direction, it was murky at best, there was zero consistency or follow-through, and anger and burnout muddled any seeds of connection. This family was in a Connection Desert, yet another source of fuel for sibling jealousy.

When jealousy causes your children to be in conflict, intervene with the collaborative spirit. In session one day, during a game of Sorry, Asher couldn't handle the fact that Andy gained another piece into his safe zone, and he accused him of cheating. Andy protested, "No, I'm winning and you're losing because you're a dummy!" Asher refused to keep playing, and things were going to escalate quickly without our support. Here's how the collaborative process played out with the brothers.

Separate: Getting through the game without a fight is not what's important. Your goal is to help your children learn how to express themselves constructively, not destructively: "Let's press pause on the game and both of you sit down and cool off for a second."

Validate + Emotion Coaching + Limits: "I see two brothers having a problem. Asher, what's your side?" He said it wasn't fair that Andy was doing better than he was: "I'm older, I should be the one who wins." Help your children recognize jealousy, where it is in their bodies, and what it makes them want to do (emotion coaching). "I hear you. You're feeling jealous. You want to win. Where do you feel jealousy the most in your body?" He said in his heart. "And all that jealousy in your heart felt so crummy that it made you flip the board so none of us can play." He put his head down and nodded in agreement. "Andy, what's your side?" He said

Asher always ruined his fun and never let him feel like a winner. "So, I want him to feel bad like me." Emotion coaching: "I hear you; you're feeling shame and you don't like it. Where do you feel shame the most in your body?" He said in his belly. "And all that shame in your belly made you feel so yucky that you called him a dummy."

Be clear, consistent, and connected with the limit: "Boys, even when you're feeling crummy inside, we still need to be careful with our words. Our words matter."

Collaborate: "Let's find more caring ways to express our feelings." I offered them two choices: "When you're angry, you can express your feelings or ask for a space break." Andy agreed to share his feelings: "That hurts me when you accuse me of cheating!" Asher took a space break.

Try Again: We returned to the moment where jealousy consumed Asher and practiced using the skills in real time.

At first, Asher and Andy were reluctant to participate in the collaborative spirit, which I expected. They had many years of repetitive patterns to correct, and change takes time. But they eventually figured it out, and the intense jealousy was eventually resolved.

Jealousy is like every other emotion. It may be uncomfortable, but children need to learn how to ride the waves of it and find their way back to the heart of their relationships—the desire to feel connected and important. When you help your children find connection even in jealous moments, you'll notice over time that they will learn to look after one another.

Physical Fights

Felix (seven years old) and Silas (five) were another set of brothers who could not resist the temptation to get physical with each other.

Their parents struggled to intervene and would often find themselves smacked in the face or kicked in the leg. As this pattern became more prevalent, both parents walked on eggshells around the boys and quickly became visibly distressed and flooded at any sign of their emotional dysregulation.

Overwhelmed by the constant physical battles, the parents asked, "Do we let them duke it out in hopes that they eventually figure it out?" No matter how hard they tried to talk good sense into the kids, they couldn't stop them from physically acting out. Of course they wanted to give up! It's tiring to have to be "on" so much, not to mention how triggering it is to witness so much aggression.

But disengaging when things feel hard with our children only amplifies the problem. Instead of seeing the physical fights as something you need to stop, shift your perspective and see them as a symptom of a deeper problem. Get curious about what's driving these behaviors. They are not happening arbitrarily, nor does it feel good for your children to get triggered into this much internal distress and chaos. Repeated physical fights between siblings might suggest your children

- Have limitations in effective problem-solving.

- Are working on frustration tolerance and impulse control.

- Have unmet needs, often in the areas of connection, sensory containment, emotional containment, and power, control, independence, and autonomy.

- May be experiencing something stressful at home or school.

- May have an undiagnosed mental health issue. By six years old, regular physical fighting—which involves hitting, kicking, shoving, punching, and so on—between children should be largely eliminated and rarely happen. This also means that older children should not physically retaliate toward younger children, even if provoked. It's age-appropriate to expect children six years and up to tap into more useful skills. If physical fights are the rule rather than the exception, you may choose to seek an evaluation for any underlying issues, such as ADHD, autism, learning differences, sensory integration differences, PTSD, depression, or anxiety. Professional support is most likely necessary in these types of scenarios.

In Felix and Silas's case, Dad was struggling with high-functioning alcoholism. Mom was unfulfilled and lonely in her marriage. Neither parent had great models for conflict resolution growing up, so their instinct was to blow up in reaction to their children. Self-reflection work was a painful process for them. Unearthing wounds they learned to bury felt physically more intolerable than accidentally getting hit in the face. Yet both knew that if they wanted to change their family dynamic, they had to L.E.A.N. into the hard. Dad had to seek help to quit drinking. Mom had to lower her guard and find security with her partner. They had to learn to sit with what made them feel uncomfortable. They had to learn how to tolerate distress, anxiety, resentment, and fear if they were to help their children with these same emotions. They had to M.O.V.E. all of that trapped shame out of their bodies to make room for a deeper connection with each other and their children. They had to learn how to better care for themselves by dousing their relentless inner critic with compassion, so they could more effectively teach their children how to care for each other.

Parenting themselves first so they could become the parents that Felix and Silas needed happened simultaneously with eliminating the repeated bouts of physical aggression between the boys. As the parents healed their inner wounds, they began parenting in more healing ways. The children's physical fights became less frequent, and the children were far more amenable to their parents' clear, consistent, and connected directive: "Felix and Silas, stop your bodies. Separate now and go cool off."

In the rare instances when the children didn't immediately follow suit, they felt more secure about breaking up the fights. Rather than hesitantly pleading for the kids to stop or being too physically rough, both parents learned to step in swiftly, confidently, and calmly. Body confidence is everything in these moments, and they held themselves assertively. They achieved this by intervening the same way, every time. The brain is an organ that loves repetition. What we repeat the most is what our children come to trust the most. Rather than repeating chaos, disorganization, and dysregulation, both parents learned to repeat calm, cool, and collected.

Navigating sibling dynamics has been one of the more challenging but rewarding parts of parenthood for me personally. Jealousy, fighting, aggression, and competition are all experiences I instinctually try to avoid. Yet there's something healing about leaning into the chaos and teaching these kids how to masterfully engage in their relationships. I hope that you find that the more you exercise the collaborative spirit with your kids, the more they will learn to internalize it and do it on their own, as I have found with my own children and my clients. As your children grow their collaboration skills, trust that their baseline will go from bickering, fighting, teasing, and poking . . . to listening, expressing, engaging, and solving.

CHAPTER 11

· · · · · ·

Aligning with Your Parenting Partner

NYONE INTIMATELY INVOLVED IN YOUR CHILDREN'S LIVES— your significant other, a co-parent, a co-parent's new significant other, grandparents, nannies, daycare, or any combination of these caregivers—is part of your parenting team. Caring for the whole family includes aligning with these caregivers. Yet it's common for my clients to reach a stage in their healing journey where they realize that they are in misalignment with their parenting partners. Although they've committed to their self-work, they find themselves reenacting the patterns and triggers they desperately want to grow out of. Unable to see their role in the cycle, they believe it is their partner who is in the wrong, and they make it their mission to get the partner to *want* to do this work.

Ultimately, this effort backfires, because parenting yourself first is a call that comes from within. Until someone is ready to get to know themselves on a deep soul level, they can't be coerced into doing the work. So I invite you to be on a *journey* toward alignment with all your parenting partners—especially your primary partner, if you have one. The end goal is not necessarily total agreement on every issue but a commitment to commonly shared values and a clear vision for your family.

Your Partner Is a Mirror into the Past

You may have noticed that your unresolved inner child wounds have worked their way into your partnership. Often, your significant other represents a parent or someone in your childhood who had a profound influence on you. Perhaps you had a mother who often reminded you of all the ways you were no good, and now you're in a relationship with someone who makes you feel small and unworthy. Maybe you had a father who left when you were young, and now you're in a relationship with someone who is emotionally unavailable. Your soul's healing comes through encountering what challenges you and finding more evolved ways to manage those challenges—and we often find that healing and growth with the people we partner with.

When we create new significant partnerships, we often carry an unconscious hope that the other person will eventually change who they are to meet our needs. Many of my clients believe (erroneously) that they can change their partner's mindset. Ultimately, we realize that no one changes themselves to meet the needs of others. The impetus for change is on *you*, and the more you commit to making little changes in yourself, the more you will disrupt whatever patterns you and your partner are engaging in. This disruption invites change. Aligning with your parenting partners depends on your openness to conflict and willingness to make changes, both of which allow for more harmony in the home environment.

Building Blocks for a Unified Approach to Parenting

It is incredibly common among the couples I treat: each person believes the other is the problem. They forget that they're on the same team and reenact their survival patterns with each other to protect themselves. Making this false assumption prevents you from seeing your part in the problem and creates more emotional distance and distress.

If the need to feel seen, heard, understood, and to be safe went unfulfilled in childhood, then you may approach your parenting dynamic with the unconscious expectation that the other will fill these important relational needs. Now that you're more confident with deconstructing your past, it's time to reimagine how you can co-construct your future.

Block One: Take Accountability for the Ways You Cause Harm

For the most part, Rafael and Yvonne got along fine with each other, until one of them triggered the other, and soon all bets were off. He knew that icing her out by staring at his phone—even during a fight—activated her deepest abandonment wounds. She knew that nitpicking and criticizing his every move activated his deepest shame wounds. They took advantage of the other's weak spots when they felt hurt, hoping to save a shred of dignity for themselves. Rarely do we feel dignified when we exploit someone's Achilles' heel. Instead, we cause more hurt to surface and create distance in the relationship.

Team parenting requires collaboration, intention, active

listening, and a joint effort from all parties. Learning to parent together is a process of learning from one's mistakes. We all have strengths and weaknesses, and it's not a character flaw to be fully human. If you learn to hide your weaknesses because you fear how your partner may exploit them, you'll ultimately suppress your true self. Chronically masking yourself to appease your parenting partner drives you further apart. Your willingness to be vulnerable with each other—as well as your commitment to not exploit that vulnerability—is the thread that bonds you together.

Resist the urge to judge your parenting partners for their mistakes, and instead focus on the ways you personally contribute to pattern reenactments. Don't wait for your partner to fix their dysfunctional behavior before you're willing to make meaningful changes for yourself. Rafael did not need Yvonne to stop nagging him for him to stop emotionally disconnecting from her in times of stress. Yvonne did not need Rafael to be perfectly organized for her to stop criticizing his missteps. True connection flourishes when you're willing to own your role in whatever disconnection you may have.

Like many of the couples I work with, Rafael and Yvonne were stuck on this hamster wheel of shifting blame onto the other to avoid any personal responsibility for their own behavior. By using M.O.V.E., rather than reacting to Yvonne's criticism and believing he was a loser, Rafael learned to tell himself, *Disagreements are okay. I can stay present.* When despair hijacked Yvonne's mind, triggering fears of loneliness, she learned to self-soothe and hold herself accountable: *He's not going to leave me. I can express my anger differently.* Then it was time for them to take the leap and enact change.

When you find yourself in a pattern of blaming, criticizing, and defending, the key is to repair these moments so you can move forward with the mission to love more deeply and to keep trying your best. Try saying, "Can we have that talk again? I realized what my part of the problem is." When you acknowledge your role, your partner can let their guard down and own their part, too. Plan what each person can do differently next time to improve your interaction. Be committed to trying your best, while also being realistic that sometimes your best is messy.

Block Two: Consistent, Small Efforts Lead to Tangible, Big Changes

My clients Amy and Marco were spread so thin between his two demanding jobs and their three school-aged children that they barely had time to connect with each other throughout the day. They felt more like roommates than lovers, and their partnership was suffering. Their interactions were fueled by criticism and defensiveness, and although they hated reenacting this pattern, they couldn't help themselves. They hoped a night away would fix their rut.

Dr. John Gottman says, "Successful long-term relationships are created through small words, small gestures, and small acts." When Amy and Marco returned from their getaway trip, burnout and detachment were waiting on their doorstep. They learned that the big moments are too infrequent to cause any real change in an already suffering partnership dynamic.

When a partnership is in survival mode for a prolonged period, it drains the emotional connection. It exposes your unresolved inner child wounds, and you're more likely to act it out rather than talk it out. Amy projected her resentment through more criticism and less affection. Marco defended against rejection by emotionally removing himself from her. Like most couples, they knew how to exploit each other's weaknesses, and doing so only further damaged their partnership.

Amy and Marco needed to take simple, tangible, and consistent action on supporting their partnership, and so they started by making a few commitments to each other. First thing in the morning, rather than looking at their phones or rushing to get the kids, they looked into each other's eyes and said, "Good morning." When Marco returned home from work, before rushing to his second job, he asked what the kids were up to and then joined in to give Amy a moment to herself. Amy offered him a shoulder rub, because although she was touched out, he was touch deprived, and this action made him feel cared for. As they made these small commitments to everyday connection—without all the bells and whistles of a fancy dinner or an expensive sitter—they found that their partnership strengthened. They started talking more, laughing more, genuinely enjoying each other more, and their emotional and intimate connection deepened.

My therapist, Dr. Hanna, once said to me, "Having a relationship is about making your beloved's life just a little bit easier." We partner up in the first place to ease the pressure and stress of living, yet we often end up feeling the opposite. It takes a conscious effort to unburden your partnership, so I recommend that you sit down with your parenting partner and discuss the little things you can do for each other and commit to doing one small act every day this week. At the end of the week, discuss if this has improved your intimacy and connection. Here are some ideas to get you started:

- Kiss your partner first thing when you walk through the door.
- Finish the dishes and wash the counter without being asked.
- Make coffee for your partner in the morning.
- Check in during the day with a loving text.

- Tell them you think they're sexy, inspiring, or fun to be around.

- Spontaneously bring them their favorite treat.

- Spend time looking at each other instead of at your phones.

- Change your schedule to help your partner out if they're having an extra busy day.

Block Three: How and When You Give Parenting Feedback Matters

Justin was sick and tired of being undermined by his partner, Chantal. At least once a day, she hovered over him as he interacted with the children. "No, we don't say things like that." "No, we don't do time-outs." "No, you're making things worse, just go away, I'll fix this." Justin occasionally lost his temper, and he was prone to using punishments like removing something the kids loved to get them to behave. Chantal, on the other hand, felt like she couldn't trust him with the kids. In her mind, he had acted out enough times and shown little awareness or desire to implement the changes they discussed in their weekly parenting therapy that she had no choice but to take matters into her own hands and correct him when his behavior wasn't aligned with her vision. She felt like he was undermining her efforts to correct familial patterns of shame, people pleasing, and feeling controlled. Like many couples, they were making the classic mistake by seeing *each other* as the problem, rather than *the problem itself* as something that needed to be addressed.

Correcting your partner's parenting in the moment with a message of "We don't do it like that" often harms your alliance. It also doesn't inspire trust and confidence in your children, who are learning how to be a good partner by watching your style of working together.

A more tactful way to support each other through these moments is by creating a Support Protocol.

1. Ask your partner how they would like you to check in with them if you notice they are heated with the kids and might need support. Let them know what you would need in a similar situation. For most of my clients, it's a helpful habit to tap their partner's shoulder and say, "Do you need any help from me?" This step cannot be discussed in a stressful moment, so take time to discuss your preferences tonight.

2. If your partner says they don't need your support, bite your tongue, and walk away. Don't insist on your way. Let them know that you're available to support them if they change their mind.

3. Debrief afterward. Ask your partner to reflect on what they were thinking, feeling, and needing in the moment. Can they connect what was happening on the inside to how they were behaving on the outside?

4. Put your heads together to reflect on the children's behaviors. What were they thinking, feeling, and needing in the moment? Any stressors?

5. Ask your partner if they're open to your feedback. If so, share how you would have approached the situation, how their actions made you feel inside, and discuss any new approaches you both might be willing to try for next time.

Note: Unless there are significantly dysfunctional behaviors taking place, do not "rescue" the children from your partner. Intervening and removing your children from the premises should be done if your partner is punching holes in walls, throwing objects, violently screaming, slamming doors, being physically aggressive toward anyone in the home, name-calling and taunting, humiliating, or engaging in harsh and unwarranted punishments. Seek immediate professional support if these problems occur in your home.

I noticed my husband, Matt, often seemed annoyed with our eldest child, who has an intensely curious personality that can sometimes feel demanding and tough to keep up with. As a child, I received similar messages that I was annoying and unwanted, and so I was aware that I was triggered by Matt's repeated eye-rolling and exasperation with our eldest.

One evening, rather than chastising Matt and making him feel bad for triggering me and mistreating our child, I said, "You seem stressed. Do you need support?" He asked me to take over for a bit, which I did. We debriefed later, and he shared that he felt frustrated that our eldest "never listens" to him. "He gets stuck on an idea, and he drains me." In the spirit of parenting yourself first, never settle for the surface understanding of your thoughts and feelings. Continue inviting yourself to dig.

His frustration wasn't with our son not listening. Our son was reflecting—like a mirror—Matt's pattern of self-denial and self-rejection. This helped Matt recognize that if he wasn't feeling heard, the feeling was probably mutual. Matt has made a commitment to protecting our son's self-image by doing his own healing work of actively nurturing his internal needs and creating more opportunities for collaboration, which our eldest loves because it gives him more freedom, power, and the chance to prove how incredibly competent he is.

This wouldn't have happened had I reacted by chastising Matt: "Stop rolling your eyes at him. Do you know how rude that is?" Doing so would have told my eldest not to trust his father . . . that he needs me to protect him from his big, mean daddy. It's far more productive to understand the meaning behind your behaviors, build more empathy for the child's perspective, and make a joint plan to move forward with more harmony and grace.

Block Four: Share in the Mental Load of Raising Children

Meera was a stay-at-home mother to four children. She loved her role, but the demands of motherhood were far greater than she had anticipated. She knew her daily routine would involve obvious physical tasks like grocery shopping, doing the dishes, packing lunches, school drop-off and pickup, and so on. But she was unprepared for the mental load of motherhood that is part of running a household and managing a family. It's all the behind-the-scenes knowledge about all the endless tasks involved in raising children, like anticipating needs (making sure the jerseys are clean in time for the kids' soccer games), planning (keeping track of the family calendar), decision-making (choosing a car seat), and delegating (hashing out who's taking the kids to the weekend birthday party). It's organizing and performing important duties like doctor visits, budgeting, holiday gatherings, school events, vacation planning, and signing up for activities. The mental load is replying to your child's hunt for their missing toy, "Check the bottom left-hand drawer of the dresser next to your bed, behind the green sweatpants and under your socks. You left it there a week ago."

Being the Knower of All Things is the most exhausting aspect of being a parent. Unfortunately, in cisgender-heterosexual partnerships, this burden almost always falls onto the mom. Right from the very start, little girls like Meera are socially and culturally conditioned to concern themselves with the needs of others. They are unknowingly indoctrinated into a life that ensures the comfort of everyone around them, often at their own expense. I am not bashing or demeaning men, but I am scrutinizing the patriarchal system that ultimately failed men by making them irrelevant in their own homes and failed women by actively oppressing them with the expectations of what they should be exclusively responsible for. A woman might be drowning, but she's learned to appear put together. Her male partner believes that she does all the work because she's good at it and she "likes" it, when in truth most women are good at it because they *do* it.

Although he wasn't a bad partner or a bad father, Meera's husband, Joaquin, contributed the bare minimum to the family. In his mind, the home and children were woman's work, and he preferred to stay out of it as much as possible. He'd reluctantly do the dishes if he were asked, but he enjoyed the more technical upkeep of the home, like repairing a light fixture. If she went out with friends for a few hours, he'd blow up her phone with texts asking where the diapers were and what time he was supposed to feed the kids. Trapped in fear of not wanting to be a burden on him, Meera found herself avoiding asking for help and doing everything on her own. She didn't want to have to deal with the guilt trips or having to teach Joaquin their family routines. It ironically took less mental effort for her to do things herself. As the years went on, the load took a toll on her mental health. Like so many of my clients, Meera felt anxious, depressed, resentful, rageful, and trapped in her own life.

If modern parents want more fulfilling connections, all parenting partners must take the steps necessary to learn about the mental load and recognize when they either take on too much or assume it's not their problem. The load itself is not likely going to change.

But how it's carried can change. Women need to give up some control of the family flow to have less cognitive burden. Men need to take on more familial responsibilities (without burdening their female partners with comparisons to what was modeled for them growing up).

A Pew Research poll in 2007 suggested that couples feel happier and more balanced when the house and home responsibilities are divided fairly. Sixty-two percent of adults surveyed reported that sharing household chores was very important for having a successful partnership. Only faithfulness and a good sex life ranked higher. Sharing chores ranked higher than compatible interests, political beliefs, and adequate income. When you take full ownership of the responsibility for a family, you tell your partner: I'm doing this *with* you, rather than I'm doing this *for* you. Taking full responsibility includes the planning, prepping, remembering, and execution—without needing oversight from your partner.

Joaquin agreed that Meera's load was too high and took on the responsibility of grocery shopping. On his first week, he called her from the egg aisle to ask if they needed eggs. He not only contributed to Meera's mental load (although unintentionally) but sent an unconscious message that he wasn't fully invested in the responsibility he took on. Meera was clear about her boundary: "I need you to do this on your own. I won't be available to provide input next time." It wasn't long before Joaquin learned to check the refrigerator and cupboards before heading to the store, create a list, buy everything, and put away the groceries when he returned home. Meera not only gained another hour to her week, but now she felt she could trust Joaquin to fully handle it. She could finally delete this responsibility from her brain, which dialed down some of the pressure she felt and alleviated some of the anxiety and depression she was experiencing.

Here are some steps to take to start divvying up the mental load:

1. Make a list of all the responsibilities for running your home, divided by daily, weekly, monthly, quarterly, semiannually, and annually. This will be tedious, but it will become a cornerstone as you map out a more balanced mental load for your partnership. Do this on a spreadsheet so it can be updated over the years as your family needs shift and change.

2. Discuss the current distribution of responsibilities and any thoughts and feelings you may have about them (especially if you're harboring resentment).

3. Discuss what an equitable, fair distribution of responsibilities looks like for your family. Meera was happy to take on about 75 percent of the home duties, whereas Chantal felt 50 percent of the home duties was what she could manage. There is no perfect distribution, as it depends on your unique situation. Plan to revisit your responsibility loads often, especially if someone appears burned out, isn't asking for help, or is becoming resentful due to the load.

4. Define who will take the lead on certain responsibilities. Who will do the grocery shopping? The meal prepping? The cooking? The laundry? The doctor visits? The holiday planning? The vacation planning? Keeping toys and closets organized? Donating old gear? Signing up for activities? Arranging playdates? Figure this out together.

5. Decide to check in once a week with each other about the mental load. How is it going? Are you managing? Do you need support? Don't stand by and watch your partner drown. You are in this together.

Don't burn yourself out trying to be perfect in how you execute basic parenting tasks. If you are spent by 5:00 p.m. and your partner is also feeling worn out, it's okay to cut corners. Use paper plates so you don't have to clean up. Give the kids an early bath. Watch an extra show as a family and get to bed early. Don't feel as if you need to be rigid with your routines and your life. It's okay to assess where you are in the moment and make your decisions based on what you *can* give, rather than what you think you *should* give.

Block Five: Couples Who Play Together, Stay Together

Playfulness is a key factor to healthy, long-lasting partnerships. Parents who are comfortable playing with each other seem to approach parenting dilemmas with more creativity and ease. They laugh with each other, look into each other's eyes, and casually touch each other when they're talking. They use a warm tone and tend to turn toward each other. They also take the time to do activities together, like bowling leagues or wine clubs. Essentially, they're intentional about spending playful, joyful time together. Playfulness increases joy, intimacy, and connection while also serving as a buffer for harder moments. When these couples have disagreements, their playful spirit usually drives a more positive, productive communication style.

Parents who aren't playful with each other tend to approach issues with more anxiety and distress, are more easily overwhelmed, and tend to be more rigid in their problem-solving. They tend to be more serious with each other. They avoid looking at each other, and there's usually not much physical contact. These couples often fall into the trap of doom-scrolling in bed or binge-watching Netflix until they pass out and wake up to do it all over again the next day. Often, parents who struggle with playfulness are inundated by too much stress. The more stressed and anxious we feel, the less creative, spontaneous, and playful we are.

I've never met a couple who says they have too much joy, play, and fun together. I have met plenty who say there isn't enough. Your children feel the playfulness you have with each other in a positive, peaceful way. They learn that loving relationships include connection, spontaneity, and joy and that relationships aren't always so serious, heavy, and hard. You can keep play alive by dancing together, preparing meals and cooking together, looking for your dream homes on Zillow, crafting together, working out together, doing morning or day dates so you're not so exhausted, having a weekly game night, and more. Prioritize this discussion with your partner and make small, incremental efforts today for big changes down the road.

Each of the five building blocks work together to help unify your partnerships by establishing a foundation for empathy, attunement, and mutual respect. The more you commit to integrating these blocks into your way of life, the easier your dynamic will feel. Keep in mind: these are relationship skills, which means both parties in the relationship need to be open and invested in learning and growing together. You will find that the blocks come tumbling down when one partner is more invested than the other. If you're struggling with a history of hurting each other, it's probably best to rebuild these blocks under the care of a licensed mental health professional.

Once you've gotten a handle on your five building blocks, you're ready to incorporate Values-Centered Partnering into your family dynamic. This key practice helps you get clear on your values, understand the barriers that get in the way of you living out your family values, and develop a plan to overcome those barriers.

Values-Centered Partnering

I developed the core components of Values-Centered Partnering out of necessity. At one stage in my career, I was leading ten mommy and me classes per week, and I heard the same question over and over: *How do we get on the same page about parenting?*

When it came to discipline, my clients Teagan and Monica were not on the same page. When Monica lashed out at the children over shutting off the television, Teagan felt hurt and took it personally. "But I thought we agreed that it was necessary to discipline?" Monica asked, befuddled. Teagan felt strongly that the children should never be yelled at; Monica thought yelling was okay if it was being used to discipline the children. They made sweeping assumptions about what they each meant by "discipline"—without any real discussion—and then made the fight about each other (instead of about the problem, which in this case was miscommunication).

Aligning with your parenting partners is the process of agreeing to live out your shared family values.

Define Your Mutual Values

What matters the most to you and your family? What do you want to see more of? What is your vision for your relationship with your parenting partner, yourself, and your family as a whole? For your convenience, I've compiled this list of common values.

- Respectful communication
- Physical health and wellness
- Shared responsibility
- Equal attention to the mental load
- Conscious discipline
- Spiritual connection
- Religious life
- Financial stability
- Social responsibility
- Cultural traditions
- Community involvement
- Environmental and climate justice
- Unconditional love
- Increased self-awareness
- Healthy boundaries
- Satisfying sex life
- Empathy and connection
- More compassion
- Joy and play
- Pleasure and contentment

There is no right or wrong way to think about your values. Your culture or family of origin or community may inform your values.

1. Write your values on a list and have your partner do the same. Then compare them. Notice where you're aligned and where you differ. Discuss the differences from a place of wanting to hear the other person's perspective. Don't try to convince each other of your point of view. Instead, try to listen and understand any differing perspectives.

2. Then, make a separate list of the common family values you both share. These will be the values you will begin to cultivate, nurture, and grow within your relationship and family dynamic.

3. Continue to discuss the values that you hold independently to eventually come to a shared understanding. For example, perhaps you wrote down conscious discipline, but your partner wrote down strict punishments for misbehavior. Part of your work together would be researching conscious discipline and punishments, making a list of pros and cons for both, sharing your personal histories and emotions attached to either style of discipline, and deciding together which approach you feel would best serve your family. Not which is "the best" but which is the best fit for your children. Getting aligned is not about parenting in a particular style. It's about finding *your* style.

Explore Your Barriers

After you've laid out your values, your next step is to consider: *What gets in the way of us living out our shared family values?* Here's a list of common barriers I gathered after doing this exercise with hundreds of families.

- Stress
- Sleep deprivation

- Poor early childhood modeling of effective communication

- Being overcommitted to work, expected to travel, and generally less available than their stay-at-home partners

- Overscheduling family activities

- Gender stereotypes, contributing to unequal division of labor and responsibilities

- Poor financial planning, overspending, or having grown up in poverty

- An underlying inner critic or highly contemptuous attitude that contributes to resentment in the relationship

- Different styles of existing in the relationship—e.g., one parent may be casual and open to risk, while the other is hypervigilant and feels extra responsible for the children's safety as a result.

This numbering continues from the previous section—it's all part of the same process!

4. **Next to each mutually held value, write out the barriers that get in the way of you living that out.** For example, let's say financial stability is a mutually shared value. Perhaps you discover that living beyond your means is the barrier. Rather than fantasizing about having financial stability, get clear on what stands in your way from achieving your vision. Or perhaps empathy and attunement are mutually shared values, and you discover that stress makes it harder for you to truly see each other. There may be buried resentments and frustrations that need to be resolved.

5. **Celebrate wins!** Give yourself a pat on the back if there are values that you feel you are embodying without barriers.

Perhaps you are masters at problem-solving and bring out the best in each other when you're stressed. Or you may feel good about how you're teaching your children to take pride in who they are.

Take Steps to Overcome Barriers

Now that you've identified the barriers, it's time to imagine what you will need to do to overcome them so your whole family can live with more alignment. In this step, you make honest, actionable changes within your dynamic. If you value healthy communication, and your burnout leads you to fly off the handle, your next step is to seriously address your burnout. Your yelling is the symptom of a deeper problem. Values-Centered Partnering is about investing your energy into resolving the core issues together.

The process of overcoming the barriers is hard work, and all your tools from Part One will support you in finding a path forward. I worked with a couple who had a shared value of quality family time. Yet the father, Armand, worked eighty hours per week and was usually gone four days a week on business trips. When Armand came home, he was understandably exhausted and stressed. He couldn't tolerate the children's chaos. He'd snap, yell, and then retreat into hiding, ashamed by his behavior and fraught with feelings of failure. Exhaustion, burnout, and unrealistic behavioral expectations were all barriers to the quality family time he envisioned.

Armand's own father dealt with stress by snapping and hiding. His mother made excuses for his dad's emotional immaturity, depriving Armand of the opportunity to witness how to stay connected even when stressed. With this awareness, Armand unlearned his old programming and found ways to calm his nerves, lower his expectations, and engage his kids in low-effort but high-reward interactions like board games and card games. With consistent changes to his own behavior, he overcame the barriers so he could authentically live out the value of quality family time.

Don't expect to overcome your barriers overnight. This process takes consistent effort and attention. Some barriers will be obvious and fixable with simple solutions; other barriers will be more complex and will take more time. Think about whether any of these solutions might help your family.

- Solicit more physical support for the children (hiring a sitter, asking a family member, swapping kid duties with a friend for an afternoon or evening).

- Get more physical support for the home (is it in your means to hire a cleaning service or get an occasional meal delivery?).

- Have better boundaries around how you spend your time ("No" is a complete sentence!).

- Go to therapy (individual, couples, family—whatever your time and budget permit).

- Spend more time in play and connection and less time working.

- Make a conscious effort to talk and engage one another.

- Spend time together as a family doing simple, enjoyable activities.

- Spend more time in nature.

- Engage in meal plan and meal prep.

- Create a concrete plan for task responsibilities.

- Define and stick to a budget that fits your means.

- Start a daily mindfulness practice to cultivate joy and warmth in the family.

- Schedule a family movie night or family game night.

Let this exercise be a launching pad for many reflective and heart-centered discussions. When you recognize that either one of you is not living out your family values, have a private conversation about it afterward and focus on the barrier—rather than the person—so you can find a solution without blame.

Look for the Good in Your Partner

I remember feeling frustrated with my husband and begging him, "Why don't you see that I'm not trying to hurt you? I'm tired of being the villain here!" His request wasn't unreasonable, and I needed to take ownership for what I had done. But if we're begging to be seen as good in our partnerships, it means there isn't enough unconditional acceptance of us, and there's a pattern of transactional love being reenacted, which triggers relational insecurity. In my case, I couldn't bear another intimate relationship where I was only seen for my faults and my badness. I had enough of that in my childhood. I needed a partner who would give me the benefit of the doubt before casting me out. Everyone needs a partner who will look for the good in them. By assuming that your partner has benevolent intentions, you give them the gift of knowing that they aren't total trash for messing up and that you still desire to connect with them, even when you don't appreciate their behavior or actions.

Looking for the good in your partner does not mean that you accept negative, destructive ways of communicating. It means that you accept that your partner is good beneath the shame and hurt they're acting out, and that you both accept full responsibility for what you say, how you say it, and how it is received. You may make a conscious choice to honor their hurt and set a loving boundary: "I know you're hurting, and I need you to know that I'm not okay with you speaking to me like that. Let's cool off and address this later, please." By committing to seeing the good in your partner, you'll see that it draws you closer together.

Lean into Conflict

Many of the clients I've worked with grew up seeing their parents fight and never seeing them make up. They have memories of hiding in their bedrooms listening to their parents' conflict. I've also had clients who, like my husband, rarely saw their parents argue and developed a belief that conflict is abnormal and should be actively avoided at all costs. Not having any conflict may be a sign of emotional distance in the same way that excessive conflict may be a sign of emotional enmeshment. I want to normalize that conflict is normal in healthy relationships.

Dr. John Gottman says that 96 percent of the time, how a conflict resolves is determined by the first three minutes of the discussion. If a conflict starts with criticism, defensiveness, avoidance, or condescension, things will turn ugly fast. Knowing how to fight fairly will strengthen your partnership by ensuring that both of your wants and needs are adequately attended to.

To help you lean into conflict with more courage, compassion, and connection, here are some basic rules of healthy conflict.

Fight Knowing Your Children Are Watching and Learning

It can be helpful for a child to witness your disagreements. It can teach them how to assert their opinions constructively or how to respectfully retract their opinion in favor of someone else's. How we fight sets the tone for how they will expect conflicts to unfold in their future relationships. We want our children to know how to navigate different personalities, communication styles, and argumentative styles, without losing sight of who they are in the process.

Dean was adamant that his children should never see him fight with his girlfriend, Mia. He saw explosive fights between his parents that traumatized him, and he never wanted his children to experience the terror he felt as a child. Mia, on the other hand, felt it was unreasonable to expect that they bottle up their feelings and put on a happy face just to save the children from feeling discomfort. Dean wasn't convinced and needed guidelines on how to fight in front of his children.

- **When you're having a disagreement, keep the style and content appropriate.** Save your explosive, aggressive fights for therapy, and protect your kids from toxic conflict. Also, it would not be appropriate to fight about intimacy issues in front of children. But it would be appropriate to fight about grocery spending if you can keep the discussion strictly about that week's budget.

- **Don't bring up the past.** If you're angry about the dishes in the sink, don't talk about every time over the last month that the dishes were left in the sink. Instead, focus on the problem in the here and now. Then, circle back to your values once you're more regulated and discuss any barriers you're noticing. In this case, you might discuss how family responsibilities are divided.

- **Hold hands when you fight.** This may be the last thing you want to do, but if you can tolerate it, holding hands serves as a reminder that you're a team. Face each other and look into each other's eyes. We're less likely to sting our partner if we're present to their humanity. As best as you can, be mindful about the words coming out of your mouth. Don't let the heat of the moment get you carried away into saying things you'll later regret.

- **If you fight in front of the kids, make up in front of them.** This will teach your children that conflicts have resolutions and people can find healthy ways to move forward. Plus, children may assume that if we don't make up in front of them then they are to blame for the fight. Children are never to blame for adult conflicts. It's usually our own wounds and habitual patterns that cause us to disconnect from each other.

Say What You *Feel* So You Can *Heal*

I was complaining about my husband's behavior to my therapist. I was feeling resentful due to all the demands I faced as a mother and felt like Matt didn't "get" it. Dr. Hanna asked me if I had shared my complaints with him. Of course I hadn't, because that would have been a mature way of handling things, and I was still an amateur at resolving conflicts in a healthy way. "Why would I tell him how I feel when I can complain about him to you?" I joked. Dr. Hanna smirked and said, "You're probably not the only one feeling this."

Although there's nothing revolutionary about this idea, the

perspective touched me. Instead of seeing that my feelings in our relationship could be mirroring Matt's, I assumed I was alone in what I felt. This belief drove me to push down my feelings and disconnect from my partnership. He read my disengagement as disinterest, which activated his insecurities of feeling worthless and unlovable. Our mutual desire not to rock the boat disrupted the water. We had to learn how to settle things down so we could grow closer together. When you learn to say what you feel in an effective, straightforward manner, without making it about your partner in a negative way, it allows you to heal within your partnership.

When I teach these skills to parents in my practice, they express their feelings like this: "I feel like you're not putting in enough effort to stay calm with the kids, and I'm having to clean up your mess because of it." Or, "I feel like you're always bossing me around, like I'm an idiot or something." Or, "I feel like you're always on your phone and you're not helping me enough." Although these statements begin with "I feel," they quickly turn onto the other person, making it about them. If you say "I feel like you . . . ," then it's a criticism, and you're inviting defensiveness into the discussion.

Instead, you want to use actual feelings words like "sad," "frustrated," "hurt," "upset," "anxious," "afraid," "angry," "annoyed," "resentful," "confused," "jealous," "rejected," and so on.

"I feel upset when I hear you yell at the kids."

"I feel insecure and want to believe that you trust me. But I'm struggling with that."

"I'm feeling burned out and under-prioritized."

It's more vulnerable to communicate this way, which is why it takes practice. Saying "I resent you" makes it about your partner. But saying "I'm feeling resentful, and here's why" makes it about your experience. Your partner will be much more engaged if they don't have to listen defensively, which will contribute to a more positive resolution. It's probably going to feel robotic and awkward at first to share your feelings like this, but you'll get there. Eventually, it will feel good to connect in this manner, and speaking critically will begin to feel forced and uncomfortable.

In addition to resisting the urge to blame your partner for your emotions, avoid using hyperbolic language, which can and usually does trigger more conflict. Words like "always" and "never" and "I can't believe you would . . ." will force your partner into defense mode and your conflict will not end well. Healthy communication between you and your parenting partner is one of the most important things you can model for your children. Parents who communicate in an emotionally present way elevate the emotional intelligence of their entire home and often raise happier, better adjusted children as a result.

Say What You Need, and Trust That Your Partner Cares

"I don't want to have to tell him what I need. I want him to know!" my client Emily announced. She wanted her parenting partner to be a mind reader. When needing others has been seen as a character flaw and is culturally shunned by our hyper-reliance on independence, it can feel pretty foreign to ask for what you need, but expecting mind reading won't cut it.

When you state your needs, be sure you are asking for what you need and not seeking to control the other person's behaviors. "I need you to be home when you say you will, because it seems like you don't care that I'm drowning" is not an effective "I Need" statement. Instead, simply state your need: "I need you to be home when you say you will." Or, "I need you to give me a heads-up if you're running late." Or, you could combine a few of the teachings from this book and state your feeling, what you need, and a boundary: "I'm feeling overwhelmed with the after-school respon-sibilities. I need more support in the evenings. Let's find a way to make it work for both of us."

Be Gentle and Intentional with Each Other

When you want to bring up a difficult discussion with your par-enting partner, do so delicately and respectfully. Frame it as you and your partner against the problem, rather than the two of you against each other. Staying grounded in this fundamental way will protect your partnership. Take these steps the next time you need to resolve a conflict or initiate a tough talk:

- **Ask if it's a good time to talk about something hard.** If it isn't, when would be a good time? If you or your part-ner tend to avoid having important talks, or if you sweep things under the rug and pretend like they're not bother-ing you, be mindful about following through with the discussion. It will be easier to ignore it and hope that things resolve themselves. But they won't. They'll build up and create more internal clutter.

- **Begin by sharing something that you appreciate about your partner.** Doing so can help your partner feel less defensive: "I see how hard you're working for this family. Thank you, it means so much to me."

- **Express your concerns succinctly, carefully, and with "I Feel" statements.** "I feel upset that the garbage has not been taken out."

- **State what actions you need from your partner.** "I need you to follow through on your responsibility of tak-ing out the trash daily."

- **State your needs concretely using "I Need" statements.** "I need more reliable support with home tasks. Can we review the list of daily chores and see where we can make some adjustments, please? It would really help me a lot."

Role-play these skills with your parenting partner with a recent conflict or made-up scenario in mind. Approaching conflict this way doesn't typically come naturally, so you'll need to intentionally rehearse them to get it into your body. Just like you have to eat and drink every day to keep up your physical health, these skills are nourishing the soul of your partnership. Deprive your partnership of them, and you will feel the effects fairly quickly. But feed it consistently, and you will flourish.

Call a Reset If It Gets Too Heated

Parents need to avoid traumatizing their children by resisting the urge to scream at each other, hurl objects, slam doors, punch walls, or engage in any explosive behavior that could frighten and scare the kids.

There are some behaviors that need strict limits and boundaries. For our kids, it's running into streets, playing with knives and fire, or driving drunk. For parents, it's aggressively losing control, regardless of where that energy is directed. Not only is this an ineffective way to communicate your anger or frustration, but it also models for your children that losing control is how you get what you want.

Notice if you're triggered, and if you are, it's not a good time to have a fair fight. Instead, call a reset. The Reset asks you to have the emotional maturity to recognize that your fight is no longer productive. This is mandatory if fighting words are being used, someone is dissociating or emotionally checking out, or the conversation has become too heated and negative, and someone needs a break. Anyone can ask for a reset, and it's important that if someone does, you respect them and agree to take some time to cool off.

Decide ahead of time how long of a break you'll need. For most of my clients, it averages somewhere between one and three hours, but this depends on each person involved in the partnership. Often, someone who needs to resolve a conflict immediately (a seeker) pairs up with someone who'd rather slowly peel off one fingernail at a time than address it head-on (an avoider). Or both partners are conflict-avoidant and might hit the reset button but then don't have a hard conversation. In some cases, clients are both eager to resolve and turn toward each other, reset, and move forward with their own timing. Have an idea of which behavior style you and your partner are. Don't try to fix or change this about yourself— or your partner. Simply recognize what your baseline is and pick a time frame that is agreeable. Sometimes you will go to bed angry (if you share a bed with your partner). It's not ideal, but that's real life.

During the Reset period, continue being cordial with each other. The break from the conversation is so you can address it later in a more constructive, healthy way. But if you have family responsibilities that you are both involved in, you can't just walk away. It takes an incredible amount of maturity to maintain politeness, kindness, and respect when you're fuming inside. Looking for the good in your partner can be helpful. Don't mope, sulk, huff, puff, or otherwise use your nonverbal language to communicate how hurt you feel or your disapproval of your partner. Doing so will only keep you stuck in insecurity and will make your partner feel responsible for your emotional caretaking.

Use the Reset period to regulate your body and emotions, so

you can maintain being in your partner's presence, even in intense, difficult moments.

- **During the Reset, think about what you're feeling and needing.** Write down what you're feeling inside, what you need from your partner, and what you need for yourself.

- **When the agreed-upon time has passed, come back together and incorporate all the skills discussed in this section.** Face each other. Hold hands. Look into each other's eyes. Breathe. Look for the good in each other. Share the feelings and the needs you wrote down. Discuss a plan for moving forward that feels mutually satisfying. Do your best to keep this interaction affectionate and loving. If the fighting happened in front of the kids, make up in front of them. You can also invite them to process what they saw and how it made them feel.

In becoming a more aligned unit, you must be invested in the well-being of everyone involved in your parenting partnership for it to be successful. If only one person is working toward healthy conflict resolution and the other is disinterested in improving the dynamic, resentment will build. I've given you a plan for minimizing resentments, enhancing connection, and improving how you interact. Your task is to implement these skills so that they become a way of life. However, if the implementation feels too complicated or difficult, I encourage you to get guidance from a licensed mental health professional whenever you need it. Caring for a parenting partnership takes a lot of effort and energy, and I know that when you dedicate the time, you'll craft a partnership that is built to last.

• • • • • •

Caring for Your Community and Beyond

W HEN I HAPHAZARDLY STUMBLED UPON MY HEALING JOUR-
ney twenty years ago, I had no idea what I was doing. It
was as if I had stepped into a pitch-black maze with only an oil
lamp in hand that allowed me to see fifty feet or so ahead of me at
a time. There were sharp turns, dead ends, and endless rough terrain. I was so trapped by my wounds that it didn't seem possible
that I'd ever escape. Thoughts of eliminating the light I carried
completely consumed me. Those were some of my darkest days,
but something within me kept whispering, *Keep going.*

With practice and repetition, I learned to trust this voice,
which revealed the fork in the road I didn't know I was searching
for. I could continue to feed the beast that I was unworthy of love,
an embarrassment to many, and inherently bad, or I could learn
how to expand my inner light by learning how to love myself and
others, accept the imperfections of all (myself especially), and genuinely feel good about who I am as a human being. I chose the latter
direction, although the former pulls me back if I'm not mindful of
myself, my surroundings, and the people I interact with. You may

be at your own fork in the road, and I commend you for your journey to get there. I know it has not been easy.

This soul excavation work becomes that much more profound when you add children into the mix. The maze becomes significantly more complicated, but the whisper of *Keep going* grows intensely louder. Kids amplify your need to continue placing one foot in front of the other, because their livelihood depends on you doing so. Otherwise, they get stuck in the mud with you, and it will be their responsibility to dig us *all* out.

I feel dragged through time when my insensitive words smear humiliation onto my children's faces. It's as if a mirror smacks me in the face, and I can't move forward without looking within. A pause is necessary. There she stands, my inner child, so full of shame and self-rejection, desperate for someone who could love her. The child within us can teach us how to support the child in front of us. My inner child is teaching me compassion and humility. And so I apologize and correct my mistake, something that wasn't modeled for me but something I will consciously embody along this healing path. Their humiliation turns to hugs, unlocking a new door of connection through failure, and allows the journey to continue onward.

It took many years for me to understand that I wasn't alone on this healing journey, although it was my solo expedition. In fact, none of us are alone. For some cosmic reason, we all chose to be here in this form at this exact time, not only to advance the healing of our individual soul through lessons of love and hardship, but the collective soul of humanity as well. The human experience is one intricately woven labyrinth: someone has stood where you stand today, and where you were yesterday another will be tomorrow. Someone has passed through the same treacherous waters, and they lived to share the secrets of getting through them. And so, when the Loneliness Shadow haunts you, shine upon it the Star of Interconnectedness, Universality, and Oneness, because this is the core of this human life we live. If you hold up your light, others will be able to find you better, and you'll be able to see just as well.

We are meant to serve one another. We are meant to uplift one another. And as you sharpen your inner compass that guides you through your personal soul work, your children will reap the benefits of your healing. You will raise them to know how to navigate their respective journeys. Instead of handing them a dim oil lamp, you'll hand them a high-capacity miner's lamp. You won't be able to control the path they choose for themselves, but at least you'll equip them with the tools they need to see further and clearer on their journey. This is the power of healing . . . we unintentionally heal those around us the more we engage in our own healing work.

While it's not my experience that the healing journey "ends" in the linear way we may desire it to, the path itself opens the more you expand your self-awareness. You won't always feel trapped and itching to escape the journey. You'll find comfortable places to set up camp, explore, roam, and enjoy. When that happens, take advantage. Don't doubt it. Don't let your wounds win and convince you that you need to prepare for doomsday. This is where you learn to trust yourself and to lean on the people in your life. Because soon enough, another storm will roll in, and it will be time to move along. These ebbs and flows are natural and it's in your best interest to learn how to roll with them.

You have given yourself the gift of healing by choosing to parent yourself first. You have gifted your children a more attuned, compassionate parent who is willing to sort through their own baggage, rather than leaving it as their inheritance. But most significantly, you have contributed to your community, your culture, and society at large the biggest gift of all: resilient, emotionally attuned, compassionate, empathic, and inclusively minded children who are genuinely invested in those around them . . . all because they feel your investment in them. Together, we can create a deeply healed world, one child-parent relationship at a time.

ACKNOWLEDGMENTS

• • • • • •

There are not enough words to express the immense gratitude I feel in my heart for every single person involved in the creation of this book. Each of you has been instrumental from conception to publication, and without you, this would not have been possible.

First, I want to thank my amazing husband, Matt, for all your love and support. You graciously took on more solo hours during the weekends and many weeknights for almost an entire year so I could get my heart onto these pages. If we can survive the book-writing process, then we can survive anything. Thank you for keeping me humble and honest and always encouraging me to grow. There's no one I'd rather do life with.

My beautiful children, Matteo and Giovanni—it is my deepest honor to be your mother. You two are my most influential teachers: You've taught me what true compassion and joy *feel* like. You are the brightest of lights and so very easy to love. I hope that if you ever choose to read this, you feel comfortable calling me out on ways I may not always live up to what I'm teaching here. Growth isn't comfortable, but I'm committed to keeping my ego out of it and learning from your innate wisdom.

To my incredible team of powerhouse women: thank you for believing in me. Michelle Howry, my editor, you took a chance on a brand-new author with a big vision for the world. And many thanks to the entire team at Putnam/Penguin Random House, including the copy editors and marketing professionals who helped to get this book's message across in a clear and inspiring way. To Sheila Curry Oakes, thank you for never judging me, for helping me organize my neurodivergent brain, and for all your contributions and support with creating this book. I'm still working on my complex of feeling like "too much," and you never made me feel like I was that. To my agent, Wendy Sherman, thank you for sliding into my DMs and encouraging me to take this next leap. If it weren't for you, literally none of this would have been possible. To be surrounded by hardworking women who uplift one another and want to see one another succeed has been healing for my soul.

To Mama SharBear, you inspired me to work with parents and young children when I started my career as a therapist. Like many eldest daughter–mother relationships, our relationship was complicated and nuanced, but there is no one else I would have chosen to be my mom. If you were alive, I'm not sure how you'd feel about this book. But I do know one thing: You'd be proud of me nonetheless. *Love you more . . .*

To Dr. Nabil Hanna, my longtime therapist: You threw me a buoy and pulled me out of some dark waters right when life was becoming unbearable. You gave me permission to get to know myself, to make sense of my past, and to break cycles of shame and self-destruction. You taught me how to love myself. And you showed me how to love others. You've probably been my biggest cheerleader in life, and I aspire to be as compassionate, nurturing, and wise as you.

Acknowledgments

To all my many private clients in the Conscious Mommy Community, as well as the moms at South Bay Mommy and Me, who I've had the privilege to learn so much from throughout the years: Thank you for giving me a platform to share this wisdom and learn in real time how it makes legitimate changes to your life. Thank you for trusting me to care for you and your children. Each of you has a special place in my heart.

And finally, to my support system (you know who you are), who have been instrumental in keeping me grounded: thank you for being the rocks I could lean on in times of high stress. It is through each of you that I learned how to counter the temptation of self-rejection through compassion and gratitude practices. When in my reflection all I could see was a bad girl, you showed me someone worth loving. It's possible I wouldn't be alive if it weren't for each of you, so thank you for sticking by me and teaching me what it means to be a friend who shows up. From the bottom of my heart, I love you all.

NOTES

• · · · · ·

Chapter 2: Break Unhealthy Family Cycles

46 **Helping her recognize that early childhood trauma:** Andrew R. Dismukes, Elizabeth A. Shirtcliff, and Stacy S. Drury, "Genetic and Epigenetic Processes in Infant Mental Health," in *Handbook of Infant Mental Health*, ed. Charles H. Zeanah Jr. (New York: The Guilford Press, 2019), https://massaimh.org/wp-content/uploads/2020/02/Chapter4Genetic AndEpigenetic.pdf.

Chapter 3: Self-Awareness Sets You Free

60 **This historical bias against children:** Elisabeth Young-Bruehl, *Childism: Confronting Prejudice Against Children* (New Haven, CT: Yale University Press, 2013).

73 **Research suggests that being able to reframe:** Claire Eagleson et al., "The Power of Positive Thinking: Pathological Worry Is Reduced by Thought Replacement in Generalized Anxiety Disorder," *Behaviour Research and Therapy* 78 (March 2016):13–18, doi: 10.1016/j.brat.2015.12.017.

Chapter 6: Demystifying Your Child's Behavior

142 **According to recent studies:** Ruthann Richter, "Among Teens, Sleep Deprivation an Epidemic," Stanford Medicine News Center, October 8, 2015, https://med.stanford.edu/news/all-news/2015/10/among -teens-sleep-deprivation-an-epidemic.html.

142 **In fact, the Centers for Disease Control and Prevention reports:** "Sleep Difficulties & Patterns Among Americans," Centers for Disease Control and Prevention, National Center for Health Statistics, June 29, 2022, https://www.cdc.gov/nchs/pressroom/podcasts/2022/20220629/20220629.htm.

142 **Specifically, six out of ten middle:** "Do Your Children Get Enough Sleep?," Centers for Disease Control and Prevention, National Center for Chronic Disease Prevention and Health Promotion, March 7, 2018, https://stacks.cdc.gov/view/cdc/56554.

142 **According to the Mayo Clinic, the hours:** Eric J. Olson, "How Many Hours of Sleep Are Enough for Good Health?," Mayo Clinic, February 21, 2023, https://www.mayoclinic.org/healthy-lifestyle/adult-health/expert-answers/how-many-hours-of-sleep-are-enough/faq-20057898.

Chapter 7: Calming Their Stress and Anxiety

164–65 **Millennial mothers reportedly experience:** Jake M. Najman et al., "Does the Millennial Generation of Women Experience More Mental Illness Than Their Mothers?," *BMC Psychiatry* 21 (July 2021): 359, doi:10.1186/s12888-021-03361-5, https://www.ncbi.nlm.nih.gov/pmc/articles/PMC8285825.

165 **70 percent of parents:** "Stress in America™ 2020," American Psychological Association, October 2020, https://www.apa.org/news/press/releases/stress/2020/report-october.

165 **A two-generation longitudinal study:** Rebecca M. Pearson et al., "Prevalence of Prenatal Depression Symptoms Among 2 Generations of Pregnant Mothers: The Avon Longitudinal Study of Parents and Children," *JAMA Network Open* 1, no. 3 (July 6, 2018): e180725, doi:10.1001/jamanetworkopen.2018.0725.

165 **Today's mothers who work:** Suzanne M. Bianchi, John P. Robinson, and Melissa A. Milkie, *Changing Rhythms of American Family Life* (New

York: Russell Sage Foundation, 2006), https://www.russellsage.org/publications/changing-rhythms-american-family-life-1.

169 **Gun violence (the leading cause of death:** Annette Choi, "Children and Teens Are More Likely to Die by Guns Than Anything Else," CNN, March 29, 2023, https://www.cnn.com/2023/03/29/health/us-children-gun-deaths-dg/index.html.

169 **the active shooter drills:** "The Impact of Active Shooter Drills in Schools," Everytown for Gun Safety, September 3, 2020, updated February 20, 2023, https://everytownresearch.org/report/the-impact-of-active-shooter-drills-in-schools.

173 **Stress can impact your child's:** Hillary A. Franke, "Toxic Stress: Effects, Prevention and Treatment," *Children* (Basel, Switzerland) 1, no. 3 (December 2014): 390–402, doi:10.3390/children1030390, https://www.ncbi.nlm.nih.gov/pmc/articles/PMC4928741.

Chapter 8: Ending Power Struggles

184 **This is the pathway toward future:** Rin Reczek, Lawrence Stacey, and Mieke Beth Thomeer, "Parent–Adult Child Estrangement in the United States by Gender, Race/Ethnicity, and Sexuality," *Journal of Marriage and Family* 85, no. 2 (April 2023): 494–517, https://onlinelibrary.wiley.com/doi/10.1111/jomf.12898.

Chapter 9: Mastering Discipline

210 **The original definition of "discipline":** "discipline (n.)," Online Etymology Dictionary, updated October 13, 2021, https://www.etymonline.com/word/discipline.

210 **It is derived from the root:** "What Does Discipline Mean?," Focus 3, accessed July 8, 2024, https://focus3.com/what-does-discipline-mean.

210 **In fact, in a Zero to Three national survey:** "National Parent Survey Overview and Key Insights," Zero to Three, June 6, 2016, https://

www.zerotothree.org/resource/national-parent-survey-overview-and
-key-insights.

212 **Of the parents who spanked their kids:** "National Parent Survey
Overview and Key Insights."

213 **Baumrind's research found that:** Diana Baumrind, "Child Care
Practices Anteceding Three Patterns of Preschool Behavior," *Genetic Psychology Monographs* 75, no. 1 (February 1967): 43–88.

213 **This style of parenting can reduce:** Kendra Cherry, "Authoritative
Parenting Characteristics and Effects," Verywell Mind, updated July 5,
2023, https://www.verywellmind.com/what-is-authoritative-parenting
-2794956.

221 **It takes about ten weeks:** "Science of Habits," University College
London, accessed July 8, 2024, https://www.ucl.ac.uk/epidemiology
-health-care/research/behavioural-science-and-health/research/energy
-balance-cancer/healthy-habits/science-habits.

221 **but it could take anywhere from eighteen:** Phillippa Lally et al.,
"How Are Habits Formed: Modelling Habit Formation in the Real
World," *European Journal of Social Psychology* 40, no. 6 (October 2010):
998–1009, https://onlinelibrary.wiley.com/doi/abs/10.1002/ejsp.674.

Chapter 10: Navigating Sibling Dynamics

242 **Many parents believe that fighting:** Darlene Lancer, "Sibling Bullying and Abuse: The Hidden Epidemic," *Psychology Today*, February 3,
2020, https://www.psychologytoday.com/us/blog/toxic-relationships
/202002/sibling-bullying-and-abuse-the-hidden-epidemic.

Chapter 11: Aligning with Your Parenting Partner

271 **Dr. John Gottman says, "Successful":** "Introducing: The Small
Things Often Podcast," The Gottman Institute, February 14, 2020,
https://www.gottman.com/blog/introducing-the-small-things-often
-podcast.

Notes

278   **A Pew Research poll in 2007:** "Modern Marriage," Pew Research Center, July 18, 2007, https://www.pewresearch.org/social-trends/2007/07/18/modern-marriage.

289   **Dr. John Gottman says that 96 percent:** John Gottman, "The 6 Things That Predict Divorce," The Gottman Institute, accessed July 8, 2024, https://www.gottman.com/blog/the-6-things-that-predict-divorce.

RECOMMENDED READING AND RESOURCES

• • • • • •

For Your Bookshelf

- *Social Justice Parenting* by Dr. Traci Baxley
- *Brain-Body Parenting* by Mona Delahooke, PhD
- *Untamed* by Glennon Doyle
- *The Explosive Child* by Ross W. Greene, PhD
- *And Baby Makes Three* by John M. Gottman, PhD, and Julie Schwartz Gottman, PhD
- *The Out-of-Sync Child* by Carol Stock Kranowitz, MA
- *Will I Ever Be Good Enough?* by Karyl McBride, PhD
- *The Blessing of a Skinned Knee* by Wendy Mogel, PhD
- *Child of Mine* by Ellyn Satter
- *The Power of Showing Up* by Daniel J. Siegel, MD, and Tina Payne Bryson, PhD
- *The Whole-Brain Child* by Daniel J. Siegel, MD, and Tina Payne Bryson, PhD
- *Conscious Uncoupling* by Katherine Woodward Thomas
- *The Conscious Parent* by Shefali Tsabary, PhD
- *Generation Sleepless* by Heather Turgeon, MFT, and Julie Wright, MFT

Recommended Reading and Resources

For Your Child's Bookshelf

- *Love Makes a Family* by Sophie Beer
- *Wilma Jean the Worry Machine* by Julia Cook
- *The Rabbit Listened* by Cori Doerrfeld
- *We're Different, We're the Same, and We're All Wonderful!* by Bobbi Kates
- *The Invisible String* by Patrice Karst
- *You Have Feelings All the Time* by Deborah Farmer Kris
- *Have You Filled a Bucket Today?* by Carol McCloud
- *Lola Reads to Leo* by Anna McQuinn
- *Counting on Community* by Innosanto Nagara
- *Marvin Gets Mad!* by Joseph Theobald
- *Sometimes I'm Bombaloo* by Rachel Vail
- *Mop Rides the Waves of Life* by Jaimal Yogis

Organizations

- Common Sense Media https://www.commonsensemedia.org
- The Conscious Mommy Community https://www.consciousmommy.com
- Sex Positive Families https://sexpositivefamilies.com
- Wait Until 8th https://www.waituntil8th.org

Apps

- Calm
- Headspace

INDEX

• • • • • •

Index

Index

Index

Index

Index